Constraining Cognitive Theories
Issues and Options

THEORETICAL ISSUES IN COGNITIVE SCIENCE

Zenon Pylyshyn, Series Editor

Constraining Cognitive Theories
Issues and Options

edited by
Zenon Pylyshyn
Rutgers University
New Brunswick, NJ

Ablex Publishing Corporation
Stamford, Connecticut
London, England

Printed in the United States of America

Library of Congress Cataloging-in-Publication Data

Constraining cognitive theories : issues and options / edited by Zenon Pylyshyn.
    p. cm. — (Theoretical issues in cognitive science)
    Includes bibliographical references and index.
    ISBN 1-56750-299-7 (cloth). — ISBN 1-56750-300-4 (pbk.)
    1. Cognition. 2. Cognitive psychology. 3. Cognitive science.
I. Pylyshyn, Zenon, 1937-   . II. Series.
BF311.C6566 1997
153—DC20   96-32728
                                     CIP

Ablex Publishing Corporation by: Published in the U.K. and Europe
100 Prospect Street   JAI Press Ltd.
Stamford, Connecticut 06901-1640   38 Tavistock Street
                                         Covent Garden
                                         London WC2E 7PB
                                         England

Contents

chapter I

Introduction: Cognitive Architecture and the Hope for a Science of Cognition*

Zenon W. Pylyshyn
zenon@ruccs.rutgers.edu
Center for Cognitive Science
Rutgers University

The research pursuits that are collectively referred to as *Cognitive Science*, or sometimes (unfortunately, in my view) as *The Cognitive Sciences*, are founded on certain (often tacit) assumptions or research-shaping hypotheses. One such assumption is that there are principles of functioning of the Cognizing Mind/Brain which, if they can be captured at all, will need to be stated in a vocabulary that is proprietary to Cognitive Science—that such principles cannot be stated in the vocabulary of biology or behaviorism, or any of the existing sciences like physics and chemistry; or technological pursuits such as engineering, communications theory, and so on. Another closely related assumption is that the understanding of mind is a task that is beyond the purview of any one of the existing disciplines—because of limitations of formal theoretical apparatus available to any one discipline, and also because relevant evidence is expected to come from a wide range of sources. A third assumption is that there are certain ancient puzzles about cognition and intelligent action that can no longer

*The conference and subsequent preparation of this volume was funded by grants from the National Science Foundation (Grant NSF BNS 91-11423), the Air Force Office of Scientific Research (Grant MIPR#91-0023) and the Office of Naval Research (Grant N-00014-91-J-1851), as well as the support of Rutgers, the State University of New Jersey, and its new Center for Cognitive Science on the New Brunswick campus. I wish to thank Carl Gillett and Paul Lodge for their help in preparing the papers for publication. Information on the Center may be obtained by writing to the director at Rutgers Center for Cognitive Science, New Brunswick, NJ 08903, or through the Internet under Rutgers University (info.rutgers.edu, or use the World Wide Web and access URL http://ruccs.rutgers.edu).

be swept under the rug: there are problems about meaning, about intentionality, and perhaps even about consciousness that either need to be addressed directly or at least circumnavigated (or gerrymandered) in a perspicuous and revealing way.

Historically, however, one additional idea brought researchers together under the new disposition and also provided the added hope for the rehabilitation of certain ancient puzzles. This is the idea of *cognition as computing*. Initially much was not clear about this union of a substantive empirical discipline with a formal (sometimes engineering) tool. The notion of computing itself was not well understood (and to some extent it is still an evolving idea today), and the correspondence between cognition and computation initially was assumed to be a weak one based on pragmatic considerations. The term often used to refer to the pursuit of the marriage between computing and cognition was "computer simulation of behavior." Slowly, however, it dawned on many researchers—I believe beginning with Newell and Simon—that more was at stake than the use of computers to execute models to derive predictions. What was special about computing is that it represented a new type of process: A process that could be described not only in abstract automata, symbol-manipulation, or information-processing terms, but at the same time had two additional properties that brought it into contact with long-standing deep problems in psychology and the philosophy of mind. In computing we had an instance of a process that could be described in terms of *rules and representations*—in terms of what its states were *about*, and at the same time avoiding the excesses of dualism by virtue of the fact that these processes were demonstrably instantiated in a physical system.

The recognition that a stronger level of correspondence between computing and cognition might exist has taken many years to dawn, and many scholars do not accept the general thesis of a deep equivalence between these two types of processes. Some of those who oppose the identification of computation and cognition continue to refer to themselves as Cognitive Scientists. Nonetheless I believe that the fundamental idea that unites cognitive scientists remains this recognition of cognition as a species of computation—at least as a working hypothesis (which is as certain as we get in science anyway). Certainly it is one of the main underlying assumptions of researchers at the Rutgers Center for Cognitive Science, where the papers included in this volume originated.

One of the reasons people are wary of accepting cognition literally as a computational process is that it seems clear that the mind/brain is quite different from typical commercial computers. This much is not controversial. But if the mind really was a computing system, the fact that it seems different from an IBM PC or other commercial type of machine could either mean that we have assumed the wrong level of abstraction for the comparison, or it could mean that the mind is in fact quite a different type of computer. These two possibilities are closely related and this is where the notion of computational or cognitive architecture becomes central.

Complex systems can always be described at various levels of abstraction. However, separate laws or principles need not exist at all of these levels. Which levels correspond to real natural kinds is an empirical matter. Cognitive science and much of AI rests on the assumption that there is an independent level of organization, which I have called the "semantic level" and Newell has characterized as the "knowledge level." This is a level of organization at which semantic principles, such as rationality or at least plausible reasoning, apply. In the case of a computational process that purports to be a model of some cognitive process, only one level of the system's organization corresponds to what we call its cognitive architecture. That is the level at which the states (datastructures) being processed are the ones that receive a cognitive interpretation. To put it another way, it is the level at which the system is representational, and where the representations correspond to the objects of thought (including percepts, memories, goals, beliefs, and so on). Notice that many other levels of system organization may be below this, but these do not constitute different *cognitive* architectures because their states do not represent cognitive contents. Rather, they correspond to various kinds of implementations, perhaps at the level of some abstract neurology, which realize (or implement) the cognitive architecture. Similarly, various levels of organization may be above this, but they too do not constitute different cognitive architectures. They represent the organization of the cognitive process itself, say in terms of hierarchies of subroutines, not a different level of the system structure.

The notion of *Cognitive Architecture* in the context of the Computational Theory of Mind (CTM) comes directly from the notion of computer architecture in computer science, where it refers to the relatively fixed set of computational resources available to a programmer in designing a program for a given computer system. Among other properties, this includes the type of memory that the computer has, the way it encodes information (the system of symbolic codes or language it uses), the basic operations that are available, and the constraints on the application of these operations (e.g., serial vs. parallel sequencing). The architecture characterizes the computer system on which the program runs, but it may reflect its physical properties only indirectly since the architecture visible to the programmer might itself be simulated in software or firmware. For this reason it is sometimes referred to as the "functional architecture" or even as the "structure of the underlying virtual machine," instead of referring to it as the "hardware" as was sometimes done.

For purposes of cognitive science, the difference between cognitive architecture and other levels of system organization is fundamental. Architecture marks the boundary between processes that can be explained in biological terms (or other physical-science terms) and those that require appeal to representations or knowledge. A fundamental working hypothesis of Cognitive Science is that there exists an autonomous (or at least partially autonomous) domain of phenomena that can be explained in terms of representations (goals, beliefs, knowledge, perceptions, etc.) and algorithmic processes that operate over these representations. Another way to put this is to say that cognitive systems have a real level of organization at what Newell (1990) has called the knowledge level. Reasoning and rational knowledge-dependent principles apply at this level. Because of this, any differences in behavioral regularities that can be shown to arise from such knowledge-dependent processes do not reveal properties of the architecture, which remain invariant with changes in goals and knowledge. This observation leads to a novel methodological proposal; namely, that the effects of the architecture are cognitively impenetrable.

Another way to view this is to recognize that a system's repertoire of potential behavioral functions—those that remain possible without changing its inherent structure, which we might call its computational or cognitive "capacity"—is constrained by its architecture. In contrast, the different regularities that we may observe in different contexts or environments can then be attributed to differences in the goals, beliefs, strategies, or rules that it adopts.

COGNITIVE SCIENCE AND THE RECONCILIATION OF INTENTIONALITY AND NATURALISM

The idea that cognition is a species of computation helps us come to terms with one very important desideratum of a science of cognition—reconciling representation-governed processes with material causation. Computation offers at least the following hypothesis for how this might be possible. A computer is a physical device that shares with mind the property that some of its regularities can be stated in terms of the semantics of its representations. We can, for example, ask why a certain function continues to produce mathematically correct results or why certain operations over expressions continue to be truth-preserving (if the operations are valid and the expressions denote true states of affairs), and the answer has to make reference to semantical notions. Similarly when certain deviations from rationality or certain systematic semantic errors occur, we can sometimes explain these in terms of the way the semantics is encoded and in terms of the architecture of the system that operates on the encodings. So for example, systematic rounding errors in mathematical functions and the way in which the complexity of the process varies with the nature of the input (e.g., the size of the numerals) would be explained by adverting to the system of codes—or to the symbol-level regularities. Similarly, further regularities require that we appeal to the physical properties of the system, particularly when the system fails in some way (e.g., the batteries are low or parts of the machine have been damaged).

This trilevel organization is precisely what we hypothesize to hold of the mind/brain. The proof of this assumption is a long-term project, but what success information-processing psychology has made—from studies of performance to studies of reasoning and psycholinguistics—is consistent with this general foundational assumption. And this, in turn, gives us some reason to hope that Cognitive Science may turn out to be a natural causal science in a certain sense which may not be true of other kinds of sciences. Perhaps this needs some clarification.

There are two extremes in styles of science in the social-biological sciences (and of course all grades in between these extremes). One style is exemplified in botany and history (which is sometimes viewed as a science). In this style, we collect humanly interesting facts and place them in taxonomies that reveal some local patterns, thereby enlightening the domain of the science. This kind of pursuit is sometimes called the "natural history" approach. But there is another style of science that attempts to find broad underlying "*causal*" principles. Because in the end, causal principles are materialist, this kind of science is committed to making contact with physics and chemistry eventually. This does not make it a reductionist pursuit since along the way these sciences may evolve a whole new set of principles based on their own vocabularies—providing the world is truly so organized. But in the end, sciences practicing this style are committed to the Unity of Science. Physiology is an example of a science that aspires to be a causal science. And so, some of us believe, is the computational heartland of Cognitive Science, as exemplified in the study of perception for example. That is why Cognitive Science pays attention to physical constraints on transduction on both the input and output side of the organism, rather than redefining the nature of the input in nonphysical terms as Gibson tried to do (and a science based on describing the input in terms of ecological categories such as affordances might well have worked after a fashion, though it would have violated the Causal Unity criterion).

We have no right to assume that all the questions of interest concerning Cognition that arise are questions that will fall under a causal-science explanation. And not all of it can be a computational science (as I tried to argue in my "Computation and Cognition"). This is not such a terrible indictment: There are plenty of very useful noncausal sciences. Linguistics, for example, is a science with a rich deductive structure and beautiful deep principles that constrain a causal science such as psycholinguistics. And there are excellent and useful taxonomic sciences. Most of social, educational, personality, and clinical studies are like that (though because the word *science* has such strong positive connotations they would deny being akin to natural history). The end-product of studies in most of psychology is a *collection* of generalizations, sometimes connected by a very loose tissue of just-so stories that serve mostly as a mnemonic framework. Psychoanalysis is such a framework, but so is almost everything in sociology and, for that matter, in economics as well (despite the high level of mathematics in the latter discipline—which just shows that formalization does not guarantee a causal science, you can axiomatize almost anything, including psychoanalysis).

There is no a priori guarantee that any particular problem, or class of problems associated with cognition will fall under a causal theory of cognition. For example, much of what goes on in cognition is what we might call common-sense reasoning and, alas, we know almost nothing about this process (by almost nothing I mean that when calibrated against what grandmother knew there has been little progress). And that's why, in my view, long-term memory has not produced a lasting scientific research program in psychology. I would not be surprised to find that molecular biology or neuroscience uncovers some useful mechanisms of LTM, but the reconstructive part of memory—the part involving reasoning that Bartlett studied—awaits an entirely new idea about reasoning. The same applies to learning, personality, and many other parts of traditional psychology: The part that lies within Cognitive Science, contrary to our earlier beliefs, either may be nonexistent or may fall under the general-reasoning problem that we don't know how to begin to analyze.

If cognitive science is to be a science like other causal explanatory sciences (and that's a big "if"—we may one day discover that all we can get out of cognitive science is a descriptive taxonomic discipline like botany) then we will have to be realists about our constructs. If we claim that the mind is computational then we have committed ourselves to a program of research whose goals are to specify what kind of computer the mind is, and what representations and codes it computes over. If that sounds like a tall order it should. We have been trying to make sense of mental activity for at least 3000 years, and this is the first time that we have any idea—however embryonic—how mindlike behavior might be produced by a material object. It may be a small and tenuous step, but it is, as Jerry Fodor would put it, the only game in town or the only straw afloat, depending on how optimistic you happen to be feeling.

THE PAPERS

The papers collected in the anthology initially arise from a historical event: The inauguration of the Rutgers Center for Cognitive Science (RuCCS) in

New Brunswick, New Jersey in October 1991. A number of the present authors were in attendance at that event and presented papers. The papers contained herein, however, were prepared much later and many of the authors of these papers were not present at the conference. Rather they are individuals who are in one way or another associates or supporters of the Rutgers Center. Taken as a whole the papers represent a range of cognitive activities that are typical of the discipline. Moreover they are in one way or another concerned with Cognitive Architecture, the original theme of the conference, and provide a variety of views about the current and potential architectures that may shape the future progress in the field.

chapter 2

On Some Parallels Between Perception Theories and Semantic Theories

Jerry A. Fodor
fodor@ruccs.rutgers.edu
Center for Cognitive Science
Rutgers University

When Zenon Pylyshyn told me—it was about six minutes ago, actually—that I would have to give a paper at this conference I became, naturally enough, faint with joy. Upon being revived, I said (well, snarled really) "What about?" and Zenon replied, airily, "Oh, anything you like, but remember it's for an interdisciplinary audience. So no data and no arguments. And, as a personal favor, no jokes." That doesn't leave me anything much except to pontificate about the Big Picture, and so I have decided to do some of that. I want to comment on what seem to me to be some interesting parallels, and also some interesting divergences, between the way perceptual theories in psychology and semantic theories in philosophy have developed over the last several decades. In the course of doing so, I will give vent to some of my sentiments about these developments; and I'll also make a few quite undetailed suggestions about what I think ought to happen next in cognitive science. The bottom line will be that most of what has been going on in theories of meaning and perception has been misguided, and for much the same reasons, and that now it all needs to be done over. If this is right, then there is plenty of work for the new cognitive science center to do. If you like, my point in what follows is to suggest an outline for its research agenda.

So, then, to commence.

The analogy to which I mainly want to draw your attention is this: The direction of modern development, both in perception theory and in semantics, has been from a more or less comprehensive atomism, to a more or less comprehensive holism. And, in both cases, the consequence of the new holism has been relativistic, so that it now seems practically truistic that both how you see the world, and what you mean by what you say, depend on your background of beliefs and theories. I will presently be wanting to remind you of the disastrous implications of these developments for epistemology. For the moment, I'll settle for a modest exercise in contrast and compare, starting with the situation in theories of perception.

Once upon a time, people had the following sort of picture of perception. Perception is a matter of matching ideas in the head to things in the world. Sometimes ideas in the head were thought of in a quasipictorial way—say as images or as templates—and the notion of "matching" was given a geometric interpretation; roughly, ideas match the things that they resemble. And, sometimes ideas were thought of in a quasilinguist way—say as descriptions or as feature lists—and then the notion of matching was given a semantic interpretation; roughly, the things an idea matches are the ones that have the properties that the corresponding mental description enumerates.

In either case, and this is the point I want to emphasize, the resulting theory of perception was *atomistic.* This is because the matching relation is itself atomistic. For example, whether something resembles your idea of a horse does not depend on what *other* ideas you have. In principle, therefore, if ideas are images, and perception is a process of matching to an image, then your being able to recognize horses as horses is compatible with your having only one idea (viz with your having in your head nothing but the image of a horse). Almost the same considerations apply to the theory that ideas are descriptions or feature lists. If your idea of a horse is the idea of something that has four legs and eats oats, and if perception is matching features on the mental list to properties of the distal percept, then your ability to perceive something as a horse depends only on your having the concepts "eats oats" and "has four legs." And if it is supposed that "eats oats" and "has four legs" are, in turn, elementary concepts, then you don't need anything else in your head to perceive something as satisfying one or the other of them.

Nothing relevant to the current considerations changed when psychologists stopped being empiricists and started being behaviorists. Suppose you think that ideas aren't things in your head after all; instead they are something like dispositions to make discriminitive responses. So, then, perceiving something as a horse is construed as making, or being disposed to make, a horse-specific response to it. Once again, perceptual capacities turn out to be atomistic since; presumably, being able to respond selectively to horses doesn't depend on being able to respond selectively to anything else. In principle, the ability to respond selectively to horses could exhaust a behavioral repertoire.

However, things did change, in a really fundamental way, with the onset of "New Look" psychologizing. Whereas empiricists and behaviorists had supposed that the basic construct in perception theory is something like matching, New Look psychologists thought that the basic concept in perception theory is something like confirmation. This goes in three steps. First you identify perceiving something as a horse with confirming the hypothesis that the thing is a horse. Then you think of confirmation not as a two-place relation between the data and a hypothesis, but rather as a three-place relation between the data, a hypothesis, and a theory; roughly, the best confirmed perceptual hypothesis is the one that achieves the 'best fit'—the best trade off—between the exigencies of the current sensory input, on one hand, and the exigencies of your background commitments on the other.

Finally, the demands that the background commitments place on perceptual hypotheses are assumed to be intrinsically conservative and global. That is, the best perceptual hypothesis is the one that accounts for the sensory data with the minimal overall disturbance of the background theory. So, to replace the matching model of perception with the hypothesis confirmation model of perception is to go from an intrinsically atomistic picture to an intrinsically holistic one. Perception is a relation between data, hypotheses and theories, and if, as we may suppose, having a theory involves having a galaxy of systematically interrelated concepts, then perception is possible only for a relatively complicated kind of mind. Only a theoretician could see a horse as a horse according to this new account of how perception works.

Though no one should underestimate the effects of mere fashion in cognitive science, I'm not meaning to suggest that the change from an atomistic to a holistic notion of perception was without persuasive empirical motivation. On the contrary, over the last three decades or so, a lot of psychologists have made a living out of experiments that demonstrate the effects of context, expectation, and the like on the speed and accuracy of perceptual identifications. Such demonstrations offered persuasive arguments (roughly, arguments that persuaded everybody but Gibsonians) of the principle that came to be known as the "poverty of the stimulus". The sensory data—however, exactly that notion is to be construed—underdetermine the subject's performance in perceptual tasks; there is, in some sense, more information in the perceptual response than in the proximal stimulation that elicits it. There must, therefore, be some source of information other than the proximal stimulus at the disposal of the perceiver. What better candidate than his cognitive background of theories and expectations?

On the other hand, as I've spent the last ten years or so remarking, the empirical situation vis a vis the holism of perception is less than utterly transparent. If there are plenty of cases where perception appears to be expectation driven or belief driven, there are also plenty of cases where perception appears to be largely recalcitrant to—or, to use Zenon's phrase—largely encapsulated from, the perceiver's conceptual background. The persistence of perceptual illusions in face of the knowledge that they are, in fact, illusory, offers the classic anecdotal example; but lots more cases are available from laboratory studies. There are, in short, poverty of the stimulus data on one side, and there are encapsulation data on the other side; the former suggest that perception must be less than fully atomistic, and the latter suggest that it must be less than fully 'interactive'. The research issues are where to draw the line and whether the line to be drawn is principled. I'll return to this presently; first, I want to take a quick look at the situation in semantics.

At the heart of the traditional atomistic account of perception was the idea that perceptual identification is some sort of a matching process. At the heart of the traditional atomistic account of semantics is the idea that meaning is the same thing as reference. Here is why, as long as you don't make a meaning reference distinction, your semantics is likely to be atomistic: Reference is, prima facie, a pairwise relation between an idea and a thing, or class of things, that the idea refers to. It therefore looks as though what one of your ideas refers to doesn't depend on what other ideas you have. So it looks like, in principle, you could have an idea that refers to horses, even if you didn't have any ideas that refer to anything else. Just as, in the psychological case, if perception is construed as matching, then, in principle, your ability to perceive a horse as a horse doesn't depend on your being able to perceive anything else as anything else, so too, in the semantic case, if representation is construed as reference, your ability to mentally represent a horse doesn't depend on your being able to mentally represent anything else. In fact, in the case of a mainline empiricist like Hume, the theory of perception and the semantic theory tend to be almost indistinguishable: the semantics says that an idea refers to whatever it resembles; the psychology says that perception is matching the idea to one of those things. The notion that semantics and perceptual psychology are much of a muchness is part of our empiricist inheritance. For reasons I'm about to explore, it strikes me as quite unlikely to be true.

I've suggested that the shift from atomism to holism in the psychology of perception occurred under the pressure of the "poverty of the stimulus" data. It's a lot harder to say what, exactly, motivated the shift from atomism to holism in semantics. Suffice it, for present purposes, that it has become received doctrine in a number of the cognitive sciences (philosophy included), that meaning is not, or not just, a matter of symbol-world relations, but also a matter of relations among symbols. Hence such slogans as that the meaning of a word is its role in a whole language; (or, to say the same thing in French, that the meaning of a word is its place in a 'system of differences'.) Or that the meaning of a theoretical term depends on the entire theory in which it is embedded. Or that the content of one of our thoughts depends on our entire belief system. And so on.

It is, as I say, remarkably difficult to find anything in the literature that constitutes an argument for these holist semantic doctrines. But some of the implications for cognitive science seem pretty clear. If having a mind is a matter of having something whose states have intentional content, then only complicated minds are possible. This is because, on one hand, nothing has content unless it belongs to a system of things that have content, and, on the other hand, systems are complicated by definition. More yet: it follows that what content a mental state has depends on what belief system it is a part of, so that it's maybe only in very rare cases—maybe it's only never—that two mental states have the same content. The paradoxical conclusions to which this line of thought leads are among the commonplaces of contemporary discussions of meaning: that, strictly speaking, translation is impossible, that, strictly speaking, communication is impossible, that, strictly speaking, no two people ever mean the same thing by what they say, that, strictly speaking, it is impossible to learn any part of a language without learning all of it, that, strictly speaking, only identical theories are commensurable, etc. Perceptual holism has correspondingly paradoxical implications for epistemology: that, strictly speaking, we see only what we expect; that strictly speaking, Ptolemaius and Copernicus saw different things when they saw the sun rise; that strictly speaking, there is no difference between seeing and thinking; and so forth. Someday, someone will write an interesting sociological dissertation on 20th century uses of the term "strictly speaking." In the present context, "strictly speaking, P" means, "well, I have a theory that entails P, but, of course, P is perfectly preposterous, so, though I go around saying that P, I am not, as a matter of fact, off my rocker, and wouldn't for the world want you to suppose that I actually think that P is, strictly speaking, TRUE."

If you put holism about perception together with holism about content, you get the kind of cognitive architecture that connectionists endorse. I take connectionism to be the legitimate offspring (as well as the reductio ad absurdum) of holism, so if you understand the mess connectionists are in, then you understand the mess we are all in insofar as we take our holism seriously. I want to say a little about this, with special attention to connectionist semantics. Then I will tell you where I think things now stand in cognitive science and what I think we should do next. Then, you will be pleased to hear, I will stop talking.

Suppose you think of concepts on the analogy of nodes in a network. Paths between the nodes correspond to interconceptual relations; inferential or associative relations as it might be. Well, as Zenon and I pointed out a couple of years ago, you had better somehow contrive that these nodes have internal syntactic structure (that the node that correspond to "brown cow" somehow has the nodes that correspond to "brow" and "cow" as constituents), because unless nodes have internal syntactic structure, they won't be syntactically productive or systematic; and if nodes aren't syntactically productive and systematic, they won't be *semantically* productive and systematic. And if nodes aren't *semantically* productive and systematic, then nodes can't be concepts (or ideas or whatever) because concepts, ideas, and the like, *are* semantically productive and systematic. This still strikes me as a damned good argument. (The more of the connectionist replies I've read, the better the argument seems.) However, notice that it's not an argument against HOLISM or against the idea that a concept is somehow a position in a conceptual network. All it shows is that if concepts *are* nodes in conceptual networks, then not all of the nodes in that conceptual network can be syntactically primitive. So, to that extent, the network must be like a language and unlike a list.

However, let's put that argument to one side, and let me tell you about another argument—one that Ernie Lepore and I have recently discovered. The new argument goes like this: Suppose you do have a network whose nodes have constituent structure. Even so you don't have all the material required for constructing a semantics in which concepts are identified with nodes in the network. This is for the following reason: Real concepts aren't only systematic and productive, they are also *compositional*; indeed, real concepts are systematic and productive only *because* they are compositional. This is an old point; one with which I assume that you're familiar. If we can entertain the novel concept "striped cow" that is because the semantics of that concept are determined when we fix the semantics of the constituent concepts "striped" and "cow" together with their syntactic arrangement.

Notice, however, that the *inferential role* of striped cow is not fixed when you fix its syntax together with the inferential roles of its constituents. Suppose that you come to believe that striped cows give chocolate milk. Then, part of the inferential role of *striped cow* in your belief system is specified by a path between the *striped cow* node and the *gives chocolate milk* node (or maybe by a path labelled *gives* that goes from the striped cow node to the chocolate milk node; the details don't matter a bit). But a moment's thought will convince you that this path isn't plausibly inherited from the paths associated with either *striped* or *cow*; if, to put it crudely, you think striped cows give chocolate milk, that's not something that follows from your concept *striped* or from your concept *cow.* It's just something *that you happen to believe about striped cows.*

So inferential roles are not, per se, compositional. So inferential roles can't be identified with concepts because concepts are per se compositional. What *is* compositional is not a concept's role in inference, but its role in analytic inference. The inference striped cow → dangerous isn't inherited from the inferential roles of striped or cow, but the inference from, as it might be, striped cow to striped animal is. That's because the inference from striped cow to striped animal is *analytic*; it's inherited from the inferential role of cow. Which, given the assumption that inferential roles are meanings, is to say that it's inherited from the meaning of "cow." Which is to say that it's analytic.

The long and short is: analyticity and compositionality are really the same thing. You can't, therefore, buy into a theory that identifies concepts with nodes in a network unless you also buy into an analytic/synthetic distinction. This conclusion is heavy with irony because connectionists are forever telling you that the good thing about their semantics is that it allows you to agree with Quine, and Rosche, and Putnam and Rorty and people like that who say that meaning is holistic because there isn't an analytic/synthetic distinction. Let me summarize this argument: if concepts are inferential roles (if, for example, they are nodes in a conceptual network), then inferential roles must be compositional. But inferential roles aren't compositional except for analytic inferences. So, either you must give up on the identification of concepts with inferential roles, or you must accept an analytic/synthetic distinction. My own view is that you ought to give up on the (holistic) notion that concepts are inferential roles; but, of course, each to his taste.

OK, now I can tell you where I think things stand in cognitive science. I think cognitive science is in a mess: and I think what made the mess it's in was a largely uncritical acceptance of holistic theses in semantics and the theory of perception. Still, I think the two cases aren't precisely symmetrical. As I remarked a while back, the rejection of atomism in perceptual psychology was empirically motivated. The poverty of the stimulus data really do make it immensely plausible that perception is more like confirmation than like matching. Whereas the rejection of atomism in semantics was, as far as I can tell, just about entirely gratuitous. I don't know of any argument that makes it plausible that the content of a concept is a function of—to say nothing of identical with—its role in a belief system and, the more one sees of (e.g., connectist) attempts to work out that sort of semantics, the more hopeless the prospects seem.

So much for where we are and how we got there; now a little about what to do next and then, just as I promised, I'll stop.

If, as I'm assuming, the poverty of the stimulus data mean what they seem to, then atomism about perception is a closed option. On the other hand, if the encapsulation data mean what they seem to, then so too is perceptual holism. The problem is to find something between the two; in effect, it's to find a line (principled if possible, de facto if not) between the background theory that can get accessed in perceptual integration and the background theory that can't. I think Zenon had the key idea in this area; the boundaries of perception are the boundaries of cognitive penetration. The interesting question is thus whether the boundaries of cognitive penetration are principled; whether we can say anything general about what kinds of mental processes can be cognitively penetrated and what kinds can't. I have some views about this, but I wouldn't trust them as far as I can throw them. The gleam of hope is that this really does seem to be an empirical research issue; one on which you can make progress by doing experiments and thinking about their results.

By contrast, the case against atomism in semantics never was seriously argued, as far as I can see; in semantics, the atomistic option remains wide open. Cognitive scientists are widely inclined to insist that at least some aspects of meaning must be intramental (must have to do with conceptual roles and the like) on pains of semantics turning out *not to be part of psychology*. However, it if the argument I sketched above is right, the cost of keeping semantics in psychology is going to be swallowing an analytic/synthetic distinction, and this looks to me like not being digestible. The analytic/synthetic distinction plays a role in semantics that is quite analogous to the role that the encapsulated/penetrable distinction plays in perceptual psychology; the function of each is to allow us to reject atomism without embracing an unbounded holism. The analytic/synthetic distinction in particular allows you to identify meaning with role in a language without relativizing meaning to a *whole* language. The catch, however, is that the encapsulated/penetrated distinction may actually work, whereas the analytic/synthetic distinction pretty clearly doesn't.

So here is my agenda for cognitive science until I retire (after that, cognitive science can do whatever it pleases). In perceptual psychology, find out if the penetrable processes constitute a natural kind. If they don't, find out if there is any other principled way of drawing the distinction between perceptually accessible background and perceptually inaccessible background. If there isn't, then give up the attempt to do perceptual psychology and get into some other line of work; because if the distinction between accessible and inaccessible background proves not to be principled, then the poverty of the stimulus problem will have inherited the frame problem, and everybody who has any sense knows that the frame problem is hopeless.

In semantics, consider seriously the possibilities for a resuscitated atomism, according to which semantic relations are exhaustively mind/world and the theory of meaning isn't part of psychology. This would really involve a fundamental rethinking of the foundations of cognitive science, and I don't have any very clear idea of where it might lead us. Certainly, it would involve giving quite different answers to questions like "What is it to have a concept?" and "What is it to learn a concept?" than the ones that cognitive scientists have thus far generally taken for granted. Whether the notion of an *intentional* psychology could, in fact, survive such a conceptual revolution is, I think, the most interesting question I know the name of.

So, then, here's my agenda for cognitive science: *deconstruct holism.* Oh, and while you're up, could somebody get me a grant?

chapter 3

Keeping Meaning in Mind

Georges Rey
rey@umiacs.umd.edu
Department of Philosophy
University of Maryland

FODOR'S EXTREMISM

For quite some time now, Jerry Fodor has been fighting the good fight against the depredations of holism on the modern mind. Specifically, he has presented theories that go some way toward localizing the crucial phenomena of perception and meaning. Quite apart from their substantial interest for psychology, such efforts come as a real relief to philosophy, which has been long suffering from the holism of the New Look's attack on the *given* and of Quine's attack on meaning. In many hands—for example, those of Richard Rorty (1979)—this holism has led to appalling consequences for the possibility of objectivity, rationality, even the existence of the world. It's good to nip such arguments in the bud.

But I sometimes have the suspicion that Fodor likes to overstate his case a little, as though what he always wanted to be when he grew up was an *enfant terrible*. Thus, he characteristically concludes his talk:

> Cognitive scientists are widely inclined to insist that at least some aspects of meaning MUST be intra-mental (must have to do with conceptual roles and the like) on pains of semantics turning out NOT TO BE PART OF PSYCHOLOGY. However, if the argument I have sketched above is right, the cost of keeping semantics in psychology is going to be swallowing an analytic/synthetic distinction, and this looks to me like not being digestible.

Unlike many of Fodor's overstatements, this one strikes me as being a very bad idea. It seems to me that semantics—a piece of the theory of concepts and conceptual competence—is inextricably involved in psychology, as is psychology in it.

I take it that Fodor is not claiming that psychology can do without semantic questions being settled by *someone*. Research into the concepts that we are born with, the course of their deployment in perception and reasoning, ways in which (just possibly) new concepts are acquired—that is, the sort of admirable research of, for example, Meltzoff, Spelke, Marr, Keil, Carey, Wellman, Leslie, Rosch, Kahneman and Tversky—presupposes *some* idea of what a concept is, and of the conditions under which an agent has it. What, after all, makes it true that a newborn has the concept of [material object] and not merely [moving shape]? or [causation] and not merely [constant conjunction]? And maybe (or maybe not) the concept of [belief]? Psychology without a theory of meaning would seem like physics without a theory of mass or charge. But it's one thing to claim that psychology *needs* a certain notion, another to claim that it's in the business of *defining* or *explaining* it. It's this latter claim that Fodor means to deny.

Some vexing terminological points need to be settled. Leaving aside theories of natural language, "semantics" as it even arises in relation to psychology involves an account of the meanings of mental states; in particular (in the present discussion) of entokenings of representations in a brain's language of thought. Philosophers usually use "concept" to mean the common *thought content expressed* by different representations, which I will indicate by enclosing words that express them in square brackets: thus, "dog," "Hund," and "chien" all express the concept [dog]. Psychologists tend to use it to mean merely the internal representation itself—the word or maybe even the image we employ in thinking. Whether this is a merely conventional issue about the word *concept* or a substantive claim about *concepts* themselves, is far from clear. Fodor, in particular, tends to use *concept* in the psychologist's way, but, as we will see, he does so on both terminological and substantive grounds.[1] Because the substantive issue is central to present concerns, I will resist this use and mean by concept thought content (prefixing it with sense- or representation as needed).

There are at least four possible candidates with which sense-concepts might be substantively identified:

1. The *mental representations* themselves (on this view, if dog and hund were internal terms, they would be different concepts)
2. The *Fregean–extension* of the terms; that is, the actual things—for example, real dogs—that satisfy the terms (here, dog, dog under ten feet tall, and dog or Swiss ocean would express the same concept);
3. The *p(roperty)–extension* of the terms; that is, the property in virtue of which something does or possibly would satisfy the term (here, dog and dog under ten feet tall would express different concepts, since there could be twelve-foot dogs; but not so water and H_2O)[2]
4. The (Fregean) *sense* of the terms; that is, the "way of thinking," or "mode of presentation" of either the Fregean or the p-extension (here, water and H_2O would express different concepts)[3]

In the case where one thinks of item 4 as involving entities distinct from the other three, I will speak of "distinctive sense-concepts."

Now, when Fodor means to exclude semantics from psychology, he, of course, doesn't mean to exclude internal representations; nor does he mean merely to exclude Fregean-extensions. Few would think that theories of mental processing have to include discussion of actual dogs.[4] The interesting cases are those of p-extensions and of senses. Semantics, as Fodor is using the term, is the theory of the relation of mental representations to *these things*, and his substantive claim about them has three claims:[5]

1. For lack of an analytic/synthetic distinction, there are no such things as distinctive sense-concepts
2. A theory of thought contents can get by with p-extensions alone
3. The theory of thought contents as p-extensions is not part of psychology

In this chapter I want to indicate reasons for disbelieving the first two of these claims (I think the third is also false, but it will lose its significance for the present discussion without the first two). Generally, the view I want to defend is that distinctive sense-concepts are needed for psychology, as psychology is needed for them, and that they are constituents of thought contents as these latter figure in psychological explanation.[6]

Fodor's main motivation for his three claims and denying this latter view is his Quiniphobia: He fears that distinctive senses were shown by Quine to be either unprincipled or hopelessly holistic; that is, so holistic as effectively to preclude cognitive generalizations across agents, or even different temporal stages of the same agent (since if, given a change in one thought is a change in all, it would be miraculous if they ever shared a thought). The only way Fodor sees to avoid such holism is to keep meanings "pure," and he and others have proposed a number of what I will call "pure externalist" theories of content that plausibly capture an important element of meaning without any mention of mentality. In particular he has proposed his "asymmetric dependence theory of content," in the spirit of what have come to be called "informational," "co-variational" or "locking" theories of meaning.[7]

There is no question that a theory of meaning needs to abstract from *some* psychological details; indeed, probably a lot more details than many meaning theorists anticipate. Insofar as meanings are part of an account of the kind of truth-valuable entities—sentences, propositions—that are communicated and thus sharable by virtually all human beings, they will need to abstract from a great many differences among human beings. For example, one person's image of a bird may be a sparrow, another's a hawk, but for all that they may both have thoughts involving [bird], they may agree, disagree, and often argue effectively about what is true or false about birds.

Not to allow for such abstraction is, indeed, to risk the aforementioned semantic holism, into which too many a theorist has recently slipped. Fodor and LePore (1992) usefully discuss ways to avoid being pushed into holism, but think that this requires avoiding mentality in semantics altogether. In a way, the issue is this: Is there a level of abstraction within psychology on which distinctive sense-concepts play a significant explanatory role? Fodor thinks not. Either semantics is into psychology up to the holistic hilt, or it has to stay clear of it entirely. Moderate positions, such as some limited a conceptual/inferential role semantics, have been rendered untenable by Quine.

In what follows, I want to save Fodor—or the rest of us—from this extremism. After a brief exposition of Fodor's view and some good psychological reasons for it in the next section, I'll consider two kinds of problems that those good psychological reasons ought to have led him to consider. I'll then discuss briefly the background worries that drive Fodor to his extreme view and suggest ways in which those worries are not so severe as he and others fear.

FODOR'S PURISM

A pure externalist locking theory is one that identifies the constitutive conditions for an internal representation's Φ having a certain content C in some fact about the causal and/or nomological covariation of tokenings of Φ with some external condition C. For Fodor, this locking relation is specified by his "asymmetric dependence" claim: Φ means C iff (1) it's a *ceteris-paribus* law that Φ gets tokened iff C, and (2) it's possible for Φ to get tokened sometimes when not-C, but when it does, it's doing so asymmetrically depends upon (1): that is, not-C's causing tokenings of Φ depends on C's causing them, but not vice versa.[8] Thus, "F" tokens in someone's brain would mean [alligator] *if* it was a cp law that they causally covaried with alligators and, although it's possible for crocodiles to cause them too, their doing so would depend on the cp law that alligators do so; but alligators doing so wouldn't depend on the crocodiles doing so.[9] Getting things wrong depends on getting them right, but getting them right doesn't depend on getting them wrong (although it does depend on the *possibility* of doing so).[10]

There are many problems with such an account that won't concern me here.[11] I will be concerned only with the problems that arise from its being, to my mind, insufficiently psychological. Ironically, I think these deficiencies can best be appreciated by considering what I regard as one of the theory's greatest strengths, the degree to which it *does* fit into psychology. I want to argue that the way in which it *is* motivated by its role in psychology is also a reason for supplementing it with features about a state or symbol's conceptual role in a person's mental life.

There actually are two somewhat orthogonal motivations at work in theories of content, which are too often run together. The usual focus of attention has been on what might be called the "vertical" issue of "naturalizing" semantic and related mental notions, showing how they can be reduced to (defined/explained/constituted by) nonsemantic, nonmental notions of the sort independently available from the other sciences. Although I think there are genuine puzzles here that ultimately need to be addressed, I am less convinced than many that we have a sufficient grasp on the varieties of intertheoretic reduction generally to be in a position yet to understand this particular case.[12] To my mind the far more interesting issue in a theory of meaning is a more "horizontal" problem of specifying a principled distinction within psychology between matters of meaning and matters of mere factual belief. For example, when do two disputants have the same concept and different beliefs versus different concepts altogether? Quine's (1953, 1954/1976, 1960) famous challenges to meaning theorists (to which I'll return in the last section) are often taken to be directed against the first issue; I think they are more interesting when directed against the second.[13]

Locking theories, too, are usually presented as solutions to the vertical problem. But, quite aside from whether they succeed at that, they offer a promising strategy for thinking about the horizontal one. They suggest a way of isolating an interesting *semantic stability* from issues of *epistemic* differences. In particular, a locking theory allows us to capture what in the world an agent is "getting at" in her use of a symbol, isolating that from her relative epistemic success or failure in reaching it. This is best brought out by Fodor's earlier paper "Psychosemantics" (Fodor 1981/1992)[14] in which we were to imagine what phenomenon would co-vary with a symbol's entokenings under "ideal epistemic conditions." As Fodor (1987) emphasizes, this suggestion by itself probably won't solve the vertical problem: Ideal epistemics is probably intentionally characterized epistemics. However, it captures quite well the previous horizontal intuition: to at least a first approximation (we'll look at a second one later), what a person means by an expression has to do with what she'd apply it to were her epistemic capacities unbounded. You and I have the same concept [alligator] iff our information about the world otherwise were complete, we would agree about what are and what are not alligators. If even under ideal epistemic conditions, we still disagreed about what are alligators, that would seem constitutive of our talking past each other, expressing different concepts by our words. The above asymmetric dependence account that Fodor offers later can be regarded as simply a way of then rendering this "horizontal" idea "vertically" acceptable.

Pace Quine (1967), belief in such a difference between meaning and mere belief need not be the result of an "uncritical mentalism," or the myth of an introspectible mental museum. For whether or not meanings are introspectible entities, their abstraction from general epistemics would seen to be essential to general mentalistic explanation: They provide a basis for beginning to predict how an agent will react to further evidence and argument, distinguishing those agents who disagree because of the differences in their evidence and reasoning from those who disagree because they really are getting at different issues, and so are not open to the same cognitive manipulations.

Locking theories are particularly interesting in this regard because they make it possible to draw this distinction between *arbitrarily divergent belief systems*. As Quine (1953) suggested, but Fodor (1987) notes more explicitly, it certainly looks as if people could believe *anything*. This is most evident in the case of philosophers: With enough intervening theory, people have convinced themselves that all is water, fire, ideas, or texts. But it arises also in comparing people across widely different cultures, different times, and different age groups (children, the senile). By confining semantics to merely to an idealized causal covariation under special circumstances, such divergencies in peoples' beliefs in actual circumstances can be tolerated as due to intervening factors limiting their epistemic positions.

But it's one thing to abstract in this way from actual beliefs, another to abstract from mechanisms of mind entirely. My only complaint with pure locking theories is that, in their anxiety to tolerate cognitive differences, they ignore deeper mechanisms that might provide for the full semantic stability that psychology requires. This can be brought out by two kinds of problems with such theories: It seems always to be possible to provide cases of locking relations with phenomena of which the agent clearly has no concept whatsoever (see the next section); and, in any case, there are further distinctions, motivated by the same interest in abstracting semantics from epistemics, that a pure locking theory neglects (see *Neglecting Distinctions* below).

FODOR'S PROBLEMS

Fortuitous Lockings

The key idea behind the asymmetric dependence theory is that the good cases make the bad cases possible, but not vice versa. This idea itself is not so novel as Fodor's audacious claim that it is this pattern of causal dependence alone, independently of psychological condition, that is sufficient for content. It is hard to quiet the suspicion that the pattern could arise in many clearly nonsemantic cases. Cases in which one condition asymmetrically facilitates another come to mind. For example, an automated relay, in which object B gets to a certain destination only if A does, but A's getting there doesn't depend on B's doing so (e.g., a troop train goes from Minsk to Pinsk only if the supply train does; but not vice versa); a lock openable in one way may asymmetrically depend on its being openable in another (so that the secretary can enter the offices only if the inhabitants can, but not vice versa); or, to take a timely case, suppose the immune system finally produces antibodies to the HIV virus only by concurrently producing them to some benign form of it, HIV* (HIV by itself destroys the system; HIV* triggers the antibodies that engulf HIV before it does so); but its producing them to HIV* might not depend on it producing them in response to HIV (break the latter by introducing one more mutation, and the former might still remain intact). Let's leave aside for a moment whether these *prima facie* counterexamples actually do satisfy Fodor's condition. Suppose that they did, or slight variants of them would. How might Fodor respond?

One strategy for him would be to allow such cases, but dismiss them as innocuous. No harm is done by supposing they are semantic, it's just that no mental system happens to be exploiting them. Aside from the affront to the philosophical claim that the condition is supposed to be genuinely sufficient, and the lack of any independent reason to believe it, we might agree.[15] But trouble brews if and when such cases arise for the psychologically relevant brain states themselves.

For if such nonexploited cases are possible, then one of my cognitive states, say, an entokening of a symbol "S," could turn out to be one of them: Suppose "S" tokens in me are locked onto cows in a standard cognitive way, entering into familiar reasonings about cows; but suppose also, unbeknownst to me or anyone, their physical constitution causes them to be locked onto a certain frequency of cosmic rays. These rays may cause tokenings of the state in me, and make the state susceptible to its being entokened by another cause (e.g., concentrations of potassium), which latter susceptibility, however, is not required for the efficacy of the rays. Thus, "S" being entokened by this other cause would asymmetrically depend on its being entokened by the rays (explaining, for example, why I often think of cows in the north, and especially after eating bananas).[16] Or suppose that when Penfield pokes at my brain with an electric probe, eliciting "S" representations of childhood cow experiences, he thereby makes them susceptible to being also illicited by pins (say, by causing a lowering of thresholds so that even the static on a pin could produce the effect). Fodor would be thereby committed to "S" having a semantics that is ambiguous between [cow] and [cosmic ray of frequency f] or [probe on area A]—just as ordinary uses of "gas" in (American) English mean either a state of matter or liquid petroleum!

Fodor (1991:262) addresses this worry briefly in his reply to Baker (1991) who also raised it. But he only wearily bites the bullet and allows that the tokenings would thereby be ambiguous, since the postulated lockings on the probes would be nominally independent of the lockings on cows.[17] He assures us that his intuitions tell him "it's OK to say that" and admonishes those of us who don't share them "to have them fixed" (p. 262).

Well, I went to have mine fixed and the doctor said (as he often does to philosophers) that there was nothing wrong, indeed, that Fodor seemed to be committed to bad psychology. In the case of "gas" it is surely important that *a speaker be disposed to recognize the ambiguity*; for example, to take the two phenomena to be in the extension of her uses of "gas." By contrast, I am not in the slightest prepared to treat the, so to say, cosmic coincidences in the same way; neither I nor Penfield nor his patients have any reason to think that their thoughts are the slightest bit ambiguous. The subjects' memories and reports, say, "I'm recalling the cows we kept," didn't have as their truth condition *either* [I'm remembering the cows we kept] *or* [My area A is being electrically probed], much less [I'm being bombarded by cosmic rays of frequency f]. Indeed, the subjects needn't have the slightest conception of either electric probes, the relevant areas of their brains, much less even the concept of a cosmic ray.

Still another kind of locking that would seem at least partly fortuitous is presented by cases of essential reliance on experts. There surely are people so mentally impaired that the *only* understanding of the word "quark" available to them (even under, for them, epistemically ideal circumstances) is "whatever those scientists call 'quarks'." They use scientists to detect quarks in the same way schoolboys may look up answers in the back of a book they don't understand. Consequently, if the scientists are thereby locked onto quarks, so are these people. But do we have any explanatory reason at all to suppose they really have the concept, that they really can have thought contents containing [quark], as opposed to a merely deferentially conferred linguistic competence?[18]

Notice that Fodor can't try treating these cases of lockings of actual symbols as involving merely "unexploited" contents, [ray], [probe], [quark]. Since the agent's brain does process "S" in ways characteristic of attitudes, and "S" does, according to the theory, mean [ray] or [poke], the agent would seem to satisfy all the conditions necessary to having attitudes with those contents. If there is a further condition for genuine exploitation, we need to hear of it. It's the condition many of us have been waiting for on something's being genuinely semantic!

In any case, as I stressed in the previous section, locking theories gain their horizontal plausibility from the fact that the reference of such terms as "cow" or "gas" involves whatever real phenomenon the people in your community are "getting at" in their uses of the terms. I doubt that Penfield's patients or anyone in my community—not even Fodor—would be at all inclined to think they've been "getting at" just any phenomenon that happens to be entirely noncognitively locked onto a state of their brain. Such causes do not give rise to any meaning intuitions, they would not enter into cognitive deliberations, and, most importantly, they would not seem to figure in any cognitive psychological laws. Cognitive manipulation by evidence or reasoning related only to the rays or pokes would not *per se* affect the entokenings of "S".[19] Worse, unlike the earlier innocuous cases, here the semantic assignments *interfere* with the psychology.

So it looks as if Fodor has to rule out all such cases. And he does provide a dazzling performance in ruling out many that have been suggested (see Fodor 1987: 110–127, 1990: 100–119, 1991a:255–277, 302–304). He might well do so with the ones I've raised here as well. The pattern he cites is an unusual one, involving simultaneously intuitions about meaning, second-order causal dependencies and internodal distances that are none too easy to sort out.[20] But even if the examples were deflected, the worry remains that it is only the obscurity of the reasonings, Fodor's ingenuity, and/or his opponent's failure of imagination that are doing the work. *For what we really want is a positive argument for believing it.*

In the passage immediately following this quote (pp. 96–100), Fodor does go on to motivate the account by consideration of how ordinary practices with words depend on fixing their extension, but not vice versa. But, as he rightly notes (1990:98), such ordinary fixings of extension involve semantically significant policies; for example, rules and decisions to use words in one way rather than another. Why think we can abstract from them and still have meaning?

It's crucial to see that all that Fodor provides at this point is a mere speculative possibility:

> Now maybe we can kick away the ladder. Perhaps the policies *per se* aren't what matters for semantics; maybe all that matters is the patterns of causal dependencies that the policies give rise to. (1991a:99)

Well, maybe, and, then again, maybe not. What's wanted here is a reason, not for thinking that semantic relations may exhibit asymmetric dependencies, which many might agree that they do; but rather *for thinking we can do away with the ladder.*[21] The apparent counterexamples I and others have mentioned can make one nervous; moreover, there seems to me a reason for thinking we can't just kick away the cognition, a reason grounded in the theoretical work that content ascriptions are supposed to perform. Consequently, mere acrobatics with the examples doesn't reassure.

Neglecting Distinctions

The second difficulty I want to discuss is that a pure externalist account is too crude. Sometimes we are interested not only in what worldly phenomena, if any, an agent is getting at, but *what way of thinking of that phenomenon* she is trying to get at as well; and we have no reason to think that the world is sufficiently rich in phenomena independently of our minds to distinguish among them. Indeed, it is notorious that "extensional" accounts like Fodor's run into standard difficulties of distinguishing among *coinstantiated concepts*; that is, concepts that are instantiated in all the same possible worlds and/or counterfactual situations. There are two kinds: those expressed by *necessarily coextensive* terms, such as "triangle" and "trilateral,"[22] "gorse" and "furze," "circle" and "point equidistant locus of coplanar points" (whatever satisfies one in each of these pairs necessarily satisfies the other); and what might be called the *necessarily codivided* ones, such as "rabbit," versus "undetached rabbit parts," versus "temporal stage of a rabbit"[23] (different things satisfy each of these three expressions, but necessarily whenever an agent is presented with something that satisfies one of them she's presented with something that satisfies the others).

Now, Fodor (1991a) does suggest a reply to cases like these:

> Actually, I'm inclined to think that "WATER" *does* mean the same thing as "H_2O." What doesn't follow—and isn't true—is that having the concept [WATER] is the same mental state as having the concept [H_2O]. (p. 114)

So differences between the necessarily coinstantiated will be differences in the structure of the mental representation that express them.[24] Here, however, it is crucial to bear in mind the terminological points mentioned earlier. What Fodor is hoping is that all the work asked of a theory of concepts as senses—in particular, the work of distinguishing among coinstantiated concepts—can be performed by concepts as *internal representations*. This is a substantive, not merely a terminological point. But there are a number of reasons to doubt that this can be brought off.

In the first place, there are many relations between the two: Different concepts can be expressed by the same type representation, because ambiguities are at least possible even in the brain; and difference type representations may express the same concept, for why shouldn't the brain have its cases of "center" and "center," "furze" and "gorse," "dog" and "hund?"

Secondly, Fodor's hope depends on coinstantiated representations having different structure; but why suppose this is always so? Why shouldn't it be possible for simple representations to be coinstantiated? Although English doesn't afford many examples, this may be due to special facts about public languages, which are, after all, conventional vehicles of communication with many mnemonic features that an internal vehicle of computation could lack. The question of just which of our internal representations have genuine causally efficacious structure is surely a question about the character of internal processing, not settled by reflection on ordinary language alone. "Triangle" may in thought be no more decomposable for an agent into "tri-" and "angle" than "breakfast" really mean breaking a fast.[25] So triangle and trilateral turn out to be simple, coinstantiables after all. In any case, why shouldn't an animal have merely one simple symbol for triangle and one simple symbol for trilateral, rather in the way that we often have several proper names for the same person?[26] Indeed, suppose an animal does have merely one simple symbol that is locked onto triangularity: which content does it have, [triangle] or [trilateral], both or some other? And why shouldn't the answer depend on facts other than orthographic simplicity, for example, on the inferences of which the creature is capable?

Consider in this connection the phenomenon of "subception," whereby many animals are able to recognize groups of things of certain (usually modest) cardinality (Gallistel 1990:chap. 10). Take a pigeon that has been trained to peck at "three-membered patterns." Along the lines of a pure locking theory, we can suppose that one of these animals actually does have an internal symbol that locks onto, say, the property of triplicity: For any sortal property, F-ness, that it can otherwise discriminate, it can also discriminate 3F-ness. Now, does this animal plausibly have the same concept [three] that I have? There's this reason to think not: The concept I (and most of us) is a concept controlled by something like Peano's axioms whereby we can be led by reasonings into understanding a potential infinity of fairly complex arithmetic truths. As Gallistel remarks:

> To discriminate on the basis of numerosity is not, however, to have a concept of number, if by "having a concept of number" we mean that an animal is capable of manipulating [numerical representations] in accord with the relational and combinatorial operations of arithmetic. (p. 348)

Humans who can actually reason arithmetically have what might be called the concept [Peano-three]. [Peano-three] and [subcept-three] certainly pick out the same worldly phenomenon; for a symbol to lock onto the one is for it to lock onto the other. But there is good reason for distinguishing them from a psychological point of view: The cognitive manipulations for the one are not the same as for the other—no amount of argument or reasoning would get a pigeon to realize that $3 = \sqrt[3]{27}$. Indeed, it may well be that normal human beings have both concepts, and that it's informative to learn that subcept-three = Peano-three.[27]

A particularly crucial set of cases of necessarily coinstantiated concepts are the necessarily uninstantiated ones: for example, [largest prime], [round-square], and arguably, [necessary causal connection]. These may not be limited to logically complex cases either. Saul Kripke (1980) has argued that unicorns could not possibly exist—usage of unicorn involved an effort to refer that, since it in fact failed, couldn't possibly succeed with the same meaning. In a different vein, Michael Slote (1975) has argued, nothing could possibly satisfy our concept, [monster]. When "Nessie" of the Loch Ness is ultimately captured, she'll quickly be dissected, analyzed, and classified by the techniques of natural science, after which she'll no longer be a monster, but just another animal (for example, a wayward dinosaur). Similar arguments have been mounted for [miracle] and [magic], and could be mounted for more philosophically interesting cases such as [free will] and [soul].[28] Perhaps some of these cases are spurious. But all that is needed is one. What is a pure locking theory to say of *it?*

Fodor (1990) briefly addresses this problem, and speculates:

> In [the case that unicorns are necessarily non-existent], it's not a law that if there were unicorns they would cause 'unicorn' tokens; laws aren't made true by vacuous satisfaction of their antecedents. Similar lines of argument suggest what appears to be a quite strong consequence of the asymmetric dependence story: no primitive symbol can express a property that is necessarily uninstantiated. (1990:p. 101)

Possibly it will turn out that there is metaphysics enough for all our primitive thoughts, a property for every primitive predicate. But it would seem pretty rash to bet one's theory of content on it.

Fodor does immediately hedge the bet, allowing that

> A syntactically primitive symbol could be . . . introduced by a definition. Whatever, precisely, *that* may mean.(p. 101)

In (1991a), he amplifies this a little further:

> This needs to be taken seriously too—there are all sorts of concepts which either don't express properties ("round cube" and the like) or don't express properties whose instantiation is nomologically possible ("phlogiston" and the like; and maybe "unicorn" depending on your metaphysical views about unicorns). One thus simply can't take the line that *all* concepts have the satisfaction conditions they do because the properties they express enter into the nomic relations that they do. Given all this, I'm tentatively inclined to a two-tiered story: There are primitive predicates (like "horse")—about whose semaniticity the information-plus-asymmetric-dependence story tells the whole and unvarnished truth—; and there are defined predicates (like

"crumpled shirt") which are introduced by definitions (=df *crumpled and shirt*, just as you'd expect. (1991a:256)

But this last concession, of course, compounds the hedge with a fudge: "crumpled shirt" by itself can't be a case of a defined predicate, since—just as indeed you'd expect—it gets its semantics compositionally. What he can't bring himself to say is what clearly follows from the earlier lines, that simple predicates expressing necessarily uninstantiated properties—like "phlogiston" and "unicorn"—are introduced by definitions. Of course, the reason he can't bring himself to say it is that such definitions would then express the very analyticities he's anxious to avoid.[29]

So it seems that, when pressed, Fodor, himself, has to concede that any locking theory will need to be supplemented with some facts about a term's inferential role. Triangle bears certain relations[30] in inference that trilateral lacks; "undetached-proper-rabbit-part," but not "rabbit" entails "is a proper part of a rabbit;" [Peano-three] is implicitly defined by Peano's axioms, [subception-three] merely by its role in discrimination; and [phlogiston], [unicorn], and [free will] by their roles in theories that turn out to be necessarily false. Moreover, I submit, it is by requiring that any locking relations be brought about as the result of the deployment of a defining inferential role that a locking theory can avoid the fortuitous lockings that we saw a pure theory invites.

Of course, we can allow that there may be a theoretically interesting use of concept talk to pick out by merely a purely p-extensional, or for that matter purely Fregean-extensional notion. Gather ye notions where there are laws, and laws wherever ye may. There may well be many different semantic interests, and so many meanings to be assigned a particular token term.[31] The point here is not to exclude extensional approaches to semantics, but to stop them from excluding intentional ones, or at any rate, an interest in finer distinctions and concepts than the pure extensionalist allows. Such concepts are senses, and it is they, for the reasons I have given, that are as indispensable to psychology as psychology is to them.

FODOR'S WORRIES

Now, it's true that supplementing a theory of meaning with an appeal to inferential role invites the notorious analytic–synthetic distinction that Quine made a generation of philosophers eschew (I believe that was the word). Quine based his objections on an attack on truth by convention, an appeal to revisability, claims of confirmation holism, and charges of explanatory vacuity. Elsewhere (Rey 1994), I argue that none of these arguments against the distinction actually work. They depend largely on a behavioristic theory of linguistic capacities and, especially, on what I call "superficialist" assumptions about meaning, that what someone means is a fact readily available in her introspections or her behavioral dispositions. Neither of these views are ones that a cognitive scientist needs to take seriously for a moment.

Indeed, I see no reason why analyses might not express rules that play a special role in controlling the deployment of predicates, but which are (in Stich's phrase) "sub-doxastic" and hence not readily available in either introspection or behavioral dispositions. From a reasonable cognitivist point of view, these are both, after all, surface phenomena involving a plenitude of underlying cognitive causes, only one component of which involves the meaning of symbols deployed.[32] Like the observation/theoretic distinction defended by Fodor (1990:chap. 10), the analytic/synthetic distinction survives best not as the superficially available distinction it traditionally has been taken to be, but as a distinction to be assessed by its role in a deeper theory of cognitive competence and processing. Just as we may not be good judges about what is "given" as opposed to imposed by us, so we may not be good at discriminating, even in our own case, between matters of meaning and matters of merely our beliefs.

The comparison invites a little bit of moralizing. In both the case of the observation/theoretic and the analytic/synthetic distinction, people have been swept up by a very general methodological picture, essentially about the revisability of everything from humdrum observation to far-reaching principles of logic. But surely we ought to be suspicious when a distinction that appears to be explanatory in a specific science is rejected on such very general methodological grounds.[33] Why should the question of whether there is a psychologically interesting distinction between matters of meaning and matters of mere belief turn on grand issues of "realism" and "confirmation holism," as Fodor and LePore (1992) insist? Given the enormous difficulties of getting the philosophy right in these quarters, isn't it far more likely that the explanatory psychology is right and we're simply confused about its connections with those grand issues? Opponents of sense on these general grounds do well to bear in mind the example of Hegel, who deduced the number of planets to be necessarily five.

In fairness to Fodor, he is not exercised only by Quine. He is as much worried by four problems that do seen to arise in framing specifically psychological explanations:

1. The problem of arbitrary divergencies in belief
2. The lack of evidence for lexical decomposition
3. The repeated failures of purported analyses
4. Externalist intuitions

However, if analytic rules are subdoxastic, these phenomena, too, would be unsurprising. Doxastic states may, after all, diverge arbitrarily from subdoxastic ones, given enough interference from other quarters. This is, of course, precisely how we might distinguish perverse philosophers like Berkeley or Hegel from the genuinely mentally impaired. And there is no reason to suppose that analytic rules are in fact deployed in all, or even most cognitive processes. Why access the rule if a handy stereotype would suffice instead? The rules may be deployed only to settle hard cases of the sort that arise in, for example, philosophy or law. Given the subdoxastic status of the rules, articulating them—providing satisfactory analyses—ought to be as hard as any empirical investigation, certainly as hard as speculations about the subdoxastic rules that govern grammar.

I suspect that it's worry, the externalist intuitions, that really convince Fodor, since they at first seem to provide an explanation of all the others. If meaning is as dependent on environmental and social factors in the way that Kripke, Putnam, and Burge have convincingly urged, then that would explain the arbitrary divergencies in belief and the lack of decompositions and successful analyses in a way that didn't presuppose an analytic/synthetic distinction that had been independently discredited by Quine.

But a moment's reflection should reveal that, insofar as the externalist intuitions are remotely plausible, these alternative stories can't be entirely nonpsychological. All of them need to include crucial psychological assumptions. It may be that "meanings ain't" entirely "in the head." But there had better be something in the head that distinguishes someone competent with a concept from someone in the same environment who isn't, for example, Einstein from his cat (or, in some cases, him from you and me). Surely that thing, whatever it is, is a fit topic for psychology. It can't be merely a predicate (which both Einstein and his cat could share) nor, for the reasons I've advanced, can it be merely a predicate locked onto a property, It must be something about how the predicate is deployed, something analogous to the "policies," the ladder of which Fodor was so eager to kick away. That is, it seems to involve something about the role of the predicate in our thought, perhaps a rule that determines that role.

Notice that appeals to subdoxastic analytic rules permit us to explain the externalist intuitions as well as their limitations. A natural suggestion is that in may cases, notably natural kind terms, the rule in the head involves—along the lines of Grice (1965) and Putnam (1975)—a "blank space to be filled in by the specialist," a kind of indexical element that permits a full semantic content to be determined by the context with which the agent interacts, much as the semantics of indexical terms like "I", "now", "this", and "that" do (cf. Kaplan, 1979).[29] The *a priori* analytic claims for such terms would, of course, be a great deal thinner than many philosophers have hoped. They probably would not include "Cats are animals" or "Whales are mammals."[34] But why think those were ever particularly compelling or important examples? Perhaps it is enough that the *a priori* analyticities in these cases involve little more than just such indexical elements. After all, someone who didn't in some way share the externalist intuitions would be someone who arguably really did mean something else by the same terms.[35]

But there are limits to externalism.[36] It certainly appears that some contents are in fact fixed, and not marked for empirical completion. At any rate, it certainly seems significantly harder to run Twin-Earth or Burge-style examples on the case of many of the traditional philosophically interesting concepts; for example, [knowledge], [justice], [piety], [free will]. Such concepts would appear to have much more "fixed" contents than the more purely empirical examples emphasized by Kripke and Putnam (as by Locke before them), which is probably why it was them and not [cat] or [whale] that have received serious philosophical attention.

In any case, the hypothesis that there are subdoxastic analytic rules seems worth exploring as an empirical hypothesis to explain both internalist and externalist intuitions. Separated from the excess philosophical baggage—particularly the superficial doxicity—with which it has been burdened, it also avoids the problems about unrevisability, divergence, confirmation practice, lack of on-line decompositions, and general unavailability that worry Fodor, as they (or some of them) did Quine. At the same time it provides a basis for ruling out the fortuitous locking and for capturing the fine distinctions that I have argued are problems for pure externalism. On this view, semantics and psychology become intertwined. But given all these virtues, who would be so prudish, or Quiniphobic, to object?[37]

NOTES

[1]Compare Fodor (1981:260), where the issue is treated terminologically, with (1991a:114 and chap. 6) and (1994:chap. 2), where it emerges more substantively.

[2]More precisely, "x is water" and "x is H_2O", properties being what correspond to predicates. For other syntactic categories (e.g. sentences) verbs, particles, there are other metaphysical entities (e.g. propositions) relations, into the complexities of which there will be no need to enter here. I will follow Fodor in using "property" metonymously to refer to the lot of them.

[3]In the present discussion, I will not be much concerned with whether Fregean senses *per se* also determine reference, or whether they constitute only a Kaplan (1979)-esque "character," determining reference only in a context. The issue will make only a short appearance in the last section.

[4]It might seem that someone who identifies senses with actual causal chains from a representation to the (kind of) object it designates would be so committed. But the main pro-

ponent of such a view—Devitt 1990—allows that psychology would in such cases deal with a "narrow" sense (i.e. those portions of such chains that are confined to the thinker's head.

[5]The first two begin to emerge explicitly in Fodor (1990:chap. 6), but get obscured by the fact that "functional role"—which many would count as "sense"—gets included as one of the relata of a belief state (pp. 167–169). (Matters are not helped either by vacillation between linking content to P-extensions and linking it to Fregean ones.) A purer version of the first of Fodor's three claims is pursued in Fodor (1994).

[6]Lest the general dialectical situation be obscured, Gabriel Segal (correspondence) has urged me not to forget how odd it is to shoulder the burden of proof in this way, since "until recently, everyone thought that you could believe that Hesperus is Hesperus without thereby believing that Hesperus is Phosphorus. And they thought that the difference between the two thoughts was not merely orthographic, since different orthographic types can express the same concept." Although, *pace* Fodor, it is important to bear in mind in this way the *naturalness* of this traditional idea, it is also worth defending it, if only to clarify the obscurities that were also traditionally attached to it, about, for example, how to distinguish change of concept from charge of belief, how what is in the head determines reference, etc.

[7]"Locking" was introduced in Barry Loewer's and my introduction to our anthology on Fodor, Loewer and Rey (1991). We discuss a number of such theories with an eye to locating Fodor's account among them. I prefer locking, since it suggests naturalistic enough radio and homing devices that seem to me analogous to what is wanted from semantics, along the lines I spell out shortly.

[8]For full details see Fodor (1987, 1990), as well his replies and our introduction in Loewer and Rey (1991). I have omitted a clause that Fodor has only sometimes included, requiring that some Φ tokens actually have been caused by C (nothing in the present paper turns on it, and many suspect that Fodor doesn't really want it).

[9]Strictly speaking, the relata here should be properties: the property of being a tokening of "F," the property of being an alligator—see Fodor (1990:102). But I spare the reader the grotesque English involved in stating it that way.

[10]Note that, as Fodor (1990:96) emphasizes, the condition is only sufficient, not necessary for meaning. Nothing in the present discussion will turn on this.

[11]For example, just what notion of "cp law" is being invoked, what reason there is to believe there are any, how meanings so individuated could be causally efficacious. See Fodor (1991b) and Pietroski and Rey (1996) for relevant discussion.

[12]I am also less terrified that others by the specter of dualism that I suspect makes them so impatient. Is there really a positive scientifically serious dualistic hypothesis in this particular domain that we need to refute?

[13]That is, where the attacks on analyticity and determinacy of translation are usually taken to be a demand for a physical (or "empirical") reduction of the notions, I prefer to think of them as a demand within a mentalistic psychology for a principled basis for claims about meaning.

[14]To be distinguished from the later book of the same name, in which he renounces this earlier view.

[15]Consider the view there really is much goodness in the world, it's just that some people lack the wherewithal to engage it. If we take such lines, we might wonder, though, why Fodor (1990:92ff)—or anyone—would be worried about "pansematicism" in the first place. It's hard not to be sympathetic to Peacocke's (1992:5) "principle of dependence" ac-

cording to which there is nothing more to a concept than its possession condition.

[16]These tokenings might even have played a role in explaining why that state often occurred in my ancestors (perhaps helping them to survive by preventing a certain form of cancer), so satisfying certain purely external teleological theories as well.

[17]He complains (p. 262) that I think civilization has been suffering from insomnia for worrying about this problem. My fear is that, in the face of such difficulties, civilization will just turn over and go back to sleep.

Note that Fodor does seem to allow the possibility—but, again, perhaps only warily, and for the sake of the argument—that "something-or-other's causing 'cow's is asymmetrically dependent on the probes causing them and not on the cows causing them, so probes cause 'cow's robustly" (p. 262). But this suggests that he intends the appeal to ambiguity quite generally, to apply to any cases generated in this fashion.

[18]Peacocke (1992:29), for example, distinguishes conditions for possession of a concept from conditions for the attribution of propositional attitudes containing it, arguing that in cases of defense dependence attributions, the latter can obtain without the former.

[19]Cases of the essential reliance on experts would, of course, involve a borderline case of these considerations, and would require subtler discussion than is possible here—but in any case than is available on Fodor's theory.

[20]Fodor (1991:117) does provide a nice nonsemantic example of symmetric dependence—air foils asymmetrically depend on Bernoulli's law—pointing out that it involves, however, laws with different effects. But, aside from the suspicion that there are probably lots more cases to consider, such examples merely invite further questions about individuating effects, and, more importantly, why in the world just those asymmetric dependencies converging on just one effect should be sufficient for meaning.

[21]To paraphrase Fodor's (1991a:255) own citations from Pooh: "Come on, it's easy" squeaked Roo—not being able to *think* of any problems. But then "there was a crash, and a tearing sound, and a confused heap" of, in the present case, semantic relations all over the ground.

[22]If you find triangle versus trilateral a little too fine for your taste, try equiangular Euclidean triangle versus equilateral Euclidean trilateral—the terms that in high school you had to prove were indeed necessarily coextensive.

[23]Quine (1960:chap. 2) deserves credit for discovering this latter, distinctive category and the interesting puzzles to which it gives rise, even if it's not at all clear that he's entitled to derive from it his sweeping "thesis of the indeterminacy of translation."

[24]Immediately following the previous quote, Fodor directs us to Chapter 6 of that work for further discussion of this distinction. Unfortunately, that discussion is far from clear as regards the issue that concerns us here. However, in Fodor (1994) the view that I set out here emerges.

[25]It would seem perfectly possible for someone learning English to think triangle meant three-sided figure, coming to notice the three angles only on reflection (I recall doing so myself).

[26]Put aside for now the thorny problems of proper name concepts themselves, which deserve (and regularly receive) papers all their own.

[27]A similar distinction could be drawn between a low-level sensory concept of redness and the more theoretically oriented one that Levine (1994) correctly notes many of us deploy.

[28]See Wittgenstein (1967) (and, I'm told, Spinoza) on [miracle], Galen Strawson (1987)

of [free will]. This is certainly one way of taking Parfit (1984) on [personal identity]. For reasons discussed in Rey (1987), I suspect it's true also of [consciousness]: indeed, what I think many of these examples have in common is a peculiar projection of our experience of ignorance (the "mysterious") on phenomena in the world, none of which could possibly have such a property in the intrinsic way we intend. But I don't expect readers to leap to agreement with this suggestion, much less as applied to the last example.

[29]One wonders, too, how the "two-tiered story"—told so to include genuinely defined predicates—sits with the Fodor *et al.* (1980) attack "against definitions." Perhaps it was that attack that was on his mind when he replied to the present argument (at the 1993 NEH summer institute on Meaning at Rutgers) by allowing even necessarily uninstantiated properties as real phenomena onto which a symbol could lock. But then he needs to address the very vacuity objection he raised in the (1990) passage previously quoted.

[30]Note carefully, I am not here in the business of specifying precisely which relations these are. I try to begin to do so in Rey (1994) but, as I emphasize there, the problem shouldn't be seen as one that can be settled independently of a detailed (empirical) theory of cognitive organization (any more than could a theory about the relations involved in, e.g., respiration or metabolism).

[31]Cf. Devitt (1996) and Eric Lormand (in press) who emphasize this source of ambiguity for even token expressions.

[32]Quine is, of course, quite aware of this, simply rejecting on his behaviorist grounds any factual basis for factoring out the one component from the other.

[33]Indeed, grounds that look very like the kinds of *a priori* grounds Quine taught us to abjure (not that, e.g., in relation to behaviorism, he practiced much of what he taught).

[34]Indeed, it is arguably a feature of normal English competence that one ought to be pulled both ways in the debate between Putnam and Katz some years ago on whether cats could turn out to be robots. On an indexical view of natural kind terms, such instability is precisely what one would expect.

This may well have the consequence feared by Block (1991) that all natural kind terms would wind up with the same narrow content (content independent of context). Perhaps the most we could hope for, at least in those cases, are wide analytic truths, which, of course, wouldn't be knowable *a priori*.

[35]This, along the lines of the general rationale for semantics I sketched previously, imagine someone who under ideal epistemic conditions is still unpersuaded, for example, that XYZ isn't water; then there would be no psychological point to ascribing to them the same concept that those of us who are persuaded possess.

[36]Her I've been influenced by Bealer (1982) and Keil (1979).

REFERENCES

Baker, L. (1991). Has content been naturalized? In Loewer and Rey (pp. 17–32).

Bealer, G. (1982). The philosophical limits of scientific essentialism. In *Philosophical perspectives I, metaphysics, 1987*, ed. by J. Tomberlin, Atascadero: Ridgeview.

Block, N. (1991). What narrow content is not. In Loewer and Rey (pp. 33–64).

Devitt, M. (1996). *Coming to our senses: a naturalistic program for semantic localism.* Cambridge: Cambridge University Press.

Devitt, M. (1990). A narrow representational theory of the mind. In Lycan, W., *Mind and cognition: A reader* (pp. 371–398). Oxford: Blackwell .

Fodor, J. (1987). *Psychosemantics*. Cambridge: MIT Press.

Fodor, J. (1990). *A theory of content*. Cambridge: MIT Press.

Fodor, J. (1991a). Replies. In Loewer and Rey (pp. 215–319).

Fodor, J. (1991b). You can fool some of the people all of the time, other things being equal: Hedged laws and psychological explanation. *Mind, Vol, C#1* (pp. 19–34).

Fodor, J. (1994). *The elm and the expert*. Cambridge: MIT Press.

Gallistel, C. (1990). *The organization of learning*. Cambridge: MIT.

Grice, H. (1965). The causal theory of perception. In R. Swartz, *Perceiving, sensing and knowing*. New York: Doubleday.

Kaplan, D. (1979). On the logic of demonstratives. In *Contemporary perspectives in the philosophy of language*. Minneapolis: University of Minnesota Press.

Keil, F. (1979). *Semantic and Conceptual Development*. Cambridge: Harvard University Press.

Kripe, S. (1980). *Naming and necessity*. Cambridge: Harvard University Press.

Levine, J. (1994). Intentional chemistry. In *Grazer philosophica* (which will appear also as *Holism: A consumer update*, ed. by J. Fodor and E. LePore).

Loewer, B. & Rey, G. (1991). *Meaning in mind: Fodor and his critics*. Oxford: Blackwell.

Lormand, E. (1996). How to be a meaning holist. *Journal of Philosophy, XCIII*(2), 51–73.

Parfit, D. (1984). *Reasons and persons*. Oxford: Oxford University Press.

Pietroski, P., and Rey, G. (1995). When other things aren't equal: Saving *Ceteris Paribus* from Vacuity. *British Journal for the Philosophy of Science 46*, 81–110.

Quine, W. (1953). Two dogmas of empiricism. In *From a logical point of view*. New York: Harper & Row.

Quine, W. (1954/1976). Carnap and logical truth. In *Ways of paradox and other essays*. Harvard University Press (first published in 1954).

Quine, W. (1960). *Word and object*. Cambridge: MIT Press.

Quine, W. (1967). *Ontological relativity and other essays*. New York: Columbia University Press.

Rey, G. (1988). A question about consciousness. In H. Otto and J. Tuedio (Ed.), *Perspectives on mind*. Dordrecht: Reidel.

Rey, G. (1994). The unavailability of what we mean I. A reply to Quine, Fodor and LePore. *Grazer philosophica* (will also appear as *Holism: A consumer update*, edited by J. A. Fodor and E. Lepore).

Rey, G. (in press). The unavailability of what we mean II.

Rorty, R. (1979). *Philosophy and the mirror of nature*. Princeton: Princeton University Press.

Strawson, G. (1987). *Freedom and belief*. Oxford: Oxford University Press.

Wittgenstein, L. (1967). A lecture on ethics. *Philosophical Review*.

chapter 4

Perceptual Constancy and the Mind's Eye Looking Through a Telescope

Bela Julesz
julesz@cyclops.rutgers.edu
Laboratory of Vision Research
Rutgers University

Itzhak Hadani
hadani@gandalf.rutgers.edu
Laboratory of Vision Research
Rutgers University

INTRODUCTION

The geometric constancies of position size and shape, during head and eye movements in space, are not fully understood, even if one accepts any of the advanced theories of visual stability that were recently published in two target papers in the same issue of *Behavioral and Brain Sciences* (Bridgeman, van der Heijden, & Velichkovsky, 1994; Wertheim, 1994). These explanations compete with the original concept of efferent copy that nulls the movement signals on the retina (von Holst, 1954), yet leave some unsolved puzzles. How is it possible that static objects, closer or farther from a static surround, appear at a standstill instead of moving faster or slower than the static surround? Furthermore, how is it possible that correcting glasses, prisms, and other prosthetic optical devices that slightly magnify or diminish the retinal image, do not affect the stability of the visual world after brief adaptation? Here, we propose that in order to achieve stability for objects at different distances from the viewer's eye, the objects may be represented as if viewed via a *1:1 magnification* telescope at (a) *optical infinity*, as if the image projected on the mind's

39

eye were collimated (Julesz, 1995), or (b) at their veridical distance (Hadani, et al., 1978; 1980a). The first suggestion diminishes the stability problem for linear shifts of the eye and provides a way to solve the rotational component. The second suggestion treats both components of eye movements computationally.

The simplest nonmagnifying collimator is a telescope that requires two lenses of equal focal length (and of course, more than two compound lenses can both collimate the input and correct for many aberrations of the first lens). We propose that one of the lenses of the mind's eye is the optics of the eye; the cascaded lens is provided by the neural computation mechanism and encompasses (a) the retinal and extraretinal signals that encode the motion of the eye and the head in space, and (b) a cortical zooming mechanism that operates at anatomical mapping of various brain areas from the fovea to V1, V2, and higher visual centers. Thus, the mind's eye can be conceived as a fictitious observer in the form of an array of spatiotopically mapped receptive fields, viewing the world through a 1:1 magnification telescope.

Visual Stability as Treated by Three Main Streams in Perception

The visual world, as described by Gibson (1950; 1966; 1979) has the property of being stable and unbounded. By stability, Gibson meant that the perceived world does not seem to move when one turns his eyes or his head around. By unboundedness, he meant that the perceived world does not seem to have anything like a visible circular or oval window frame. Thus, the phenomenal world seems to stay put, to remain upright, and to surround us completely. This experience, according to Gibson, is what a theory of perception must explain (Gibson, 1966). Another difficulty for any theory of perception is the fact that the organism cannot scrutinize his retinal image directly, but only after some major transformations have taken place by early and unconscious mechanisms of visual processing. Pure projective geometry considerations tell us that the two-dimensional retinal image is optically inverted, distorted (due to the spherical structure of the eye), and constantly moving and jumping across the receptors (due to the combined motion of the eyes in the head and the head motion in space). Yet, neither these expected image distortions, nor the retinal slips (or the resultant blur) are normally perceived. Moreover, objects are also perceived monocularly out there and at different distances from the eye.

Attempts to address the problem of objects' constancies (or the problem of visual stability) can be classified into three main categories:

1. The traditional inferential approach
2. The Gibsonian direct perception approach
3. The computational approach

The traditional inferential view regards visual stability as a large problem that is solved by several subsystems and with the aid of a great number of cues (see Shebilske, 1977). Different explanations suggest that we perceive static environment as static, depending on the outcome of the following mechanisms: (a) the elimination mechanism that uses subtraction; (b) the translation mechanism (the take-into-account explanation) that uses compensation; (c) the evaluation mechanism; and more recently, (d) the calibration mechanism. (For a detailed discussion on the differences between the various mechanisms, see Shebilske, 1977; Bridgeman, et al., 1994.)

Two general notes on the inferential approach: First, most explanations concentrate on eye movements (pure rotations) relative to the head, leading, at best, to egocentric representation that is not time invariant. This drawback was remedied partially by the direct approach (Gibson, 1966; 1979) and has received an important role in Wertheim's (1994) model. Second, the role of distance of objects from the eye in visual stability is underestimated. Therefore, depth perception and visual stability were treated separately.

The second category includes the Gibsonian direct perception and Wertheim's theory. Gibson (1950) has pointed out that the retinal projections contain considerably more information on the visual world than has been assumed by the traditional inferential approach. The transformations that successive retinal projections of the same rigid object are undergoing during locomotion of the observer contains some "higher-order" variables, that are candidates for the extraction of signals that could specify eye movements. Thus, the Gibsonian approach assumes that the perception of ego and objects' motion is derived exclusively from retinal afferent information, and explanation of visual stability does not need the concept of extraretinal signal (Wertheim, 1994). Although Gibson (1966) recognized that vestibular and somatosensory afferent may also contribute to the percept of egomotion, in a later paper (Gibson, 1968), he takes these signals as having only a role of confirmation. A major point of difference between the direct and the inferential approaches is that the former assumes that in normal vision, perception is veridical.

Attempts to bridge the gaps between the first two approaches include the Dual Mode model and the Wertheim model. The Dual Mode theory (Mack, 1978; Matin, 1986) has developed from concepts originally formulated by Wallach (Wallach, 1959) to explain the phenomenon of center-surround induced motion. According to the Dual Mode theory, there exist two modes of visual perception: (a) A direct mode, in which extraretinal signals play no role, and that yields veridical percepts, and (b) An inferential mode, which makes use of extraretinal signals, and that may yield illusions of motion. The theory assumes that there are two kinds of cues that may generate a percept of motion: *object-relative* and *subject-relative* cues. The object-relative cues stem from motion of objects relative to each other. The subject-relative cues stem from object motion relative to the observer. Wertheim (1994) presents evidence that shows the logic of the Dual Mode theory is flawed because the empirical criterion for distinguishing between the two modes is questionable. In turn, Wertheim (1994) presents a more comprehensive theory of visual stability in which retinal and extraretinal signals are combined and create a reference signal that encodes the movement of the retinal surface in the inertial space. An important point in Wertheim's theory is the recognition of the fact that extraretinal signals are partial or inaccurate and therefore, cannot serve as a reliable source for visual stability (Wertheim, 1994; see also Howard, 1986). The later argument provides the retinal signals a crucial role in establishing object constancies.

Common to most explanations of visual stability is the consideration of the visual stimulus as a homogeneously moving pattern in the fronto-parallel plane. Differential motion of surface points, as well as a surface's egodistance, is not usually considered. In our view, this oversimplification is a serious drawback of both approaches and leads to qualitative models of restricted nature. The drawback can be remedied by the rigorous computational approach where the frame of reference of the reconstructed objects is explicitly specified (see Hadani & Julesz's commentary in Wertheim, 1994). However, computational analysis of the stability problem led to a different theoretical deadlock, which is the *indeterminacy* of the obtained solutions. The only determinate solution in the computational approach was obtained by a navigational theory of space perception advanced by one of us (Hadani, et al., 1978; 1980a; Hadani, 1991; Hadani, et al., 1994) and is now called the Space Perception In Navigation (SPIN) theory (Hadani, 1995). In general, the computational approach has no metaphorical window to elucidate what 3-D reconstruction, or what shape from motion computations, means with respect to the mind's eye. Therefore, in the following sections, we discuss various computational solutions and suggest the type of metaphorical window that can represent them.

Computational, navigational models differ from the two earlier approaches by also considering, within the context of visual stability, the egodistance and the 3-D structure of objects. (Hadani, et al., 1978; 1980a; Longuet-Higgins & Prazdny, 1980; Bruss & Horn, 1983). Because of the complexity of the stability problem, the computational models are usually restricted to static (rigid) objects and the perceptual constancy problem is reduced to the analysis of the ability to recover from the optic-flow the six motion parameters of the eye (the reference signal), the egodistance, and/or the structure of objects. Bruss and Horn, (1983) call this capacity *Passive Navigation*, a notion that we take as equivalent to the direct perception concept, with the exception that rigorous mathematics have been added. Several approaches are used to address the issue: the *discrete approach* (Longuet-

Higgins, 1981; Hadani, et al., 1980a; Meiri, 1980; Nagel, 1981; Tsai & Huang, 1985), the *differential approach* (Koenderink & van Doorn, 1976; Longuet-Higgins & Prazdny, 1980), and the *least squares approach* (Prazdny, 1981; Bruss & Horn, 1983). Works in the discrete and differential approaches are also characterized by analyzing the minimum conditions under which an ideal observer can solve the passive navigation problem. These minimal conditions are given in terms of a number of points and views. The most rigorous solution was advanced by Tsai and Huang (1984). They show that seven points and two views are required to recover the distance and the motion parameters (but up to a scalar in the translation vector). Longuet-Higgins and Prazdny (1980) show that the structure of object and motion parameters can be recovered from a single point and its near neighborhood (again, up to a scalar in the translation vector). Thus, the solutions in the computational approach face a scale ambiguity problem.

In contrast to the common view in computational vision, and in line with the concept of direct perception, the SPIN theory claims that the passive navigation problem has a unique solution, and this claim is supported by showing an existence proof (Hadani, et al., 1994; Kononov, 1996). Furthermore, the SPIN theory suggests three intrinsic "hard-wired" measures: (a) the radius of the eyeball, (b) the fixed distance between the head system origin and the eye system origin, and (c) the Interocular Distance—as metric units to scale the objects in physical units. The general solution offered by the SPIN theory for both passive and active navigation (without or with extraretinal signals, respectively) was possible because of the clear distinction that was made between retino-centric, head-centric and object-centric representations (Hadani, 1995). The analysis attaches to each system a separate coordinate system and utilizes linear transformations to exchange representations between the different frames of references. For example, to solve the isolated passive navigation problem, there is no need to consider the head system, but only the eye and space systems as frames of reference. Then, the 3-D coordinates of objects are projected onto the retina through a pinhole and get a 2-D retino-centric representation. Optic-flow analysis is then applied to calculate the egodistance of each image point and the six motion parameters of the eye in space. The egodistance of each point, with its 2-D retinal location, accomplishes a 3-D retinotopic representation. Knowing the relative orientation between the eye system and the object system enables the projection of the retino-centric representation into object-centric representation. The object-centric representation reflects the "out-thereness" of the perceptual experience. Furthermore, because linear transformations are invariant to the position of static points as well as to the distance function, then position, size, and shape constancies are preserved in mental representation. Because this solution relies only on retinal information, a question is raised as to how such a system can confirm the veridicality of its solution. The consideration of this question in the context of normal and prosthetic vision led us to the statement of the magnification and distance paradoxes to be described in Section 4. Let us first examine, however, the meaning of visual perception offered by the three approaches as reflected by their metaphorical windows.

THE DIFFERENT WINDOWS METAPHORS AND
THE TELESCOPE

To explain to novice students the essence of visual perception, investigators in the inferential approach introduce the concept of a projection plane in front of the observer (Goldstein, 1996; Cutting, 1986) as shown in Figures 4.1a and 4.1b. In Figures 4.1a,b the window is static with respect

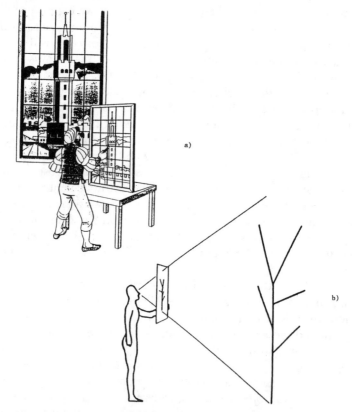

FIGURE 4.1.   Two illustrations of Alberti's window metaphor.
(a)   An artist painting a perspective using the Alberti's window method (From Goldstein, 1996.)
(b)   Schematic illustration of the Alberti's window utilized in a "structure from motion" treatise (From Cutting, 1986.)

to both space and the observer's vantage point. In our view, this ancient metaphor, called *Alberti's window*, is misleading. First, it does not account for many of the static features of the retinal image like spherical distortion, inversion, etc. Second, if the window or the observer moves, the position of the objects' representations in the window will change. Thus, position, size, and shape constancies are not preserved. Third, the image would be blurred by motion. Fourth, no veridical space perception can be recovered from a static image. Furthermore, this kind of interpretation of space perception leads to the most ambiguous theoretical situation where, in principle, an infinite family of spatial objects of different shapes and of different orientations may have the same retinal representation, or conversely, the same retinal image may evoke the percept of an infinite number of real objects having different shapes and orientations as illustrated in Figure 4.2.

The analogous metaphor in direct perception attaches the window to the observer's head. Figure 4.3, which illustrates this metaphor, is depicted by Gibson as an upgrading of one made by Mach (1959), was entitled *The Visual Ego* (Figure 4.4). *The Visual Ego* metaphor better represents the dynamic nature of vision. Gibsons' improvisation of the Visual Ego is comprised of three snapshots (Figure 4.3). Each snapshot is made for a different heading direction. However, the three snapshots may not immediately

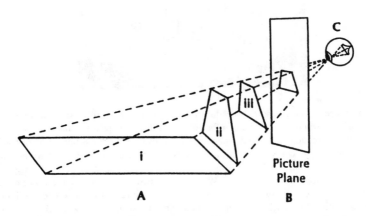

Note: Different layouts (i, ii, iii) in different orientations project the same two-dimensional patterns in the picture plane B that represent Alberti's window, and consequently on the retina of the eye C. (From Hochberg, 1971).

FIGURE 4.2.   The common view in visual perception regarding the uncertainty in object reconstruction.

Note: The three drawings show three different snapshots of Gibson's study as seen by his mind's eye while sitting on a comfortable chair. Each snapshot is made for a different heading direction. The three snapshots demonstrate the "out-thereness" of the perceptual experience. Note that Gibson's nose is shown in all three drawings occupying the same position. The TV set, which is one of the external static objects, occupies different positions. The question is: Which of the two, the TV set or the nose, has time invariant representation in Gibson's mind's eye? The reader can easily test and answer this question himself by rotating her head about a vertical axis while fixating a static object and attending to her nose. The reader will realize that the external static objects are perceived as static while her nose is perceived as moving relative to the static object. (From Gibson, 1979.)

FIGURE 4.3. Gibson's improvisation of the *Visual Ego* metaphor originally advanced by Mach.

Note: This metaphor is named by Mach as the *Visual Ego*.

FIGURE 4.4.   The world seen by the left eye as depicted by Mach.

reflect what Gibson meant by his conception of the mind's eye. Let us suggest our interpretation of these drawings. In our view, they demonstrate, in the first place, the "out-thereness" of the perceptual experience, e.g., that objects are perceived out there in space and not on some internal 2-D neural screen. Moreover, the reader may note that Gibson's nose is shown in all three drawings occupying the same position. Gibson's nose is an object that is attached to his head, and in this respect, it is egocentered. The TV set shown in all three drawings is an external static object, but occupies different positions. Thus, the pertinent question here is: Which of the two, the TV set or the nose, has a time invariant representation in Gibson's mind's eye? The reader can easily test and answer this question by rotating his head about a vertical axis while fixating, monocularly, a static object and attending to her nose. The reader may realize that the external static objects are normally perceived as static, while her nose is perceived as moving relative to the static object.

The meaning of the Visual Ego metaphor is that perception can be conceived as a process that turns the eyeball into a transparent window in front of the mind's eye, which is situated inside the skull. This analogy makes objects to be perceived as being stable and as to be viewed as out there and presumably, at their veridical distances. The transparent window metaphor apparently eliminates the need to compensate the retinal image shifts against head movements because the window is firmly attached to the head (though it still requires stabilization of the image against eye movement). This kind of representation, as the SPIN theory analysis can show, leads to egocentric (or head-centric) representation, which is time variant, and does not represent what we normally experience when we observe the world through the Visual Ego. As mentioned earlier, the visible top of our nose is seen as moving relative to the stationary environment as would be expected in object-centric representation. Only with attentional effort can we perceive the objects moving relative to the nose, had the representation been head-centric. (Note that the ability to switch between the two modes expands the Dual Mode theory in the sense that different external objects—body centered, stationary, or moving—can be perceptually selected as our world's static frame-of-reference). In order to get a prolonged static (time invariant) percept of objects, one has to transform a retino-centric or head-centric representation that one may have at some stage of early computations, into object-centric representation. This can be done navigationally by integrating the "reference signal" (Hadani, et al., 1994; Hadani, 1995). Integration is obtained by updating the transformation matrices that describe the momentary relative position of the eye–head and head–space systems. Although Gibson was not aware of the available mathematical tools required to elucidate this point, we believe that he intuitively realized the object-centric character of perception because he had indicated that direct perception is not characterized by egocentric representation (Gibson, 1979, p. 201). Moreover, the SPIN theory disagrees with the interpretation given to direct perception by computational investigators, regarding it as a look-up table (Ullman, 1980). The SPIN theory analysis suggests that Gibson was theoretically correct about the notion of direct perception by showing that passive navigation can be obtained analytically. The question is, whether it can be obtained empirically (see Discussion).

What is the analogous metaphor of the computational approach? Practically, the retinal image is taken as the effective window, as shown in Figure 4.5. However, the indeterminate solution means that on the sole basis of retinal signals we cannot perceive absolute depth, but only relative depth. Therefore, indeterminate solutions cannot achieve veridical object's constancies. The theoretical implication of this kind of indeter-

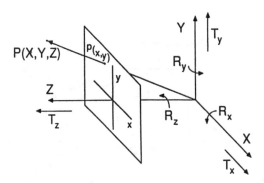

Note: The cartesian coordinate system is attached to the moving eye where origin is coinciding with the pinhole (exit pupil). Thus, the window shown is also attached to the eye
and is positioned in front of the pupil. (From Simpson, 1993.)

**FIGURE 4.5. A standard window "metaphor" utilized by the computational
approach to define the optic flow.**

minacy is illustrated in Figure 4.6 by a family of parallel trapezoids. The
reader should note that the degree of perceptual ambiguity obtained in
the inferential approach (Alberti's window) is greatly reduced by the
computational approach because the family of possible objects that can
be reconstructed is limited to affine (or zooming) transformation. In
other words, this means that we cannot perceptually distinguish between
a near, but small object and far, but large object (Ullman, 1979, p. 199;
Bruss & Horn, 1983). Moreover, it means that Wertheim's reference signal cannot be uniquely recovered and that visual stability can be obtained
only with extraretinal information because they also encode the motion
parameters of the eye in space. However, as noted earlier, the extraretinal
signals are partial and inaccurate; thus, they cannot conceivably serve as a
reliable source that supplement visual stability during fixations. They presumably serve the role of filling in the reference signal during saccades,
e.g., when retinal signals are ineffective (see Hadani, et al., 1994; Hadani,
1995).

 This discussion naturally raises the following question: Given that the
retinal image is not a good metaphor for mental representation, what kind
of metaphor could better represent the computational approach? As a first
approximation, we would like to adopt the Visual Ego, suggested by Mach
and elaborated by Gibson, for head movements. However, analysis of space
perception in the context of prosthetic vision (Section 4), brought us to
arrive at the telescope metaphor to be presented next.

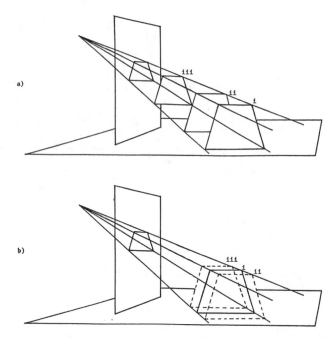

Note: The three trapezoids represent an infinite family of parallel objects having a size scaled by the distance from the vantage point (compare with Figure 4.2). (b) The degree of uncertainty, further diminished by the SPIN theory from infinite family of objects to a single object at the veridical depth (trapezoid i).

Note: The ambiguity interval in reconstructing egodistance on sole basis of motion parallax cue is depicted by the dashed trapezoids (ii, iii) that are flanking trapezoid i.

FIGURE 4.6.   (a) The solid trapezoids (i, ii, iii) demonstrate the reduced uncertainty in object reconstruction obtained by the computational approach.

THE TELESCOPE METAPHOR

The simplest nonmagnifying telescope requires two lenses of equal focal lengths (and of course, more than two complex compound lenses can both collimate the input and correct for many aberrations of the first lens). We propose that one of the lenses of the telescope is the optics of our eye; the cascaded lens is provided by the retinal and extraretinal signals and some neural circuits that can zoom (scale) the size of the perceived objects with their perceived distances. One of the features of these neural circuits may be the cortical magnification factor in anatomical mapping of various brain areas from the fovea to V1, V2, and higher visual centers that may provide several computational simplifications. The other feature is a neural zooming mechanism that operates at early stages of visual processing. The mind's eye, in this metaphor, is the collimated image at the output of the telescope that is captured by an array of spatiotopically mapped receptive fields.

The importance to space perception of the cortical magnification factor, in the form of a multiple logarithmic transformation, has been suggested by Schwartz (1980) in order to perform some affine transformations that seem to simplify operations that occur in form perception [e.g., retinal polar coordinates are transformed on V1 to the conceptually simpler cartesian coordinates]. Here, we argue that this factor, which may seem to introduce severe deformations in the representation of objects in the visual cortex, presumably, may play an additionally important role in visual stability by enabling a simple (similar) matching between two spherical systems that play a role in the control of eye movements: the fixed-with-respect-to-the-eye retinal polar system and fixed-with-respect-to-the-head orbital system. Both systems, being spherical, may be best represented with polar (or spherical) coordinates. Then, simple matching between the two systems can be obtained only when the eye is in the primary position and both systems coincide. However, when the eye maintains a secondary or tertiary position, there is no match between the two. Had the attention-driven, oculomotor-control mechanism utilized polar coordinates, more complicated computations to calculate the ballistic trajectories of saccades from one orbital position to another would be required. Much simpler computations may be required if the retinal and the orbital coordinates are similar. This can be obtained, as suggested by Schwartz, by multiple logarithmic transformations converting both systems into cartesian. Then, rotations between the two systems are converted into translations.

The other feature, suggested as a mechanism for the cascaded lens, is the neural zooming circuits. The conjecture that such mechanisms are used is supported by the size constancy phenomenon, stated as Emmert's law. Indeed, objects are perceived as having constant size even as their retinal image increases manyfold when they are viewed at reduced range. It can easily be shown with afterimages or with a tiny monitor attached to one's spectacles frame that the perceived image on the monitor, or the afterimage, shrinks as one inspects surfaces at increasingly closer ranges in order to achieve size constancy. Obviously, some cortical zooming mechanism at a rather early stage must perform this zooming operation. Furthermore, it has been suggested that infinitesimal affine transformations (also called Lie-germs, after the mathematician Sophus Lie) performed in the visual cortex can produce size and shape constancies (Hoffman, 1970; Dodwell, 1983) and emulated as a model on the Connection Machine by Papathomas and Julesz (1989).

Our suggestion that the retinal signals with the extraretinal signals and/ or neural zooming circuits might be used to supplement the eye's optic by acting as a telescope in the viewer's perceptual system (what we call the mind's eye). We think this is novel and can explain many seeming para-doxes of visual stability. Whether this hypothesis can be experimentally confirmed remains to be seen, but as a possibility, it has some heuristic appeal.

THE MAGNIFICATION PARADOX

Analysis of realistic visual situations by utilizing the Visual Ego metaphor leads to several perceptual puzzles, particularly its inadequacy to account for prosthetic vision. These puzzles become more enigmatic when observ-ers use low power prosthetic optical devices, such as correction glasses that modify the effective magnification of the retinal image without affecting the stability of the perceptual experience. However, when the power of the optical device is high, such as a binocular with 3× magnification or higher, the observer can hardly adapt to the impairment in stability (Demer, et al., 1991). One of the aims of the present article is to state these puzzles and to suggest ways to resolve them with the help of the telescope metaphor. Because visual stability is basically a monocular phenomenon applicable to static objects, we will ignore problems of binocular vision and the percep-tion of real motion.

Perceptual constancy, however, does hold under two puzzling circum-stances:

1. When objects are in front or behind a reference plane (platform), and therefore, should move faster or slower than the platform, respectively, and with increased (or decreased) velocities as their distances from the platform become larger (or smaller), they are seen as stationary. For those workers in perception who do not believe in the percept of abso-lute depth, this perceived stability of the stationary, visual world—regardless of distance—is particularly enigmatic. We call this the *Dis-tance Paradox.*

2. When optical devices are attached to the head in front of the viewer's eye with magnifications slightly larger or smaller than 1:1, one would assume that the stabilized platform at 1:1 magnification would drift faster (or slower) than the observer's head and eye movements as the optical magnification is larger (or smaller) than 1:1. Nevertheless, although new prescription glasses might cause momentary errors of visual stability, the visual system quickly adapts to the new glasses result-ing in complete stability. Readers who wear bifocals, can verify that there is always a visible shear motion in the boundary of a bifocal lens. Only one side of the two half lenses can be stabilized at a time. We argue that

perceptual phenomenon obtained in the unadapted aperture creates a *Magnification Paradox.*

In the sequel, we propose that both paradoxes can be resolved by the telescope metaphor (a) when the retinal projection is a collimated and stabilized array; thus, effectively originating from a projection center at infinity, and (b) when the objects are perceived at their veridical distances. We also propose that in normal uncorrected vision or after adaptation to an optical device, the effective magnification of the visual world at the mind's eye is 1:1 and the scene is perceived as stable in spite of eye and head rotations. However, when the magnification of an optical device is high and cannot be adapted, the perceived distance of the scene changes too.

Some Observations on Visual Stability with Prosthetic Vision

In order to better understand the magnification paradox, one may imagine a situation in which a visual scene is observed monocularly through a high magnifying monocle (1:3 or higher) that is attached firmly to the head (a monocle of a magnifying binocular can serve for that purpose). Alternatively, in the case of low power devices, where adaptation is fast, one may try to monocularly view the visual scene via a bipartite field (e.g., through both parts of bifocal glasses or through the border of simple correcting glasses). Then, rotating the head results in visible shear motion at the border. If the magnification imposed by the optical device is smaller than that of the unaided eye (as is the case with a single negative correction lens), then that part of the scene observed through the lens, and not adapted, will move in the same direction of the head movement while the other part will remain stationary. If the magnification imposed by the optical device is larger than that of the unaided eye (as is the case with positive correction lens), then the scene will swing in a direction opposite to the head rotation. When the whole scene is observed via a high power device, the magnified image cannot be stabilized by adaptation and the image will move in the opposite direction of the head. (The inverse effect occurs by inverting the binocular and observing the scene via the objective lens.) These image swings actually mean an impairment to the visual stability that any observer, with noncorrected vision, normally experiences. Furthermore, with bifocal or single-lens corrective glasses, one can easily observe that it is possible to stabilize either part of the visual field voluntarily and almost without practice, but it is impossible to stabilize both parts simultaneously.

It can be shown that an observer can adapt to different whole field magnifications introduced to the two eyes. This capacity indicates that the visual system can adapt to small magnification variations, and that this adaptation is probably carried out by independent monocular mechanisms.

Having pointed out situations in which a magnifying device impairs visual stability in one direction of the head rotation and an image diminishing device impairs stability in the opposite direction, let us define *unity magnification* as the magnitude of the apparent magnification of the perceived scene viewed with a normal, unaided eye when no impairment of visual stability is observed. The last definition is different from the magnification of the optical apparatus of the eye—the cornea and the lens—in the sense that it refers to the apparent magnification at the mind's eye. Adopting the definition of unity magnification, one can visualize the mind as a fictitious observer (say, an array of spatiotopically mapped receptive fields) situated inside the skull, observing the world through a unity magnification telescope. Unity magnification means that the scene observed by the mind's eye is not distorted as would be expected from the high refracting power of the eye's optics and from the cortical magnification factor. Indeed, unity magnification also means that the angular velocity of the perceived image is opposite but equal to the angular velocity of the head. Then, for a stable scene, the ratio of the perceived image-angular velocity to the head-angular velocity equals one and the difference between the two (the amount of instability) equals zero.

Now, imagine a situation where the head of a human observer rotates by an integral rotation about a vertical axis while the eye maintains the primary position at the beginning and at the end of the head rotation. Then, pure kinematical considerations show that the observer's eye rotated exactly by an integral rotation in space about a vertical axis (for better realization of the physical situation of integral rotation of the eye in space, one may consider the observer's eye fixed to his or her head throughout the whole rotation). The magnification paradox becomes obvious when one considers two cases of a rotating monocular observer: (a) the observer has normal uncorrected vision and is equipped with a cross-hair in front of her eye; the cross-hair is attached to her head and centered at the optical axis in the primary position, and (b) the observer is equipped with a magnifying device having a reticle with a central cross-hair. In case (a) the observer should not experience any image instability. In case (b), however, the visual scene observed, via the monocle, is perceived to be continuously moving relative to the head. As we indicated earlier, the magnitude of the image movement is sign dependent and is a monotonic function of the magnifying index of the monocle (Case b). It should be zero for the unaided eye (Case a). However, in both cases, when the integral head rotation is accomplished, he or she will see, coinciding with the cross-hair, exactly the same visual point that was overlapped by the cross-hair at the initiation of the rotation. The enigma here is that a spatial point viewed via a magnifying device with the head performing one integral rotation (that makes the point to be perceptually moving via the metaphorical window at an angular velocity different than the head), ends up with perceiving the same point at the same position, as when the head rotation had been started. This result is in contrast with the expectation that the positional error of the unstable image will reset itself as some point of the integral rotation, or alternatively accumulate and create a positional error at the end of the rotation. Yet, the reader can verify that no reset occurs and positional error is not integrated. Thus, image instability creates a magnification paradox.

DISCUSSION

Essential differences between three approaches in cognitive psychology, all dealing with the problem of perceptual constancy, were examined in this chapter with the help of their representative metaphors. This examination required, in the first place, identification of the metaphor that best represents each of these approaches. Thus, our choice may be disputable and needs justification. The Alberti's window did not create a problem because it is extensively used in old and modern treatises of sensation and perception (Goldstein, 1996). As for the visual ego, we argue that although Gibson himself used Alberti's window in his latest book to illustrate the ambiguity that perspective projections creates to vision (Gibson, 1979), we believe that the visual ego is a better representation of Gibson's view, at least, it is at the latest evolutionary stage of his theory. Moreover, different improvised Mach's visual ego appeared in his 1950 and 1966 books, and indicate that this provocative metaphor of the mind's eye attracted his attention and motivated him to add his own interpretation that also appeared in his 1979 book (Figure 4.3). Our choice of the retinal image as a tentative metaphor for the computational approach was based on the standard definition of the optic flow (Bruss & Horn, 1993; Simpson, 1993). However, as indicated earlier, the nature of the effective window, after the computations are carried out, remains ambiguous, leaving room to suggest the telescope metaphor as one that may inspire the computational approach.

The telescope metaphor has all the advantages of the ego metaphor and more. Being attached to the head, it emulates the need to compensate for rotational head movements. The input to the mind's eye in this metaphor is taken as the image that is created by the cascaded neural lens at the exit of the telescope. Thus, static objects in front of a static platform are seen as static when the eye moves because motion parallax is diminished for this collimated image—and may provide an answer to the distance paradox. The zooming mechanism emulates adaptation to correcting glasses, prisms, and other optical devices, making the metaphor a suitable model for both normal and prosthetic vision. It may provide an answer to the magnification paradox with the assumption that the ratio of the perceived and veridical distances equals the magnification of the telescope, and that unity magnification may yield veridical perception of distance. Moreover, a standard telescope generates linear shifts, rotations, and zooming, that are analogous to global affine transformations of translation, rotations, and dilation/contraction, respectively. Thus, visual stability in this model can be obtained by compensating just for this subgroup of the Lie transformations. Indeed, all these features of the telescope are presumably accomplished by the hypothetical cascaded lens that emulates neural processing of retinal and extraretinal signals. In conclusion, the telescope metaphor suggests that the perceptual problem of visual stability (or object constancy) can be metaphorically reduced to *geometric optics*.

The consideration of the metaphorical windows, as a reference for comparison between the three approaches, provided a simple way to illustrate the differences in the uncertainty of object reconstruction embedded in the different models. This uncertainty is shown to be the greatest in the inferential approach, it is considerably narrowed by the computational approach, and diminished by the direct perception approach. In the SPIN theory, it is reduced to a measurement error. In this context, we note that Ullman's interpretation of the ambiguity entailed in the computational approach, e.g., that "we cannot perceptually distinguish between a near but small object and far but large object" is correct but may have additional meaning. Here, we would like to suggest an alternative theoretical interpretation to the scale ambiguity in the computational approach which is more relevant to the core issue of this chapter. The scale ambiguity in the solution of system of differential equations, derived by the computational models, stems from the fact that the number of unknowns is greater (by one) than the number of equations. Yet, a navigational–computation scheme (integration) can be applied even with this handicapped system of equations by assigning, as an initial condition, an arbitrary value for one of the unknowns such as egodistance or motion. The interesting consequence of this "trick" is that the system would produce a solution that retains position size and shape constancies across time. However, the reconstructed world and the motion parameters given by this solution would not be veridical except when the initial value assigned is veridical. Moreover, such a system may retain this nonveridical solution without sensing its contradiction with the physical world. An active system, on the other hand, can use the vestibular signals that are anchored to the inertial space to confirm the veridicality of its solution (Gibson, 1968) and to set the initial value to a veridical one. In humans, when a disparity between the visual and vestibular signals exists, they evoke the physiological unpleasant feel-ings of motion sickness. The fact that we normally do not experience motion sickness may suggest that in normal vision, there is an agreement between visual and vestibular signals and perception is veridical.

The previous arguments tap the crux of the difference between the views of the two authors, as were reflected in the two versions of the telescope metaphor. The first view (BJ) is in agreement with the consensus in computational vision about the perceptual implications of the scale ambiguity problem. Thus, this view adheres to the perception of relative depth. The second view (IH) is grounded on the SPIN theory's derivations and agrees with Gibson's claim about the veridicality of space perception. Thus, this view adheres to the notion of absolute depth perception. Indeed, this kind of dispute should be resolved empirically by conducting a crucial experiment that will decide between the two views. Because no such experiment is yet envisioned, we would like to present an additional observation involving prosthetic vision that may lead to the design of such a crucial experiment. The suggested observation becomes meaningful with the following two premises: (a) The same object cannot simultaneously occupy two different locations in space, and (b) In prosthetic vision, the perceived distance of a scene varies with the magnification of the device.

The observation requires a simple negative lens (a correcting glass for myopia may suffice) that is mounted on one's head a few centimeters in front of the eye and covers only part of the visual field. The scene should be static. Due to the optical interference, some of the objects, viewed close to the border of the lens, create double images (e.g., monocular diplopia). The first question raised by this observation is: Which of the two perceived double representations of the same object better represents its veridical position? Applying small head rotations may reveal that one, or both, of the images may be perceived as drifting contingent with the head rotations. As noted earlier, it is likely that one of the double images may be adapted to yield a stable percept. Thus, the second question is: What is the meaning of the stability perceived under these circumstances? Or equivalently, what is the perceptual meaning of the notion of unity magnification? The significance of this kind of observation in resolving the dispute of relative–absolute depth perception stems from the fact that the two parts of the diplopic object have the same extraretinal signals.

In summary, Alberti's window is an ancient metaphor that does not faithfully represent that state of the art in perception. Gibson's version of Mach's inspiring visual ego metaphor better represents the dynamic nature of vision and the problem of perceptual constancy. The newly derived and more sophisticated telescope metaphor may account for both normal and prosthetic vision and is suggested here as a challenge for the computational approach. Our observations on perception, using prosthetic vision, lead to certain paradoxes that should be resolved empirically and may provide an answer to the dispute on relative–absolute depth perception.

ACKNOWLEDGMENTS

The authors wish to thank Alex Kononov for collaboration in the mathematical derivations of the SPIN theory; to Drs. Harry L. Frisch and Gideon Ishai for consultation on theoretical issues; and to Carol A. Esso for editing and for her competence in word processing. This project is sponsored by AFOSR Grant No. 93–NL–165.

REFERENCES

Bridgeman, B., van der Heijden, A. H. C., & Velichkovsky, B. M. (1994). A theory of visual stability across saccadic eye movements. *Behavioral and Brain Sciences, 17*, 247–292.

Bruss, A. R. & Horn B. K. P. (1983). Passive navigation. *Computer Vision, Graphics, and Image Processing, 21*, 3–20.

Cutting, J. E. (1986). *Perception with an eye for motion.* Cambridge: MIT Press.

Demer, J. L., Goldberg, J., Franklin, I. P., & Schmidt, K. (1991). Validation of physiological predictors of successful telescopic spectacle use in low vision. *Investigative Ophthalmology & Visual Science, 32*(10), 2826–2834.

Dodwell, P. C. (1983). The Lie transformation model of visual perception. *Perception and Psychophysics, 34*, 1–16.

Gibson, J. J. (1950). *The perception of the visual world.* Boston: Houghton Mifflin.

Gibson, J. J. (1966). *The senses considered as perceptual systems.* Boston: Houghton Mifflin.

Gibson, J. J. (1968). What gives rise to the perception of motion? *Psychological Review, 75*, 335–346.

Gibson, J. J. (1979). *The ecological approach to visual perception.* Boston: Houghton Mifflin.

Goldstein, E. B. (1996). *Sensation and perception.* Pacific Grove, CA: Brooks/Cole.

Hadani, I. (1991). The corneal lens goggles and visual space perception. *Applied Optics, 30*(28), 4136–4147.

Hadani, I. (1995). The SPIN theory—A navigational approach to space perception. *Journal of Vestibular Research, 56*, 443–454.

Hadani, I., Ishai, G., & Gur, M. (1978). *Visual stability and space perception in monocular vision: A mathematical model.* (Tech. Rep. No. TSI 07–78). Technion-IIT, Location: The Julius Silver Institute of Biomedical Engineering Sciences, Haifa, Israel.

Hadani, I., Ishai, G., & Gur, M. (1980). Visual stability and space perception in monocular vision: Mathematical model. *Journal of the Optical Society of America, 70*(1), 60–65.

Hadani, I., Gur, M., Meiri, A. Z., & Fender, D. H. (1980). Hyperacuity in the detection of absolute and differential displacements of random-dot patterns. *Vision Research, 20,* 947–951.

Hadani, I., Ishai, G., Frisch, H. L., & Kononov, A. (1994). Two metric solutions to the three-dimensional reconstruction for an eye in pure rotations. *Journal of the Optical Society of America, 11*(5), 1564–1574.

Hochberg, J. (1971). Perception II. Space and movement. In J. W. Kling & L. A. Riggs (Eds.), *Woodworth and Schlosberg experimental psychology* (3rd ed. 475–550). New York: Holt.

Hoffman, W. C. (1970). Higher visual perception as prolongations of the basic Lie transformation group. *Mathematical Biosciences, 6,* 437–471.

Howard, I. P. (1986). The vestibular system. In K. R. Boff, L. Kaufman, & J. P. Thomas (Eds.), *Handbook of perception and human performance, Volume 1—Sensory processes and perception* (pp. 11-1–11-30) New York: Wiley.

Julesz, B. (1995). *Dialogues on perception.* Cambridge: MIT Press.

Koenderink, J. J. & van Doorn, A. J. (1976). Local structure of movement parallax of the plane. *Journal of the Optical Society of America, 66*(7), 717–723.

Kononov, A. (1996). *SPIN theory and indeterminate scale problem.* Unpublished Master's thesis. Rutgers University, New Brunswick, NJ.

Longuet-Higgins, H. C. (1981). A computer algorithm for reconstruction a scene from two projections. *Nature, 293,* 133–135.

Longuet-Higgins, H. C. & Prazdny K. (1980). The interpretation of moving retinal images. *Proceedings of the Royal Society of London, B 208,* 385–387.

Mach, E. (1959). *The analysis of sensations.* New York: Dover.

Mack, A. (1978). Three modes of visual perception. In H. L. Pick & E. Saltzman (Eds.), *Models of perceiving and processing information* (pp. 171–186). Hillsdale, NJ: Lawrence Erlbaum Associates.

Matin, L. (1986). Visual localization and eye movements. In K. R. Boff, L. Kaufman, & J. P. Thomas (Eds.), *Handbook of perception and human performance, Volume 1: Sensory processes and perception.* ch. 20. New York: Wiley.

Meiri, Z. (1980). On monocular perception of 3-D moving objects. *Institute of Electrical and Electronics Engineering Transactions on Pattern Analysis and Machine Intelligence,* PAMI-2, 582–583.

Nagel, H. H. (1981). On the derivation of 3D rigid point configurations from image sequences. Paper presented at the IEEE Conference on Pattern Recognition and Image Processing, IEEE PRIP-81 Dallas, Texas, August.

Papathomas, T. V. & Julesz, B. (1989). Lie differential operators in animal and machine vision. In J. C. Simon (Ed.), *From the pixels to the features: Proceedings of the COST 13 Conference.* North-Holland, invited chapter, 115–126.

Prazdny, K. (1981). Determining the instantaneous direction of motion from optical flow generated by a curvilinear moving observer. *Computer Graphics and Image Processing, 17,* 238–248.

Schwartz, E. L. (1980). Computational anatomy and functional architecture of the striate cortex: A spatial mapping approach to perceptual coding. *Vision Research, 20,* 645–669.

Shebilske, W. L. (1977). Vasomotor coordination., visual direction and position constancies. In W. Epstein (Ed.), *Stability and constancy in visual perception: Mechanisms and processes* (pp. 23–69). New York: Wiley.

Simpson, W. A. (1993). Optic flow and depth perception. *Spatial Vision, 7*(1), 35–75.

Tsai, R. Y. & Huang, T. S. (1984). Uniqueness and estimation of 3-D motion parameters and surface structures of rigid objects. In S. Ullman & W. Richards (Eds.). *Image Understanding 1984* (pp. 135–172). Norwood, NJ: Albex.

Ullman, S. (1979). *The interpretation of visual motion.* Cambridge: MIT Press.

Ullman, S. (1980). Against direct perception. *Behavioral and Brain Sciences, 3*, 373–415.

von Holst, E. (1954). Relations between the central nervous system and the peripheral organs. *Animal Behavior, 2,* 89–94.

Wallach, H. (1959). The perception of motion. *Scientific American, 201,* 56–60.

Wertheim, A. H. (1994). Motion perception during self-motion: The direct versus inferential controversy revisited. *Behavioral and Brain Sciences, 17,* 293–355.

chapter 5

Analogical Representations

Bart Selman
selman@research.att.com
AT&T Bell Laboratories

INTRODUCTION

The notion of *analogical representations* or *analogues* was introduced by Sloman (1971) in order to make a distinction between representations consisting of a description in some language, and representations that are more direct models or pictures of the things represented. Sloman uses the term *Fregean* representations for the first category, and analogical representations for the latter. An example of a Fregean representation is a set of sentences in first-order logic. Some examples of analogical representations are maps, pictures, diagrams, linked lists, and flow charts. In recent years, Fregean-style representations have become the dominant form of representation in most work on knowledge representation. In certain applications, however, analogical representations appear to be more natural, and allow for faster information retrieval than their Fregean counterpart.

In this paper, we will discuss the foundational work on analogical representations, and describe their use in various artificial intelligence (AI) systems. We also briefly describe related research in psychology on *imagery* and *mental models*. And, finally, we consider a closely related form of representation, called a *vivid representation* (Levesque 1986).

FOUNDATIONS

In this section, we review the foundational work on analogues. Each subsection describes one of the main characteristics of analogues: *structural correspondence, internal constraints*, and *operational correspondence*.

Structural Correspondence

Sloman (1971) was the first to address the issue of analogical representations. Analogues were contrasted with Fregean representations in an attempt to describe essential differences between the expressiveness of these forms of representations. In a later paper, Sloman (1975) critically reviews his 1971 paper, and challenges a number of previous claims, made by himself and by others, on the differences between analogical and Fregean representations. In his later paper Sloman proposes the following characterization of an analogical representation. If R is an analogical representation of D, then the following properties must hold:

1. There are parts of R representing parts of D, as dots and squiggles on a map represent towns and rivers.
2. It is possible to specify some sort of correspondence, possibly context dependent, between properties or relations of parts of R and properties or relations of parts of D, for example, size, shape, direction, and distance of marks on a map may represent size, shape, direction, and distance of towns.

With this characterization Sloman intends to capture what he considers one of the main properties of analogues, namely some form of correspondence between the (syntactic) structure of the analogical representation and that of the represented domain.[1] An important shortcoming of this characterization is that the correspondence relation is not further specified. Sloman states only that this correspondence can be quite complex; for example, in the case of a two-dimensional sketch of a three-dimensional scene. However, from the examples Sloman discusses, it is clear that he does not want to allow for arbitrarily complex correspondence relations. In fact, it appears that the definition would become vacuous if unrestricted forms of correspondence were allowed.

To see that Fregean representations in general do not satisfy the requirements previously stated, we note that in such representations none of the parts or relationships need to correspond to parts of or relations within the objects denoted. This is best illustrated with an example. Consider the phrase "The city 53 miles north of Brighton." Although it contains the word "Brighton" as a part, the object denoted by the whole phrase, that is, London, does not contain the city of Brighton as a part.

Internal Constraints

Another characteristic property of analogues is given by Palmer (1978). He describes the nature of analogues as part of a discussion on fundamental aspects of cognitive representations. Palmer argues that analogues fall within a special class of representations by virtue of the way in which certain relations in the domain are represented. He refers to this class of representations as *intrinsic*. The complement of this is the class of *extrinsic* representations.

A representation is called intrinsic whenever the representing relations have the same internal constraints as the represented relations. Palmer illustrates these notions using an example of representing the taller-than relation on a set of physical objects. As an example of an extrinsic representation, he considers representing these objects by nodes in a directed graph. In this representation, the fact that a is taller than b is represented by a directed edge from a to b. In this representation, the transitivity and asymmetry of the taller-than relation are not inherent in the representation, that is, we can represent states of affairs where these constraints are violated. As an example of an intrinsic representation, we would associate with each object a number, and taller-than would correspond to the greater-than relation on numbers. This representation exploits the transitivity and asymmetry of the ordering relation on the numbers. Note that it is not possible to violate these constraints.

As a second example, Palmer considers the representation of distances between N cities. This information can be represented in an $N \times N$ matrix in which each entry specifies the distance between two cities. Alternatively, consider a list of two-dimensional coordinate pairs that represents the location of each city, where distances follow from the standard Euclidean distance measure. The latter scheme again does not allow for inconsistencies (in this case, in the set of distances).

These examples illustrate the basic intuition behind intrinsic representations: they capture some of the constraints in the domain they represent in their *internal* structure. Such representations often also allow for fast information retrieval. For example, in the analogical representation of the taller-than relation, two objects can be compared by directly comparing their associated numbers.

The constraint nature of analogues makes them good candidates for consideration in a formal framework introduced by Mackinlay and Geneseroth (1984) for analyzing properties of specialized languages. A specialized language is any language with limited expressive power relative to a general first-order language. They show how statements (messages) in such languages can be translated into sentences of first-order logic. Internal constraints of the language are also formulated in first-order logic. Examples of some of the languages they consider are: maps, diagrams, and organizational charts.

Mackinlay and Geneseroth define a message as an arrangement in the world intended to convey meaning. For example, a particular configuration of blocks on a table can be a message. They define a language as the set of *conventions* that a speaker and hearer have for constructing and interpreting messages. To be able to describe these conventions in first-order logic they introduce the following definition:

> Let $\bar{f}$ be a formula in first-order logic describing a message, expressing a fact f, in the specialized language. Then, a fact f is stated in language l in situation s if and only if the associated message formula $\bar{f}$ is satisfied in s:

$$Stated\ (f,\ l,\ s) \Leftrightarrow Satisfied\ (\bar{f},\ s)$$

in which s is a situation (McCarthy and Hayes 1969): a complete state of the world including the statement in the specialized language. The argument s allows us to talk about different states of affairs. In this formula and subsequent ones, variables are given in lowercase and constants are given in uppercase. Free variables are universally quantified.

As an example we consider the specialized language describing a schedule for computer science courses and their interrelation in the form of a *layered tree* (see Figure 5.1). The conventions of this language can be expressed as follows:

$$Stated\ (\texttt{Prereq(x,y)},\ \texttt{LAYERTREE,s}) \Leftrightarrow Satisfied\ (\texttt{Connected(x,y),s})$$

$$Stated\ (\texttt{Concur(x,y)},\ \texttt{LAYERTREE,s}) \Leftrightarrow Satisfied\ (\texttt{SameLayer(x,y),s})$$

in which Prereq means that one class is a prerequisite for another and Concur means that two classes can be taken concurrently. Note that, for example, Connected($\bar{x},\bar{y}$) is a description of a message in the specialized language. Because of the special way in which the relations are encoded in the diagram, they have certain inherent properties. For example,

$$\texttt{SameLayer (x,y)} \Leftrightarrow \texttt{SameLayer (y,x)}$$

$$[\texttt{SameLayer (x,y)} \wedge \texttt{SameLayer (y,z)]\ SameLayer (x,y)}$$

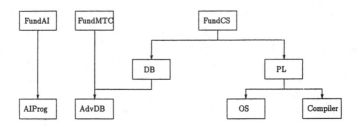

FIGURE 5.1. A layered tree representation (from Mackinlay and Genesereth 1984).

Mackinlay and Genesereth propose the following definition to character-ize the expressiveness of a language:

> A set of facts *fs* is *expressible* in language *l* if there exists a situation *s* that states every fact in *fs* and does not state any other fact:
>
> $$Expressible(fs, l) \Leftrightarrow \exists s([\forall f \in fs\ Stated\ (f,l,s)] \wedge [\forall f \notin fs \neg\ Stated(f,l,s)])$$

Based on this definition of expressibility and considerations of the cost of storage and retrieval of facts, they formulate a set of criteria for choosing an appropriate specialized language. Their criteria are tuned towards choosing languages for graphical displays and therefore incorporate measures of the speed of retrieval of facts from the display by human subjects.

Mackinlay and Genesereth's framework provides a good formalism for describing specialized representations, such as analogical representations, but it does not deal with the actual implementation of the representation language. Given that one generally hopes to derive some computational advantage of the use of an analogical representation, it is important that there is an efficient way to implement the language. In particular, the internal constraints of the language should be easy to enforce and maintain. Some of the main methods for maintaining constraints are:

1. Choice of topology. Often, choosing an appropriate topology is sufficient. One example is the representation of distance as a derived notion, as discussed previously. Another example is the representation of concepts in a distributed form, in which a concept is represented in terms of a set of primitive features, called micro-features (Hinton *et al.* 1986). The set of micro-features representing a concept that is a generalization of another concept will form a subset of the more specific concept. So, transitivity comes for free.
2. Additional features. One can introduce additional features in the representation with the sole purpose of maintaining constraints. The work by Schubert *et al.* (1983) is an example of this approach. They use numbers to implement an efficient mechanism for determining relations between objects organized in a semantic network. Consider a hierarchy of types. The basic idea is to assign an interval on the integers to each object such that *b* is a subtype of *a* if and only if the range of integers assigned to *b* is a subrange of those assigned to *a*. It is clear that transitivity again will come for free in this representation. This approach can be characterized more generally as one using specialized data structures to maintain constraints.
3. Procedural. The use of a set of special procedures is the most general approach towards maintaining internal constraints. The efficiency of

these procedures often determines whether using a specialized language is appropriate. Below, we will encounter examples of this approach in spatial reasoning and qualitative physics.

Operational Correspondence

In a classic experiment, Shepard and Meltzer (1971) studied the rotation of a mental image. They concluded that when people try to determine whether or not two pictures display the same physical object under a different rotation, the mental image of the object used by the human subjects goes through a number intermediate states corresponding to those a real physical object would go through when rotated. Shepard identified this phenomenon as an *analogical process*, which he described as follows:

> By an analogical or analogue process I mean just this: a process in which the intermediate internal states have a natural one-to-one correspondence to appropriate intermediate states in the external world. (Shepard 1978, page 135)

Although Sloman's notion of analogical representations is intended to capture a structural correspondence between the representation and what it represents, Shepard tries to capture the temporal aspect of the represented process in a direct manner. An analogical process need not involve an analogical representation. In practice, however, we often encounter both aspects of "analogical" together.

Qualitative simulation (Bobrow 1984) as used in the work on qualitative physics is a prime example of an analogical process studied in artificial intelligence. We will return to the work on qualitative simulation below.

THE USE OF ANALOGICAL REPRESENTATIONS IN AI SYSTEMS

Geometry Theorem Proving

We find the first use of an analogical representation in a program called the *Geometry Theorem Proving Machine* by Gelernter (1959; and also Gelernter et al 1960). The program proves theorems in elementary plane geometry. Gilmore (1970) gives a detailed description of the axiomatic theory underlying the Geometry Machine and analyzes the various aspects of the use of the diagram and other heuristics.

The Geometry Machine utilizes a diagrammatic representation of the theorem to be proved. The diagram is represented by a list of Cartesian coordinates of the points mentioned in the theorem to be proved. The diagram is a model (in the Tarskian sense) of the premises of the theorem, so any statement that does not hold in the model cannot be a consequence of the premises, and therefore cannot be part of a proof of the theorem. The program exploits this property of the diagram by pruning its search space. The approach is sound because the diagram is used only for pruning. A statement such as "segments AB and CD are of equal length" is checked in the diagram by computing the lengths of the segments from the coordinates of the points. Since round-off errors could result in this statement being mistakenly classified as nonvalid, causing the theorem prover to ignore certain consequences of the premises, the approach is incomplete.

To what extent does the use of a diagrammatic representation enhance the performance of the theorem prover? Gelernter et al. (1960) provide experimental evidence showing that the diagram is crucial to their approach. An attempt was made to prove a number of basic theorems without the use of a diagram: on the average, 1000 subgoals were generated at each state, versus an average of 5 subgoals when using a diagram. The performance of the theorem prover does, however, degenerate when extra points have to be introduced in the diagram. The Geometry Machine could handle problems up to the level of difficulty of high school examinations.

Model-Based Reasoning

The Geometry Machine uses semantic information to guide the theorem proving process. The semantic information is given in the form of a model of the formal system under consideration. A model can be viewed as an analogical representation of the problem under consideration.

Reiter (1976) enriches rules for natural deduction, similar to those by Bledsoe et al. (1972), with semantic information based on models. In this approach models are used to reject subgoals, and intermediate states of the proof suggest changes to the model. Also, certain rules suggest "good guesses" that is, a model is used to suggest a possible substitution of variables by terms involving only function symbols. Reiter emphasizes the smooth transition between the use of semantic information and deductive syntax during the theorem proving process, since the syntactic and semantic modules interact continuously. The method subsumes Gelernter's theorem prover, and provides a domain-independent mechanism to guide the theorem-proving process with semantic information.

Another example of the use of a model or a partial model can be found in the system FOL by Weyhrauch (1980). FOL is an interactive proof constructor using rules of natural deduction and semantic attachment. The logic used is first-order predicate calculus with equality and allows for sorted variables. In FOL we can map predicate and function symbols to a procedural representation of their intended meaning. For example, we can assign to each numeral (symbol in the language) and the function symbol "+" their natural interpretation. This is realized in the system by a call to the LISP function for addition. These semantic attachments form a (partial) model of the theory under consideration. Weyhrauch calls these (partial) models *simulation structures*. So, the semantic attachment can now be used to evaluate certain quantifier-free expressions, provided all the symbols in the expression are assigned an interpretation. In general, this is much more efficient than reasoning from first principles, for example, by using Peano's axioms. One of the problems is of course that one has to be able to specify an appropriate simulation structure. Also, the limitations are quite apparent. For example, a simulation structure cannot be used to determine that $[\alpha \vee prime(X)] \wedge [even(X) \vee \beta]$ implies $(X = 2) \vee \alpha \vee \beta$, since this would require an enumeration over the infinite domain of the simulation structure (α and β are formulas in first-order logic, *prime* and *even* are unary predicates with their standard interpretation, and expressions are universally quantified). For a generalization on Weyrauch's approach, see Stickel (1985).

Spatial Reasoning

An important early example of the use of an analogical representation can be found in Funt's spatial reasoning system, called WHISPER (Funt 1976, 1980, and 1983). WHISPER deals with simple stability problems in a blocks world. It is able to predict how an unstable configuration of objects will fall over. WHISPER uses a general-purpose reasoner (called the high-level reasoner), which interacts with a module that contains a diagrammatic representation of the current state of affairs. The system contains a set of procedures that make observations in the diagram, for example, whether one object touches another, and procedures that compute consecutive states of affairs, such as *rotate*, which rotates an object over a predefined angle in the diagram.[2]

Figure 5.2 illustrates the main idea behind the program. In this figure, M stands for the physical blocks world, and T is a logical theory consisting of two parts: a general description T_{gen} of the dynamic behavior of blocks, and a description T_{init} of a specific initial state of affairs. M' is a model that satisfies T (in general many such models will exist). The main thrust of WHISPER is that in many situations we can use M' to obtain information about M. For this to be the case, it is necessary that certain predicates, functions, and individuals of M' correspond to predicates, functions and individuals of M in such a way that the results of applying these predicates and functions to individuals in M' can be transformed into results of apply-

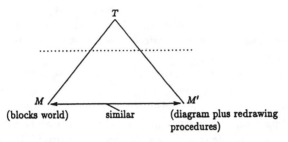

FIGURE 5.2.   Theoretical framework of WHISPER (from Funt 1980).

ing the corresponding predicates and functions to the corresponding individuals in *M*. Thus, what is needed is a certain similarity between *M* and *M'*. This similarity guarantees that certain experiments and observations made in *M'* yield similar results in *M*.

It should be noted that Funt does not give an explicit specification of *T* and *M*—much of the knowledge is represented in a procedural form. Also, time is not explicitly represented; in fact, only the current state of affairs is represented, and procedures compute consecutive states of affairs. This approach is very much like the one taken in STRIPS (Fikes and Nilsson 1971; Lifschitz 1986). Such a representation is appropriate here, since a state of the diagram determined solely by its previous state.

The high-level reasoner executes routines that check for instabilities, and decides which objects to rotate. Objects in the diagram are stored as sets of points in a two-dimensional array. This allows for a straightforward representation of irregularly shaped objects. Instead of representing all relations and functions explicitly, many can be computed efficiently by special procedures. For example, *touche*(*A*,*B*) determines whether objects *A* and *B* touch each other, and *center_of_area*(*A*) returns the coordinates of the center of area of the shape of object *A*. There is also a procedure that computes how far an object can rotate before a collision with some other object occurs. The procedures that calculate these particular relations and functions are parallel algorithms, employing a special representation of the diagram in polar coordinates (referred to as the retina).

WHISPER'S diagrammatic representation has a number of interesting properties. First, we observe that the computation of the *touches* relation is essentially independent of the number of objects in the blocks world, a reasonable property when we consider how an agent would determine this in the real world. The correspondence of the time complexity of these operations indicates some form of operational correspondence between the computation of *touches* and the process of determining this in the real world. The implementation of the function *free_rotation* is a good example of an analogical process. The procedure rotates the object over a series of small steps, while observing whether a collision occurs. During this process the object will go through a sequence of states similar to those a rotating object in the real world goes through. Consistency constraints, such as that objects cannot occupy the same space, are maintained by the routines that manipulate objects in the diagram. Other constraints, such as the transitivity of the *above* relation, are again implicit in the representation.

Under control from the high-level reasoner, WHISPER constructs a sequence of diagrams. When no more changes in the diagram occur, the system has found a stable state. According to Funt, the high-level reasoner performs reasoning at a level above the dotted line in Figure 5.2. However, it seems that the program, during its computation, can also be viewed as directly computing the model M'. The model-based view is warranted in this case, since starting from a particular configuration, all relevant aspects of the subsequent configurations are completely determined. This is a consequence of the deterministic nature of the macroscopic physical laws that govern the process. Consequently, M' is isomorphic to M with respect to the relevant predicates.[3]

Closely related to the approach taken by Funt is the work by Forbus (1980, 1983). His program FROB deals with the "Bouncing Ball World" (i.e., it analyzes the motion of a ball bouncing on an arbitrarily shaped surface). This program also uses a diagrammatic representation of space, albeit stored in a different form than Funt's. Basically, Forbus integrates a metric representation with a more qualitative description of the domain, that is, a set of relationships between various regions in the diagram. FROB also keeps track of the velocity of objects.

Both WHISPER and FROB deal with *complete* spatial information. In general, spatial reasoning systems will also have to deal with incomplete information. The question arises as to whether a representation that is limited to relatively complete information, such as a diagram, is still useful when dealing with incomplete information. McDermott and Davis (1984) address this issue in their work on planning routes through incompletely specified domains.

The system by McDermott and Davis maintains two representations of spatial information: a relational one describing topological information, such as (in person4 bldg55), and an analogical one consisting of a *fuzzy* map containing metric information, such as the fact that the distance between New York and Los Angeles is greater than 3000 km. A fuzzy map is like a regular map except that uncertainty about the exact location of objects can be expressed by assigning a region on the map to each object. The system actually maintains a collection of such maps to allow for different frames of reference, however this aspect is not relevant to our discussion here. The topological information consists mainly of overlap and inclusion relationships. This information is stored in a semantic network of an indexed set of assertions.

As Brooks (1981) observes, deductions following from a set of general metric constraints quickly become computationally infeasible when the number of constraints grows. McDermott and Davis therefore store metric information in a fuzzy map. The idea is not to store the metric facts per se, for example, as a set of sentences in first-order logic, but as a map in which these facts hold. This way inference becomes often a matter of "just looking" on the map.

Although a fuzzy map can deal with certain forms of incomplete information, an arbitrary set of facts cannot be faithfully represented. For example, consider information that A and B are located somewhere in the USA. This information can be represented by assigning two "fuzz boxes" of the size of the USA to each of the objects. Now consider the additional fact that B is two miles from A. The new set of facts cannot be expressed precisely in the fuzzy map representation. Thus, we lose some expressive power, but gain in computational efficiency.

Simulation

In a simulation, we start with an initial description of the system under consideration and compute its subsequent states based on a causal description of the system. Much work on reasoning about physical systems (Bobrow 1984) is based on simulation. A simulation is an analogical process, since it will go through a sequence of intermediate states that have a one-to-one correspondence to the states of the process that is being modeled.

Funt's and Forbus's approaches, as discussed previously, are examples of the use of simulation in a spatial reasoning task. Another example is the work of Gardin et al. (1986) on modelling the behavior of liquids. Their system represents a liquid by a set of molecules of some finite grain size. The behavior of the molecules is governed by six local rules, for example "a free molecule moves down until it either encounters another molecule or a rigid body, in both cases becoming constrained" (gravity), and "a molecule can change its position to a neighboring one if that one is not occupied by either another molecule or a rigid body" (nonpenetrability). The system is implemented using an object-oriented programming style. Molecules are represented by actors that exchange messages between neighbors. Gardin et al. report good qualitative results on a wide variety of tasks such as filling a container from a tap. To our knowledge, their system is the first implementation handling these tasks correctly. Their representation is analogical according to the characterization by Sloman and the computation can be characterized as an analogical process as defined by Shepard.

For examples of the application of simulation in nonspatial tasks, see Kleer and Brown (1983; 1984), and Forbus (1984).

ANALOGICAL REPRESENTATIONS IN COGNITIVE SCIENCE

Imagery

People often report that they can form *mental images* of an object that resemble the object's actual appearance. To answer questions about the objects they seem to inspect the image in much the same way they would inspect the real object. Although there are many open questions concerning the nature of mental images, it appears that they possess several of the characteristics of analogical representations. We therefore review some of the work exploring the nature of mental images and their role in cognition.

We first consider the resolution of a visual image. Through introspection it seems that features of a small mental image or one of a distant object are harder to distinguish than features of a large image or one of a nearby object. Several experiments (Kosslyn 1981; Finke 1986) confirm that indeed the resolution of a mental image of an object decreases as does that of a visual image.[4] Even effects of asymmetry in our perception, such as the fact that the resolution in the vertical direction falls off more rapidly than that in the horizontal direction when an object is moved away, are found when dealing with mental images. This is just one of the findings that indicate that the very same mechanisms are operative in imagery as in perception, and that the mental image is in some sense like a visual image (Shepard 1978; Finke 1986).

Another aspect of mental images is how we transform them. Shepard (1978) takes the stance that many operations involving images are analogical processes. This stance is based on his early findings on rotating mental images as described previously. (See also Hinton 1979.)

Kosslyn (1981) describes a now classic experiment on scanning a mental image. A subject is asked to inspect a configuration of objects (such as landmark items on a map), form a mental image of the configuration, and "focus" in on one of the objects. Subsequently, the subject is given the name of a second object and asked to mentally scan the image along a direct path from the first object to the second. Kosslyn consistently found that the time required to complete the mental scanning was directly proportional to the physical distance between the objects in the imaged scene. Thus the scanning is very much like scanning the actual configuration of objects.

Pylyshyn (1981) has criticized many of the conclusions relating properties of mental images to those of pictures. In the debate on the nature of mental images, he identifies as the main issue which properties of mental images are *inherent* in the functional architecture of cognition. (Pylyshyn considers the notion of internal constraints, as discussed previously, the main characteristic of analogical representations.) Although it seems clear that the underlying representation of the mental image has certain internal constraints (e.g., we cannot image any arbitrary object whose properties can be described), Pylyshyn argues that it is far from clear what exactly the constraints are; that is, which aspects of the mental image are analogical. For example, he argues that reaction times in mental scanning processes are a result of our tacit knowledge of perception: the subjects simply simulate the scanning process using their knowledge of perception. In other words, the mental scanning process is cognitively penetrable. Pylyshyn claims that most aspects of mental images are cognitively penetrable, and therefore should be described in terms of our beliefs about perception. This claim is challenged by others, such as Kosslyn and Finke, who propose the opposite view: that most of the aspects of mental images are inherent.

Aside from the question of the nature of mental images, there is the issue of what role these images play in human cognition. Shepard (1978) cites a number of prominent scientists that claim to have used images in their work. Apart from this anecdotal support for the possible role of images in cognition, Larkin and Simon (1987) provide more direct support. They analyze the problem solving process for a number of elementary physics problems (concerning the stability of certain configurations) and some basic geometry problems. They compare two forms of problem representation: a sentential one, in which the information is ordered as a list of sentences, and a pictorial one, in which the information is represented using a spatial index. In their analysis they formulate the problem first in terms of a neutral representation, called the propositional representation. This is basically a knowledge level (Newell 1982) description of the problem. Subsequently, they represent the information in a sentential and a pictorial form and compare the problem solving process in terms of information processing operators that act on these representations.

The most important distinction between sentential and pictorial representations found by Larkin and Simon is the difference in the efficiency of the search for information. In the pictorial representation, information for a logical step is often found at a single location and cues for the next logical step are often found at an adjacent location. Problem solving can therefore proceed through a smooth traversal of the diagram. These findings are an indication of the potential importance of pictorial information in cognition.

Mental Models

Johnson-Laird (1983) introduces a theory of *mental models* to explain higher processes of cognition, in particular, natural language understanding and inference. Johnson-Laird has done extensive research on the ability of human subjects to draw logical inferences. The mistakes people make led him to challenge the use of mental logics in cognitive theories (in its most extreme form the idea behind mental logic is "that reasoning is nothing more than the propositional calculus itself [Inhelder and Piaget 1958]). As an alternative, he proposes the use of mental models in higher cognitive processes.

A mental model is an analogue in the sense that the structure of a mental model is analogous to that of the corresponding state of affairs in the real world—as we perceive or conceive it. However, the structure of mental models may still vary considerably. Certain models introduce only a minimal degree of analogical structure, such as the use of separate elements to stand for separate individuals.

Consider, as an example, that you want to draw conclusions from the following premises:

All the artists are beekeepers
All the beekeepers are chemists

Johnson-Laird proposes to construct a mental model of the following sort (we use a slightly modified notation):

$artist_1$	$beekeeper_1$	$chemist_1$
$artist_2$	$beekeeper_2$	$chemist_2$
$artist_3$	$beekeeper_3$	$chemist_3$
	$(beekeeper_4)$	$(chemist_4)$
	$(beekeeper_5)$	$(chemist_5)$
		$(chemist_6)$

in which roles are assigned to certain, hypothesized individuals, for example, $artist_1$ asserts that $individual_1$ is an artist. This model expresses the following facts: There are three (distinct) individuals, each with three roles, namely artist, beekeeper, and chemist, and two individuals with two roles, namely beekeeper and chemist, and finally there is one individual who is a chemist. Note the implicit closed-world and unique-name assumption. For example, since $artist_4$ is not asserted it is the case that the fourth individual is not an artist. The parentheses indicate that these facts are possibly, but not definitely true; for example, $chemist_6$ asserts [chemist($individual_6$)∨ ¬

chemist(individual$_6$)]. The numbers of individuals with the different properties are chosen arbitrarily. Therefore, no conclusions concerning the numbers of individuals can be based on this model.

When asked whether it follows that *All the artists are chemists*, you can readily inspect the mental model and determine that this conclusion is indeed true. The approach is potentially unsound, since we consider only one particular model. But, most interestingly, Johnson-Laird found that the kinds of mistakes that are made using this approach are very similar, if not identical, to those made by human subjects in syllogistic reasoning tasks.

Based on the success in explaining inferences, and his work on natural language understanding, Johnson-Laird postulates mental models—and thus a kind of analogical representation—as a main form of mental representation, in addition to the general sentential form.

VIVID KNOWLEDGE REPRESENTATIONS

Levesque (1986) introduced the notion of a *vivid* representation. The basic idea behind the notion of vividness is to constrain the logical form of the knowledge base in such a way that deduction becomes computationally efficient. Levesque mentions pictorial representations as an important source of vivid information. It is therefore not surprising that vivid representations share many properties of analogical representations. We will first consider an analysis of the logical form of pictorial representations. This discussion will provide some of the intuitions behind vivid representations. We will then return to the notion of vividness and its relationship to analogical representations.

An Example: Pictorial Representations

Sober (1976) argues that pictorial representations can best be viewed as an impoverished form of linguistic representations. As the main aspects that distinguish pictorial representations from general linguistic representations, Sober mentions their specific logical form, their apparent specificity, and the fact that their interpretation requires the notion of a point of view.

Sober limits his discussion to so-called representational pictures that give it to be understood that a certain state of affairs obtains. So, if a picture is *true*, the state of affairs *does* obtain. We identify each representational picture with an existential hypothesis that posits the existence of certain specified objects. To facilitate the discussion of this reduction, Sober introduces an interpretation function I, which maps pictures into sentences.[5] We can say that given a picture p, I(p) specifies the information p provides.

Sober considers whether sentential connectives have counterparts in pictorial representations. For example, does there exist a binary operator * mapping pictures p and q into an interpretation corresponding to the conjunction of the interpretations of p and q; that is, I(p * q) = I(p) ∧ I(q)?

The pictorial juxtaposition operation roughly corresponds to the conjunction operation on sentences (as an example, imagine a picture of a table juxtaposed with a picture of a chair). Some obvious difficulties with this correspondence are in representing the information regarding relative positions between objects, and pictures that have highly context-sensitive interpretations.

The notion of picture containment roughly corresponds to the sentential implication operator. However, the only clear examples are those based on the fact that a conjunction of two propositions implies each conjunct. More interestingly, Sober observes that there is no pictorial operation corresponding to the sentential negation operation. From a picture of a river, consider how to obtain a picture with *precisely* the interpretation of the presence of a "nonriver". Note that it is not sufficient to give a picture of, for example, a table, since besides indicating that there is something that is not a river, such a picture also implies the existence of a table, which does not capture the *general* notion of nonriver. In general, Sober claims that given some predicate P and a picture representing ∃x P(x), there will be no pictures that give it to be understood (merely) ∃x ¬ P(x). Thus, if a certain predicate can be expressed in a pictorial system its negation cannot.

Logical disjunction is another sentential operator that appears to be missing in the pictorial domain. Consider an ambiguous picture as a possible candidate for a picture obtained from two unambiguous pictures. We take the canonical example of an ambiguous picture: the Necker cube. Observe that, although this picture has two different interpretations, its interpretation is not simply given by the disjunction of these two interpretations since one perceives the two alternative interpretations at different moments in time, and not as a true disjunction at any particular point in time. Sober postulates that, in general, if two predicates occur in an interpretation then their disjunction will not. For this to hold we must be somewhat more precise about the notion of interpretation. For example, suppose that limes look precisely like lemons. In that case, could there not be a picture with a sentential counterpart ∃x (lemon(x) ∨ lime(x))? Sober claims that in such a case the *preferred* interpretation will contain only one predicate for example, ∃x yellow_ellipsoid_fruit(x). Sober admits that his arguments against disjunction, although intuitively appealing, need further analysis.

Another interesting property of pictorial representations is their *specificity*. Consequently, the sentential counterpart of a picture cannot be arbitrarily weak. For example, there is no picture whose *full* sentential counterpart is $\exists x$ `fire_engine(x)`. Somehow, we can only justify a picture of a fire engine by being able to point to subparts of the picture and justifying them as representing subparts of a fire engine; that is, there is some form of structural correspondence between the representation and that which is represented. Therefore, a representation of a complex object will necessarily be complex.[6]

The specificity of pictures makes them relatively complete with respect to the presence and/or absence of objects. The two main sources of incompleteness are due to the *granularity* of the representation and *blind spots*. The incompleteness introduced by the granularity of the representation is of a special form, namely one related to the notion of *similarity* with respect to physical shape. The incompleteness due to blind spots is mainly a result of the occlusion effect. Blind spots prevent us from drawing conclusions about what is not present in the depicted scene (e.g., there might be a dog behind the barn).

In summary, Sober's analysis captures the logical properties of the relatively large class of representational pictures. (See Howell [1976] for a discussion of some of the shortcomings of the analysis.)

A Characterization of Vividness

We have seen how pictures can be viewed as *limited information bearers*, allowing only for certain logical operations. Vivid representations are more a general characterization of such restricted information bearers. Levesque (1986) postulates that such representation will play a central role in computationally efficient knowledge representation systems.

A first requirement of a vivid knowledge base is that it contains complete knowledge with respect to the set of objects and relations with which knowledge base (KB) deals.[7] This requirement eliminates all forms of incomplete knowledge in the KB, which are often a source of intractability (Levesque and Brachman 1985). A knowledge base is said to contain complete knowledge if and only if it has a unique model (up to an isomorphism). Relational databases without null values are examples of such KBs (Reiter 1984).[8]

Completeness is a rather strong requirement. We might wonder whether this requirement by itself is a sufficient condition for tractability. In general, the answer is no. For example,[9] the complete theory of Presburger arithmetic contains formulae with proofs that grow superexponentially with the length of the formula to be proved (Fischer and Rabin 1974). As an example from propositional logic, consider an algorithm that, for any complete set of sentences, returns the satisfying truth assignment, and for other sets of sentences, returns an arbitrary truth assignment. Valiant and Vazirani (1985) show that this problem is NP-hard under randomized reductions, and therefore not tractable unless NP=RP (considered unlikely).

To guarantee that the unique model of a vivid KB can be computed easily, certain constraints are placed on the form in which the knowledge is encoded. These constraints are captured by the following two main properties of a vivid KB:

1. There will be a one-to-one correspondence between a certain class of symbols in the KB and the objects of interest in the world.
2. For every simple relationship of interest in the world, there will be a type of connection among symbols in the KB such that the relationship holds among a group of objects in the world if and only if the appropriate connection exists among the corresponding symbols in the KB.

The notion of a connection among symbols in the KB is intended to capture a certain syntactic relation among these symbols. If we allow for any arbitrary syntactic relation then the second part of the characterization would simply state that our representation is complete with respect to the set of relations and objects in the real world; that is, a relationship holds among a group of objects in the world if and only if such a relationship logically follows from the entire KB. However, we are interested in a much more limited form of connection, hence the qualification *appropriate.* Levesque mentions as a possible further specification that it is a connection that can be tested for locally, and therefore independently of the total number of facts present in the KB.[10]

Figure 5.3 illustrates the two main properties of a vivid KB. The vivid KB represents a world with two individuals and their relationship; more precisely, the symbols Jack and Jill represent the individuals and the husband relationship is represented by connection involving a co-occurrence in the sentence of the form ...is married to... (with the husband in the first position of the sentence).

Another example discussed by Levesque is based on two KBs of the following form:

KB_1 contains the sentences

```
Dan drank exactly 7 ounces of gin.
Jack drank exactly 6 ounces of gin.
```

and KB_2 contains the sentences

```
Jack and Dan together polished off a 13 ounce bottle of
    gin.
Dan had precisely one more drink (1 ounce) than Jack.
```

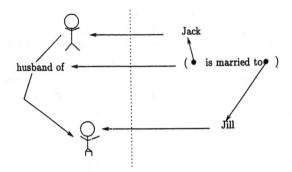

FIGURE 5.3. An example of vivid knowledge representation (from Levesque 1986).

According to this characterization, KB_1 is vivid with respect to the *amount* Jack and Dan drank individually, since the representations of both individuals are directly connected with the representations of the amount they drank. KB_2 is not vivid by the same criterion.

Being tractable by itself is of course not enough to explain why we should care about vivid knowledge. However, presumably much of the information we encounter is in a vivid form, with pictorial information as the main source.

Finally, let us briefly consider the relationship between analogues and vivid representations. Levesque discusses how vivid representations are an analogue of the domain in that operations on the representation are like operations on the domain itself. As an example, he considers how to determine the number of objects in the vivid KB with some specific property. As in the database case, this operation involves simply counting a set of tuples (i.e., no general inference) and is thus similar to the operation one would perform on the domain itself. This property corresponds directly to the operational correspondence property of analogues. Also, the two conditions placed on the form of the vivid KB lead to a form of structural correspondence between the representation and the domain, like that of analogues. However, the notion of internal constraints that we encountered for analogues is not a characteristic aspect of vivid representations in general. The concept of a vivid representation can therefore be viewed as a generalization on the notion of an analogical representation.

SUMMARY AND DISCUSSION

We discussed analogical representations or analogues. We described their main characteristics, namely a structural correspondence between representation and domain, internal constraints, and a correspondence between operations performed on these representations and those in the domain. We also described several applications of analogues. There are several different approaches to the use of analogues in reasoning. The use of a diagram in theorem proving (Gelernter 1959) is an example of a sound approach; the diagram is used only to prune search space. The use of fuzzy maps in route planning (McDermott and Davis 1984) is an example of a technically unsound, but computationally efficient method: general inference is replaced by direct look-up of information on the map. Simulations, as used in spatial reasoning (e.g., Funt 1976) and other reasoning tasks about the physical world (e.g., DeKleer and Brown 1983), are examples of analogical processes.

As for the role of analogues in cognition, we discussed work on mental imagery and mental models. Larkin and Simon (1987) show the possible role of pictorial representations in problem solving tasks. Johnson-Laird (1983) discusses the use of mental models in an explanatory theory of syllogistic reasoning, and postulates that they play an important role in higher cognition Finally, we briefly discussed vivid representations (Levesque 1986), which are closely related to analogical representations. Both analogical and vivid representations have good computational properties, and therefore hold promise for use in large knowledge-based systems.

NOTES

[1]Whereas the structure of a spatial domain naturally corresponds to its spatial properties, the nature of structure in nonspatial domains is less clear. Connell and Brady (1987), in their work on learning general descriptions, use a more generally applicable notion of correspondence; they require their representation to be such that a small change in the representation corresponds to a small change in the represented domain.

[2]The actual situation is slightly more complex; WHISPER contains a separate module, the retina, in which certain observations and potential changes in the diagram can be tested in a parallel manner.

[3]The actual situation in WHISPER is slightly more complicated, since rotations of objects are executed in sequential order. Therefore, there will be states of affairs that do not correspond to the states in the real world.

[4]In an example of such an experiment we have to imagine a relatively big object and a relatively small object, e.g., an elephant and a mouse, in one image. It turns out that subjects can detect more easily details of the large object than of the small one.

[5]You could trivially represent a picture, given in the form of a two-dimensional array of pixels, in a sentential form by a conjunction of predicates specifying the gray-levels of the pixels in the array. However, here we will be concerned with the actual interpretation of the picture, or in other words what a picture is taken to *represent*.

[6]Why can't we simply stipulate that a certain homogeneous red canvas (i.e., noncomplex) represents the Empire State Building? Sober claims that in this case it is not clear that we are still dealing with a pictorial representation; such a stipulation seems to violate the principles governing the conventional use of pictorial representation.

[7]This requirement is akin to the specificity of pictorial representations.

[8]From the characterization given below, it follows that a relational databases without null values is an example of a vivid representation of information.

[9]Examples are from Jim des Rivières and Ray Reiter.

[10]If we assume that we can access individual symbols in constant time, than it follows that in a vivid KB one can determine a (relevant) relationship between a group of objects in constant time.

REFERENCES

Bledsoe, W. W., Boyer, R. S., & Henneman W.H. (1972). Computer proofs of limit theorems. *Artificial Intelligence, 3,* 27–60.

Bobrow, D. G. (1984). Qualitative reasoning about physical systems: an introduction. *Artificial Intelligence, 24,* 1–6.

Brooks, R. A. (1981). Symbolic reasoning among 3-D models and 2-D images. *Artificial Intelligence,* 17, 285–348.

Connell, J. H. & Brady, M. (1987). Generating and generalizing models of visual objects. *Artificial Intelligence, 31*(2), 155–184.

De Kleer, J. & Brown, J. S. (1983). Assumptions and ambiguities in mechanistic mental models. In D. Gentner & A. L. Stevens (Eds.), *Mental model.* Hillsdale, NJ: Lawrence Erlbaum Associates, 155–190.

De Kleer, J. & Brown, J. S. (1984). Qualitative physics based on confluences. *Artificial Intelligence, 24,* 7–83.

Fikes, R. E. & Nilsson, N. J. (1971). STRIPS: a new approach to the application of theorem proving to problem solving. *Artificial Intelligence,* 2, 189–208.

Finke, R. A. (1986). Mental imagery and the visual system. *Scientific American,* March, 88–95.

Fischer, M. J. & Rabin, M. O. (1974). Super-exponential complexity of Presburger arithmetic. Proceedings AMS Symposium on the Complexity of Real Computational Process, vii, 27–41.

Forbus, K. D. (1980). A study of qualitative and geometric knowledge in reasoning about motion. Technical Report AI.TR.615, Massachusetts Institute of Technology, AI-lab, February, 1981.

Forbus, K. D. (1983). Qualitative reasoning about space and motion. In D. Gentner and A. L. Stevens (Eds.), *Mental model.* Hillsdale, NJ: Lawrence Erlbaum Associates, 53–74.

Forbus, K. D. (1984). Qualitative process theory. *Artificial Intelligence, 24,* (1986), 85–168.

Funt, B. V. (1976). WHISPER: A computer implementation using analogues in reasoning. Doctoral dissertation, Department of Computer Science, University of British Columbia, Vancouver, Canada, March.

Funt, B. V. (1980). Problem-solving with diagrammatic representations. *Artificial Intelligence, 13,* (1980), 201–230. Reprinted in *Readings in knowledge representation* by R. J. Brachman & H. J. Levesque (Eds.), Los Altos, CA: Morgan Kaufmann, 1985, 441–456.

Funt, B. V. (1983). Analogical Modes of Reasoning and Process Modeling. *IEEE Computer,* October.

Gardin, F., Meltzer, B., & Stofella, P. (1986). The Analogical representation of liquids in naive physics. *Proceedings of the Seventh European Conference on Artificial Intelligence,* Brighton, U.K., July, 154–159.

Gelernter, H. (1959). Realization of a geometry theorem-proving machine. In *Information processing: Proceedings of the International Conference on Information Processing,* UNESCO, 1959. Reprinted in *Computers and thought,* E. A. Feigenbaum & J. Feldman (Eds.), New York: McGraw-Hill, 1963, 134–152.

Gelernter, H., Hansen J. R., & Loveland, D. W. (1960). Empirical Explorations of the Geometry Theorem Proving Machine. *Proceedings Western Joint Computer Conference, May 1960.* Reprinted in *Computers and thought,* E. A. Feigenbaum & J. Feldman (Eds.), New York: McGraw-Hill, 1963, 153–163.

Gilmore P. C. (1970). An examination of the geometry theorem machine. *Artificial Intelligence, 1,* (1970), 171–187.

Hayes, P. J. (1974). Some problems and non-problems in representation theory. *Proceedings of AISB Summer Conference,* University of Sussex, 1974, 63–79. Reprinted in *Readings in knowledge representation* by R. J. Brachman & H. J. Levesque (Eds.), Los Altos, CA: Morgan Kaufmann, 1985, 3–22.

Hinton, G. E. (1979). Some demonstrations of the effects of structural descriptions in mental imagery. *Cognitive Science, 3,* 231–250.

Hinton. G. E., McClelland, J. L., & Rumelhart D. E. (1986). Distributed representations. In *Parallel distributed processing* by D. E. Rumelhart, J. L. McClelland, & the PDP Research Group, Vol. 1, 71–109. Cambridge MA: Bradford/MIT Press.

Hobbs, J. R., Blenko, T., Croft, B., Hager, G., Kautz, H. A., Kube, P., & Shoham, Y. (1985). *Commonsense Summer: Final Report,* Report No. CSLI-85-35, Center for the Study of Language and Information, Stanford University, October.

Howell, R. (1976). Ordinary pictures, mental representations, and logical forms. *Synthese, 33,* 149–174.

Inhelder, B. & Piaget, J. (1958). *The growth of logical thinking from childhood to adolescence.* London: Routledge and Kegan Paul.

Johnson-Laird, P. N. (1983). *Mental models.* Cambridge, MA: Harvard University Press.

Kosslyn, S. M. (1981). The medium and message in mental imagery: A theory. In N. Block (Ed.), *Imagery* (pp. 207–244). Cambridge MA: Bradford/MIT Press.

Larkin, J. H. & Simon, H. A. (1987). Why a picture is (sometimes) worth ten thousand words. To appear in *Cognitive Science.*

Levesque, H. J. (1986). Making believers out of computers. *Artificial Intelligence, 30,* 81–108.

Levesque, H. J. & Brachman, R. J. (1985). "A fundamental tradeoff in knowledge representation and reasoning (revised version)." In R. J. Brachman & H. J.

Levesque (Eds.), *Readings in knowledge representation* (pp. 41–70). Los Altos, CA: Morgan Kaufmann.

Lifechitz, V. (1986). On the semantics of STRIPS. *Workshop on Planning.* Timberline.

Mackinlay, J. & Geneserth, M. R. (1984). Expressiveness and language choice. Proceedings of the Fourth National Conference on Artificial Intelligence, 226–232 Austin, TX.

McCarthy, J. & Hayes, P. (1969). Some philosophical problems from the standpoint of artificial intelligence. In B. Meltzer & D. Michie, *Machine Intelligence, 4,* 463–502. Edinburgh University Press.

McDermott, D. V. (1987). Critique of pure reason. To appear in *Computational Intelligence.*

McDermott, D. V. & Davis, E. (1984). Planning routes through uncertain territory. Artificial Intelligence, 22, 107–156.

Newell, A. (1982). The knowledge level. *Artificial Intelligence 18*(1), 87–127.

Palmer, S. P. (1978). Fundamental aspects of cognitive representation. In E. H. Rosch & B. B. Lloyd (Eds.), *Cognition and categorization* (pp. 259–303). Hillsdale, NJ: Erlbaum Press.

Pylyshyn, Z. W. (1981). The imagery debate: Analogue media versus tacit knowledge. *Psychological Review 88,* 16–45.

Reiter, R. (1976). A semantically guided deductive system for automatic theorem proving. *IEEE Transactions on Computers, C-25*(4), 328–334.

Reiter, R. (1984). Towards a logical reconstruction of relational database theory. In M. L. Brodie, J. Mylopoulos, & J. W. Schmidt (Eds.). *On Conceptual Modelling Perspectives from artificial intelligence, databases, and programming languages* (pp. 191–233). New York, NY: Springer-Verlag.

Schubert, L. K., Papalaskris, M. A., & Taughter, J. (1983). Determining type, part, color, and time relationships. *IEEE Computer,* October, 53–60.

Shepard, R. N. (1978). The mental image. *American Psychologist, 33,* 125–137.

Shepard, R. N. & Meltzer, J. (1971). Mental rotation of three dimensional objects. *Science, 171,* 701–703.

Simmons, R. G. (1982). Spatial and temporal reasoning in geological map interpretation. *Proceedings of the Second National Conference on Artificial Intelligence,* 152–154. Pittsburgh, PA.

Sloman, A. (1971). Interactions between philosophy and AI—The role of intuition and non-logical reasoning in intelligence. *Advance Papers of the Second International Joint Conference on Artificial Intelligence.* London, U.K. Reprinted in *Artificial Intelligence, 2,* 1971, 209–225.

Sloman, A. (1975). Afterthoughts on analogical representations. *Proceedings Theoretical Issues in Natural Language Processing.* 164–168. Cambridge, MA. Reprinted in Readings in Knowledge Representation by R. J. Brachman and H. J. Levesque (Eds.), Los Altos, CA: Morgan Kaufmann, 1985, 431–440.

Sober, E. (1976). Mental representations. *Synthese, 33,* 104–148.

Stickel, M. E. (1985). Automated deduction by theory resolution. *Proceedings of the Ninth International Joint Conference on Artificial Intelligence,* 1181–1186. Los Angeles, CA.

Valiant, L. G. & Vazirani, V. V. (1985). NP is as easy as detecting unique solutions. *Proceedings of the Seventh Annual ACM Symposium on the Theory of Computing,* Providence, Rhode Island, May, 458–462.

Weyhrauch, R. W. (1980). Prolegomena to a theory of mechanized formal reasoning. *Artificial Intelligence, 13,* (1980), 133–170. Reprinted in *Readings in knowledge representation* by R. J. Brachman & H. J. Levesque (Eds.), Los Altos, CA: Morgan Kaufmann, 1985, 309–328.

chapter 6

Possibilities and Real Possibilities for a Theory of Reasoning

Luca Bonatti
luca@lscp.msh-paris.fr
Laboratoire des Sciences Cognitives et Psycholinguistique, Paris

SQUEEZING PHILOSOPHICAL JUICE FROM A THEORY OF REASONING

What happens when we become convinced that tigers are dangerous animals, that Gödel's proof is right, or that we ought to fight against starvation in the third world? Here are three statements. One is about the world and certain objects in it; the second one states a mathematical fact; and the last one goes beyond the theoretical sphere, committing us to a certain course of action. Is there a common explanation, a common system contributing to the fixation of kinds of beliefs that are so different? Let us call this question Question P, as a shortcut for "Philosophically very interesting question to which psychologists pay very little attention nowadays."

Since these topics have been at the center of philosophical interest for centuries, it would seem that the relevant theoretical options are unmanageably many. However, if one takes a naturalized standpoint about epistemology and the morals, answers to such questions turn out to depend on the state of development of specific empirical theories. There are many possibilities, but *possible* explanations of reasoning are not enough; what we need is the space of *real* possibilities, as they now appear to turn out. And once the current theories about reasoning and the mind are taken into account, the options will turn out to be surprisingly few. The present paper intends to chart that space, thus filling in a precondition for answering Question P.

I will make a negative and a positive point. In a nutshell, my negative point is that we know much less than is generally admitted on reasoning, and that most evidence does not afford precisely the kind of information

85

we would need in order to decide between alternative theories. My positive point is that the little we know about the notion of *natural logical consequence* may be sufficient to at least frame an answer to Question P.

I proceed in the following way. I start by identifying the broad landmarks of the space to explore. I then briefly argue that as of now, among the merely possible theories, the really possible options are all representational in nature. I present the basic ideas behind them, get rid of nonreal differences between them, and show what the real difference consists of. I then argue for my negative point: most of the available evidence is mute on such a difference. Finally, I briefly return to Question P, and argue for my positive note.

THE OPTIONS

At least three models of reasoning either suggest different naturalistic solutions to Question P or imply that no solution can be given.

One way to answer is to hold that our reasoning processes are governed by a mental logic. Briefly, according to this view, the content of our beliefs is represented in a certain syntactic form, and rules or procedures manipulating their syntax derive other beliefs. Particularly attracted to this view, which I will call the *mental logic hypothesis*, are those who are sensitive to the apparent similarity between the inner processes leading from beliefs to other beliefs in different domains, and to our ability to handle problems arising in new or unfamiliar situations.

Another possible answer is that reasoning is a content- (or situation-) driven process. According to this view, rather than applying general rules acting on the syntax of mental representations, the mind exploits certain features of the situations it represents. Here reasoning is not, strictly speaking, *inferential,* but is like imagining "what happens after" in a movie. Our ability to carry on such a process will depend on the content of the particular scene we are inspecting, and on what we already know about similar situations. Thus partial to this view are those who are struck by our unequal problem solving skills, which seem to decrease in inverse proportion to the abstractness of the problem at hand. According to this line—I will call it the *mental models hypothesis*—there still is a structural description of reasoning, but lo and behold the key factors will be content and/or familiarity, rather than form.

A third possibility, put in an extreme way, is that we don't reason at all. Our good performance at solving certain classes of problems could be entirely due to our attunement with the environment, progressively refined through evolution. To have a sense of how this position differs from the previous ones, let's imagine that we are dealing with our nutrition system. The two first hypotheses would explain nutrition by appealing to the existence of a stomach transforming food *via* digestion. But we might indeed be organisms living in an environment made up of a sort of pre-munched soup containing all the proteins and vitamins necessary for us. Thus, without any need for a stomach, nutrition might be a direct passage of the nutrients from our mouths to our bodies. We might have enough plasticity to adapt to small variations—so we find, say, groups who survive by eating slightly different types of premunched soups—whereas natural selection may have taken care of eliminating all the really unfit creatures.

Ascending from stomachs to brains, according to the third hypothesis we carry out what we improperly call a reasoning process as a sort of direct response to situations in the environment, more or less like we react appropriately to our ecological niche when we intuitively care for our offspring and we intuitively don't care for cockroaches. Attracted to this view are those who feel strongly about our apparent good problem-solving abilities only in environmentally sound situations, and who are uncontrollably nervous about talk of inner representations, competence, cognizing, and similar notions.

TRIMMING THE OPTIONS

The first two images of the human processor are both structural in nature. They both postulate a reasoning box that transforms representations into other representations. As such, they have to take representational talk seriously: laws of reasoning are laws quantifying over representations, and by standard Quinean reasons this is ontologically committing. In striking contrast, the third option *prima facie* does not need to postulate any specific reasoning processor. In an important sense, for it to reason is the same as to tell apart a triangle from a circle: there is really no reasoning, but only pattern recognition:

> Some believe that the existence of inferences implies a kind of logical system similar to that employed in conventional symbolic-processing models. I have become increasingly convinced that much of what we call reasoning can better be accounted for by processes such as pattern matching and generalization, which are well carried out by PDP models. (Rumelhart 1980, p. 28)

Nor is such option committed to any particular view of mental representations, and in fact it promises to be able to dispense with them. Hence the nonstructural view is apparently the simplest and the most radical one, and it should be taken as the null hypothesis.

Yet, it is not a *really* possible option. The troubles with it are twofold. There is first a principled problem, which can be expressed thus: shapes come in all sorts of shapes. In particular, the shape of a contradiction is just slightly different from the shape of a logical truth: it suffices to add a little negation. But that addition makes all the possible differences with respect to all sorts of problems we can raise about the mind. Pattern matching is a general mechanism, totally indifferent to the *kinds* of patterns being matched. On the contrary, what we want to know from a theory of reasoning is why certain patterns, and not others, are causally responsible for drawing the inferences that we consider *good* inferences. An explanation of reasoning based solely on pattern matching, and not on the logical nature of the patterns being matched, is bound to miss the main point about reasoning.

The second trouble concerns the state of development of the hypothesis. A psychologically plausible theory of even a fragment of deductive reasoning *which respects the ideology of the nonstructural view* does not exist. There seems to be a trade off between psychological adequacy and antistructural ideology: some proposals respect the ideology but cannot be considered a model even of a fragment of human reasoning, and some others are serious options, but do not respect the ideology.[1]

Bechtel and Abrahamsen (1991) offer a good example of a theory of the first kind. Moved by the fact that undergraduates have difficulties at mastering abstract logical systems, they argue that there is no natural system of logic and treat propositional reasoning abilities as an emergent property of a connectionist network. To show how such abilities could arise out of sheer training, they present a network that separates valid from invalid arguments out of a group of 194 test problems roughly performing as undergraduates do. To obtain such levels of correctness (84%), the network needed 960,000 training trials on 384 trial problems. Bechtel and Abrahamsen feel entitled to conclude that their network is psychologically plausible because it "clearly exhibited one of the prominent characteristics of student performance; it required a good deal of practice and error correction before it could solve most of the problems" (p. 171). They add that "the network did a credible job of learning to recognize argument forms and evaluate the validity of arguments" (p. 171).

Now, to evaluate the seriousness of such conclusions it is enough to look at some details. Consider first the competence aspect. *All* the arguments (the 384 training arguments plus the 194 test arguments) were obtained by only 12 argument schemes like "If p then q, p; therefore q" by substituting p and q with of the letters A, B, C, D and their negations, and the network required 960,000 training trials to master them. Presumably, another great deal of training is necessary to extend its ability to handle the same schemas when substitutions with the letter E are allowed. By contrast, subjects' competence, say, on *modus ponens* is a totally different phenomenon: when the rule is understood in one case, its generalization to all its substitutions is immediate. Or consider the learning aspect. If we take seriously the psychological reality of their network and we assume, for the sake of the argument, a learning period of ten years, we should conclude that without taking any day off, and by practicing 266 times per day, children finally master 12 argument schemas and can apply them to up to four different contents! Clearly neither the kind of training nor the kind of "know how" acquired by the network has any remote connection with any kind of human logical ability. To stick to a strict antirepresentational ideology, Bechtel and Abrahamsen abandon any psychological plausibility.

On the other end of the spectrum, Shastri and Ajjanagadde (1993) present a network aimed at implementing the fast and almost reflexive reasoning typical of most human verbal (and nonverbal) interactions, in a parallel architecture constrained by biologically plausible parameters. Their network, SHRUTI, intends to model how dynamically generated facts (facts that the system is given on the spot, without consulting its internal memory) can interact on-line with long term structures and quickly generate inferences. For example, when people are told "John gives a book to Mary," presumably they are able to derive the consequence "Mary owns a book" immediately. In essence, Shastri and Ajjanagadde account for such abilities by wiring in the relevant meaning postulates connecting the relevant predicates, and by using temporal synchrony between nodes in order to get the right thematic role assignments in the inferences.

Shastri and Ajjanagadde's very ingenuous solutions, which cannot be reviewed here, are a good example of how a parallel architecture can handle nontrivial inferential problems. But for our purposes it is important to notice that SHRUTI also turns out to be committed to a fair amount of representational ontology—a fact that the authors would be willing to admit—and thus is not an alternative to the ontology of the structural view. There are at least two levels at which SHRUTI is committed to representations of explicit rules. The first one is already there: meaning postulates are already explicitly represented. The second one would be there if SHRUTI were developed enough to account for data on deduction. SHRUTI does apply some *modus ponens* inferences without explicitly representing an abstract logical rule for it. However, it does so only locally, in effect by specifying *modus ponens* predicate by predicate. If SHRUTI were to be extended to account for people's logical abilities at drawing abstract inferences, then the natural way to do so would be to follow precisely the same solution Shastri and Ajjanagadde used for representing inferences among predicates. Connections between nodes representing antecedents and consequences of abstract rules should be wired in, and in this way SHRUTI would end up incorporating an ontology for reasoning similar to that of the structural options.

In sum, the nonstructural, antirepresentational view, attractive as it may look, is not presently in the running. We have to look somewhere else.

THE STRUCTURAL OPTIONS

The real possibilities for a theory of reasoning are restricted to the mental models and mental logic hypotheses. Although both structural in nature, their differences are apparently so marked that they are generally presented as radical alternatives. However, finding out exactly what they say, why they are incompatible, and what evidence could settle the issue, is a far from trivial task. The nature of the opposition has been described in various ways, as the alternative between analog and digital representations; between semantic and syntactic methods; between form and content; between explicit rules and implicit inferential ability; and between abstract and concrete reasoning. In fact, all such differences, on which most of the debate between models and logic has focused, are largely artifacts of imprecise pictures of the two hypotheses. I will first get rid of the most misleading contrasts; I will then identify the real difference between the two hypotheses; and finally, I will argue that most of the empirical data are mute on such a difference.

WHAT THE CONTRAST BETWEEN MODELS AND LOGIC IS NOT

It is important to see that the hypotheses have much in common. First, they are both varieties of a representational theory of mind. They are both about the nature of the internal representations of deductive processes. Hence, if there is a fight, in an important sense it is a family fight.

Second, both hypotheses recognize that before reasoning proper, many other representations must be computed. For example, if the input is a spoken text, both hypotheses admit that at least phonetic, phonological, prosodic, and syntactic forms, as well as the literal meaning of words and sentences, must be computed. So from sound waves until reasoning both hypotheses presuppose the same representational ontology; in particular, they both recognize that propositional representations of the input are computed before reasoning proper takes place (see, for example, Johnson-Laird & Byrne 1991, ch. 9).

Third, neither hypothesis accounts for the role of pragmatics in reasoning. According to both architectures, the input relevant to reasoning is not the first semantic analysis of a text, but the propositional representations of the message *once all contributions of pragmatic factors have been integrated.*

Supporters of the mental logic hypothesis explicitly admit that comprehension processes are prior to reasoning (Braine et al. 1984; Braine & O'Brien 1991). It is more difficult to see that the same holds for the mental model hypothesis, since often we find the opposite claim in the literature (see for example, Byrne 1991; Byrne & Johnson-Laird 1990; Johnson-Laird et al. 1993), but an analysis of the mechanism of model construction makes it clear. In a nutshell, according to the model hypothesis, a set of procedures sometimes called procedural semantics acts on a propositional representation of the premises of a text and outputs models. But if a roughly Gricean picture of language is correct, and communication is loaded with conversational implicatures, then procedural semantics cannot act on the *verbatim* propositional representations of the text: if it did, it would miss the correct implicatures and would deliver inappropriate models. The right input for procedural semantics must be disambiguated input; hence, pragmatics must have exerted its influence before the first models for a linguistic message are constructed (see Bonatti 1994).

Fourth, both hypotheses hold that there are two different kinds of reasoning: a fast and almost automatic process occurring during text comprehension proper, and another process based on more complicated reasoning strategies and structures. In the mental model hypothesis, this difference is captured by assuming that understanding a problem involves the construction of the minimal number of models compatible with its premises, whereas reasoning proper consists in the construction of further models that are possible counterexamples to the conclusion. Unlike first understanding, a search for counterexamples is supposed to be costly and optional. In the mental logic hypothesis, the same distinction is captured by the difference between two kinds of rules. For example, Braine's theory of propositional reasoning assumes that a (presumably innate) routine— the Direct Reasoning Routine in Braine et al. (1984)—is available to subjects effortlessly and almost automatically, and supposedly is the origin of our ability to draw many sudden inferences when we explicitly solve problems or when we are engaged in everyday verbal interactions. The logic corresponding to such routines is not complete, but is sufficient to account for quite an extended inferential ability. Other secondary routines and strategies account for individual differences. The theory supposes that reasoners resort to them only when the direct reasoning routine fails. They have a higher computational cost, are not easily available, and may not ever be available to certain subjects.[2]

If we keep in mind such commonalities, some of the contrasts that have motivated the opposition between mental logic and mental models turn out to be misleading. One, particularly pernicious, describes the contrast as the opposition between semantic and syntactic methods, or between contentful and formal methods. Generally the opposition is constructed in the following way. A mental logic theory is meant to be a description of the mechanism driving inferences in reasoning and text comprehension. Hence, it is a syntactically-based theory. By contrast, mental models are alleged to be "semantic:"

> Formal rule theories lack the machinery to deal naturally with meaning— they are, by definition, theories that depend on the form of inferences (...) In contrast, the model theory *has the machinery to deal with meaning*—it is a theory that depends on the semantic procedures that construct models. (Byrne 1991, p. 77)

> The bare idea of a sentential engine does not, as I have said, explain the nature of intentionality; (...) sentences qua syntactic items do not have their semantics written into them. This makes for a stark contrast with the modelling theory, since models are *already* intrinsically semantically significant— they have the mechanism of intentionality engraved right on them. (McGinn 1989, p. 202)

But there is no basis for these claims. The same argument that led us to conclude that models don't explain the role of pragmatics in reasoning applies for the role of meaning as well. Models are built after the surface and the disambiguated semantic analysis of the message have been retrieved, and hence presuppose meaning precisely as mental logic does.[3] This shouldn't surprise anybody: theories built around the mental model hypothesis are theories about the structure of certain internal representations. If they are true, they clarify *how* we reason—in virtue of which mechanisms we solve certain problems and yet are unable to solve others. But a theory of the *mechanism* for reasoning, just as any other theory of mechanism, *is syntactic through and through.*

So mental models are as formal and syntactic as mental logic is, in the sense of Stich (1983). And in fact, the very same literature supporting models is based on such assumption. Most of the best empirical evidence for models consists of studies that investigate how subjects perform when solving totally formal problems, such as syllogisms (Johnson-Laird & Bara 1984), or problems containing different types of quantifiers (Johnson-Laird, Byrne & Tabossi 1989). And rightly so: if the model theory is right, the mechanisms it describes must work equally well whether subjects are given problems with or without content.

It may still be said that still models can make better room for the role of content in reasoning, whereas mental logic cannot. But even this argument is misleading. Surely there are many places for a model-like theory in which to factor in content. For example, the content of a message can be sufficiently plausible to stop the construction of further models, and hence can induce errors in reasoning—or, vice-versa, can stimulate search for counterexamples (see for example Oakill, Johnson-Laird & Garnham 1989). But a mental logic theory could make the exact same room for content. We may say that content can elicit more sophisticated strategies of proof, or that when it biases a certain conclusion, it forces the system to bypass all nonmandatory inferences. Even with respect to the possible role of content, the hypotheses are on the same footing.

My conclusion leaves us somewhat puzzled. If I am correct, the two hypotheses have much in common; furthermore, some of the central motivations opposing them turn out to be unfounded. Should we conclude that, surface differences notwithstanding, the two hypotheses are in reality one?

No. There is a real difference; it lies, I claim, in the *structure* of the representational device on which reasoning is defined. Yet, once again, most of the debate between models and logic is not about this real difference, but turns around a misleading contrast. I now turn to show this point.

PURE AND IMPURE REPRESENTATIONS: THE REAL NATURE OF THE DISPUTE[4]

Scientists are humans and are endowed with the psychological equipment typical of every other member of their species. For some unexplained reason, humans are irresistibly attracted to the elegance of clear-cut distinctions. *Qua* humans, scientists too are happy when they find some clear landmarks that allow them to chart the territory of their interest more clearly. To detect such landmarks more easily, it is often useful to see the problems from a certain distance, as philosophy teaches us to do: from such a vantage point, differences seem much more defined. The trouble is that distance may also induce errors of perspective that may get us lost when coming back to normal, everyday work. On balance, if we want to get around safely, we will be better off abandoning philosophical elegance and getting a closer look at the actual territory. This, I think, is the best course of action for the case at hand also.

The basic intuition of the mental logic hypothesis is clear: at a certain level of analysis a logical form of the propositional representations contained in the input message (not specific to the natural language in which the message is encoded) is computed, and acting over it are procedures implementing logical rules which derive further logical forms. Notice that such a picture is compatible with the existence of some domain-specific inferential mechanisms which, in certain cases to be specified, draw inferences on the basis of nonlogical features of the representations.

Seen from a distance, the intuition behind the mental model hypothesis seems clear and attractive also, so attractive that one may lose interest in getting any closer. Roughly, it claims that reasoning (and text understanding) consists in the manipulation of tokens representing concrete samples of entities in the world, and in the construction of alternative arrangements of tokens. Deduction doesn't need any abstract rules: the intrinsic properties of the representation will suffice.

Thus, at least at first blush, although mental logic seems to require naturally a language of thought on whose formulas abstract rules or procedure apply, mental models seem to be able to dispense with discrete manipulation of proposition-like objects in favor of analog simulations. What keeps reasoning processes and the world in phase are not operations over linguistic entities, but the existence of a special relationship between world and internal representations: the representations in the head are isomorphic to the situations in the world. So the theory of mental models promises to be not only an alternative to mental logic but also, to the extent to which the two are linked, to the language of thought (e.g., McGinn 1989; Garnham 1993).

Once the intuitive picture behind models is accepted, it seems natural to describe a thinking system as a simulation engine:

> A thinking system, we might say, is a *simulation engine*—a device that mimics, copies, replicates, duplicates, imitates, parallels reality. The basis of the intentional relation consists in the relation of literal modeling. And the procedures that operate on these models themselves model external processes: mental causal processes replicate worldly causal processes, mental laws imitate physical laws. There is a kind of isomorphism between the world and the mind (or its tectonic basis). (McGinn 1989, p. 176)

In short, models would differ from the kinds of representations postulated by mental logic because the latter ones are purely linguistic, discrete entities not directly related to the world, whereas the former ones are purely nonlinguistic, analog, and are governed by laws that simulate the laws of the world (see also Selman, this volume). That would seem strong enough a contrast to justify the opposition between the two hypotheses. They contrast two opposite kinds of representations: two incompatible, though equally pure, representations.

This is the intuition. But what happens when we get a closer look at the actual scientific theories? You will have noticed more than one resemblance with the case of mental imagery. Images are also described as nonlinguistic, analog representational devices that put in the mind a faithful reproduction of the world. But with the resemblances, the criticisms come as well. So if models are to be the basis for a theory of reasoning and text understanding, we cannot take *seriously* the idea that such pure representations provide the desired ontology, for at least two of their features. First, precisely like images (see Fodor 1975), they are not expressively rich enough. A model of Mary loving John is also a model of Mary not loving Mark, of Jack and Karl being left out of Mary's life, and so on, but these are all different potential premises or conclusions of different arguments and must be kept distinct. Hence, pure models can't provide the right ontology for reasoning and text comprehension. Second, if models simulate the world, and they simulate analogically, then they have to exploit properties of the architecture of the mind, this being the only way to make sense of the notion of analog simulation (Pylyshyn 1984). But then the same properties will be exploited whenever the same kinds of architectural structure invoke the same laws (see the thorough arguments in Pylyshyn 1980; 1981; 1984), and hence we should expect that the same inferential pattern will go through in those cases. But that will lead to absurdities right away. Consider an example. It is argued that people draw the inference 'John is to the right of Karl' on the basis of the premises 'John is to the right of Mary' and 'Mary is to the right of Karl' not in virtue of the existence of a meaning postulate governing the spatial relations 'To-the-right-of', as a logic-like theory would suggest, but because models are constructed in working memory with a structure whose laws *simulate* the spatial deployment of John, Mary, and Karl in the world (see Johnson-Laird & Byrne 1991; Johnson-Laird 1983). Hence, by a property of the architecture of working memory, transitivity is guaranteed. But architecture is architectural, that is, stable. If it were the case that the laws governing the mechanisms sustaining the representation are responsible for the inference, we should conclude that in all cases similar representations trigger similar inferences, and therefore, that the architecture constrains us to derive that John loves Karl from the premises that John loves Mary and Mary loves Karl.

To dispose of such absurdities, we are obliged to qualify when the laws of the architecture mimicking transitivity are relevant for the inferences to be drawn. We have to say that in the case of a model for spatial premises they are, whereas in the case of a model for 'Love', they are not. But this is to say that the laws governing models and the mechanisms involved in handling them are irrelevant, *except when they satisfy the logical properties of the relation they represent,* and this amounts to the denial that the analog properties of the representations can dispense with the logical properties of the relations (see Pylyshyn 1980, p. 125). Models don't speak for themselves: somehow the logical properties of the relations must indicate which features of the representation are to be recruited to guarantee the relevant inferences without resorting to purely symbolic manipulations.

Such considerations may lead us to seriously doubt the soundness of the intuitive picture behind pure mental models. And, in fact, once we look at *the real* mental models more closely—the ones developed, to a certain extent, in actual theories of deductive reasoning—we find quite a different picture. Models are not just arrangements of tokens isomorphic to the world. They contain many linguistic elements that make them quite different from sheer replicas of the world. Consider, for example, negation. For modelists, or image theorists, or direct realists, it is a delicate matter indeed. The reason is simple: there is no negation in the world, and therefore there is no negation in images, models, or anything directly extracted from the world. How is it possible to overcome this limitation? Johnson-Laird and Byrne claim that models can do it quite easily. If the model for 'There is a triangle' is

$$\Delta$$

then the model for 'There is not a triangle' is

$$\neg\Delta$$

where the added tag "is a propositional-like tag representing negation" (Johnson-Laird & Byrne 1991, p. 44; see also Johnson-Laird et al. 1992, p. 422). So, at least for atomic sentences, negation is represented *directly within models* in its propositional form, rather than being an operation over models.

Or, again, models represent quantifiers by means of specific representative samples of the domain of quantification. As a consequence, quantified sentences turn out to be always existentially entailing (see Boolos 1984): for any predicate in a quantified sentence there will be at least one token instantiating it in the corresponding mental models. This implies that the model of 'All men are mortal', is also a model in which 'There are men', and "There are mortals" are true. But then also from "All unicorns have wings" we should derive that there are unicorns and they have wings. Therefore, apparently, mental models cannot represent sentences such as "Unicorns don't exist". Now, we may overcome the problem by enriching models with another linguistic element. We may add another "propositional-like" tag that acts like an existence predicate of a free logic, thus distinguishing real tokens from imaginary tokens.

Or, again, it is constitutive of "pure" mental models that they don't contain variables, but only tokens representing individuals, and indeed a *specific* number of tokens. But then they are too poor to explain nonfinitary reasoning and reasoning with big cardinalities. Once again, the shortcoming is not a fatal one. We may imagine putting individual tokens to double duty, treating them as representatives for classes and thus mimicking variables in logical forms. This can be achieved by adding further linguistic labels stating something like "This token is really there for all its friends." Likewise, to explain numerical reasoning we could add labels for big cardinalities, as Johnson-Laird himself suggested. So the representation for "There are 50,492 individuals in the stadium" contains tokens for individuals to which labels are attached "functioning as a propositional-like label attached to the model" (Johnson-Laird 1983, p. 443) and representing the number 50,492. But then surely we also need to introduce operations over tags. For clearly when the model needs to be updated because only 43,014 individuals remain in the stadium after 7,478 left, the only way to do it is to operate a subtraction directly over the linguistic label in the model. In other words, it is necessary to reproduce within models *the same operations that would be needed if models did not exist in the first place* and the representations were expressed linguistically.

Pure mental models are plagued by many other similar limitations, and the way to overcome them is also similar. Thus, once we move from the intuitive idea to a real theory, we have to begin quickly polluting the original purity of the representations by introducing linguistic labels and operations over them. Real mental models are not "pure models," but a sort of mixed form of representation partly linguistic and partly alinguistic. This means that the intuitive picture behind models does not correspond to any really possible theory. The ambitious version of the model theory, which was supposed to offer a "*radical* alternative to the language of thought" (McGinn 1989), is not a real possibility: in reasoning, we cannot do without an internal language.

Now we can finally see what the real controversy is about. It does not concern *alternative kinds* of internal representations, as the intuitive pictures lead us to think. It is a much less exciting, wholly empirical enterprise of *assessing how many linguistic elements are needed in the representations of the various domains of reasoning under investigation*. Hence, to do justice to the hypotheses, we must assess *case by case* which elements of the representations—whether the symbolic ones or the "modelic" ones, if any—bear the burden of the explanation. The puzzle I want to raise in the next section is that much of the evidence generally considered to decisively rule in favor of models is in fact mute on the real dispute.

HOW MUCH DOES THE CURRENT EVIDENCE SAY ON THE REAL DISPUTE?

Today, to one degree or another, almost every psychologist, linguist or semanticist makes working use of mental models, without paying too much attention to the nature of the entities she postulates. So one may easily get the impression that everybody really means the same thing when talking about models. As Johnson-Laird puts it,

In some domains theorists have emphasized the *content* of mental models. [...] In other domains, such as perception, discourse, and reasoning, theorists have emphasized the *structure* of models and how they are constructed by mental processes. Yet the theorists are talking about the same beast. (1989, p. 490)[5]

In fact, I will argue, the notion is multiply realized. Furthermore, I will show that in some cases the senses of mental model are not appropriate for a psychologically plausible theory of reasoning, and in some other cases the evidence gives no information about the real controversy between models and logic or, if anything, suggests that a mental logic theory is correct.

Nonpertinent Uses of Models

We should first dismiss all the uses of the notion that have no psychological value. These can be found especially in the program of psychologization of intensional semantics. A tradition originated with Montague has elaborated sophisticated formal analyses by using model and modal theories. Partee (1979) proposed to develop a semantics with a human face, a theory with both the expressive capabilities of a linguist's semantics and the desired psychological plausibility.

After initial enthusiasm, the program stalled. This was partly due to the restricted range of application of the original Montagovian semantics, but a deeper difficulty exists: it is not at all clear that we can have it both ways. To gain adequate descriptive power, intensional semantics seems to need formal tools clearly beyond the reach of human mind. It seems that a choice is called for between a psychologically plausible semantics and a linguistically satisfactory semantics.

Maybe the future will bring better insights on how to bridge the gap between the two domains. However, for the moment the sense of mental model currently used in natural language semantics is not psychologically relevant. In any case, if progress were made and the linguist's models became psychologically credible, they would not coincide with the current notion of mental models used by psychologists of reasoning. Consider, for example, type distinctions: they are essential in Montague-like theories, whereas there is no space for them in psychologists' mental models. Once again, it is possible to add types to mental models by enriching their linguistic component with further labels, but then the linguistic elements within mental models would acquire further importance and the distinction with a mental logic theory would become even more watered down.

Mental Models as Clusters of Beliefs

Studies on naive and expert representations of specific domains of knowledge apparently offer more direct psychological evidence for models (see especially Gentner & Stevens 1983). I will claim however, that in most cases they are not informative about the nature of internal representations, and are in fact perfectly compatible with a program of mental logic. As usual, I will argue by reviewing some representative examples.

Generally, studies in this area deal either with how people interact with machines or objects in the world, or with how people master particular domains of knowledge. They often include some psychological experiments (mostly, protocol analyses of "work sessions") and, where the domain is not too complex, some computer simulations. For our purposes, an immediate difficulty is their explanatory span. A general theory of reasoning must account for people's ability at handling certain general-purpose inferences, whereas general reasoning abilities, such as propositional or predicative inferences, or more broadly deductive reasoning, are not even in the conceivable explanatory domain of the theories offered.

But the main problem for the question I am addressing has to do with the kind of evidence provided when compared to the kind of problem that needs to be addressed. It is hard to find arguments or data that show that even the limited domains investigated by such studies *require* nonpropositional, pure model-like, knowledge representations. With only few exceptions (see *Analog Simulations*, later), if we eliminated the word "models" and substituted it with "naive theories," or "clusters of beliefs," nothing would be lost in the explanations offered.

Consider Norman (1983). His studies on man-machine interaction aim at finding out what kind of "model" of a machine produces subjects' typical behaviors while interacting with it. He reports that, for example, when people use a hand calculator, they often press the Clear or Enter buttons more than necessary. Protocol analysis reveals that certain typical beliefs are behind such uneconomical behavior. People justify their behavior with explanations like "You never know, sometimes it doesn't register," or "It doesn't hurt to hit extra." Norman concludes that "(t)hese behaviors seem to reflect some of the properties of mental models (...)" (p. 10). He takes mental models seriously: for him, "mental models are what people really have in their heads and what guides their use of things" (p. 12). But clearly here, far from being psychologically real, models don't bear any explanatory role. It is enough to say that people have beliefs, more or less justified, and act according to them. In their actions, they follow heuristics or rules of thumb that they can often spell out perfectly well in propositional terms. No insight on the internal form of the representation is given by Norman's findings.

On the basis of their studies on naive conceptions of space, McCloskey (1983) and Clement (1983) argue that people's reasoning about space is surprisingly similar to a pre-Galilean conception of physics. Subjects make many errors, which decrease with increased level of physics education, but remain constant in type across groups. Protocol analysis revealed that such errors are not casual, but that "subjects relied heavily upon a well-developed naive theory of motion in arriving at answers to the problems," and that all of them "held the same basic theory" (McCloskey 1983, p. 306), which roughly conforms to the medieval notion of *impetus*.

These are extremely interesting findings, but even in this case we may uniformly substitute the word "models" with "clusters of beliefs" without losing one single result. Yet, in interpreting similar findings, Clement writes:

> We have seen that deeply seated mental models in the form of physical intuitions can be very compelling and resilient, even in the face of potentially contradictory evidence. (...) They appear to have become "embedded into the system" at a perceptual-motor ("gut") level rather than at an abstract level. However, it is not yet clear how we are to go about modeling the way such deep notions are represented mentally. The usual method is to represent them as lists of symbols in the form of rules or propositions. This leaves unanswered the question of the locus of meaning underlying each symbol. Such models fail to capture the representational richness that is suggested by the resistance of preconception to change, by subjects; reference to "picturing", imagining and feeling, by spontaneous hand motions simulating forces and movements, and by expressions of necessity and intuitive conviction during explanation. These phenomena may eventually be more fruitfully modeled in terms of visual and kinesthetic representations of a more analogue character. (Clement 1983, p. 337)

Clement hints at a philosophical difficulty for propositional, mental logic-like theories: representing naive physical knowledge in terms of rules and propositions "leaves unanswered the question of the locus of meaning underlying each symbol." This is surely true, but there is no reason to suppose that mental models, or other analog representations of knowledge, shed any more light on the problem. In fact, neither theory has a way to address questions about the origin of meaning (see Bonatti 1994; Bonatti, MS). Clement looks for an alternative to propositional-like representations because he finds that subjects' intuitive theories of motion are resistant to advanced instruction, as if some kind of deep preconception blocked the installment of a correct theory. However, once again, deep preconceptions need not be nonpropositional in form to be resistant. The world is full of people holding beliefs explicitly represented in propositional form that turn out to be deep preconceptions.

In sum, in studies of this kind the notion of a mental model can stand perfectly as a shorthand for "theory," or "cluster of propositions." Every result is compatible with both the mental logic and the mental model hypotheses. Ingenious as they may be, such studies cannot provide the evidence required to address the detailed elements of the internal representations that are needed to settle what's really at stake.

Analogical Reasoning and Mental Models

Prima facie, studies on analogical reasoning seem to offer a better case for types of analog knowledge representation and/or for mental models. Analogies are often presented as mappings between different internal models. However, even these studies don't and can't provide the right evidence needed for making progress in the dispute between mental logic and mental models. To show this, I briefly examine the most developed theories of analogical reasoning.

Gentner (Gentner and Gentner 1983; Gentner and Toupin 1986; Gentner 1989) argued that analogies aren't simple rhetoric devices used to speed up familiarity with new areas, but engage specific psychological mechanisms. Gentner and Gentner (1983) tried to gather evidence for these mechanisms by investigating common reasoning about physical systems. By testing how novices solve unfamiliar problems once cued to use an analogy with a domain they know better, Gentner and Gentner showed that analogies may have a role in problem solving. Furthermore, the transfer of knowledge from the base (the known) domain to the target (the unknown) domain follows some systematic principles. Subjects import only certain elements from the base to the target. For example, electricity flows at a certain rate, like water, but is not wet, unlike water. Why, when using the flow of a river as an analogy to understand electricity, do people import the first piece of knowledge and not the second? Gentner proposes the hypothesis that reasoning by analogy exploits a structural mapping from the base domain to the target domain that keeps constant some of the *relations* holding among objects of the base domain, but none of their *predicates*. Consider how knowledge about the solar system can bear on problems about atomic structure. There is a base-structured domain of knowledge, involving planets and their laws, and a largely unknown target area to be investigated. The schema organizing knowledge in the base domain may be as shown in Figure 6.1, where "the nodes represent concepts treated as wholes and the predicates express propositions about the nodes" (p. 104).

Subjects can use the base schema by mapping its nodes (Sun, Planet, and so on) onto the nodes of the target domain (Atom, Electron, and so on), while leaving the relations linking the nodes in the first network (say, Revolves around) unchanged. More precisely, an analogy consists in a mapping *M* so characterized:

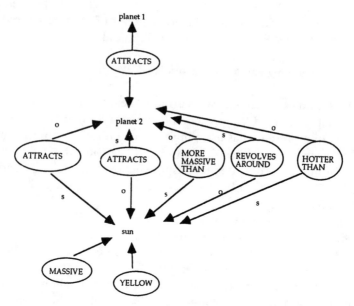

Note: Words in circles represent n-ary predicates, lowercase words represent nodes, and low-
        ercase ss and os represent thematic roles.

FIGURE 6.1.   Organization of knowledge in a domain (from Gentner & Gentner 1983).

- M: $b_i \rightarrow t_i$
- M: $(R\,(b_i,\,b_j) \rightarrow R(t_i,\,t_j))$

where *b*s are objects in the base domain, *t*s are objects in the target domain, and *R* is a relation holding in the base domain. A principle called *systematicity principle* by Gentner states the following: generally, the imported relations are those already connected in systems of relations within the base domain, and governed by higher order relations. So for example, "Is hotter than" and "Has more mass than" are both relations defined within the objects in the solar system, but the former stands somewhat on its own, and the latter participates with other relations in the relevant laws of the system. Simply put, it is because an object *a* has more mass than an object *b* that *a* attracts *b*; therefore, the relation "Has more mass than" is causally efficacious in the base domain, or equivalently, the relation is subsumed under the higher-order relation of causality. For Gentner (1989) the hierarchical structure of the relations is explicitly represented, by and large as shown in Figure 6.2.

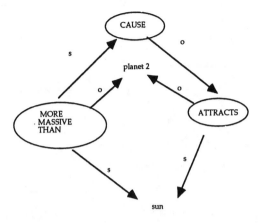

FIGURE 6.2.   Hierarchical structure of relations in a knowledge base.

A reasoning program can identify the relations to be preserved by inspecting the presence of superordinate relations linking them. Thus the mapping would bring the objects of the base domain into the objects of the target domain, and preserve the relations selected according to the systematicity principle, as shown in Figure 6.3, finally creating the new schema in Figure 6.4. It is assumed that a further step of analogical reasoning consists in checking the validity of the potential inferences on the target domain.

In sum, analogical reasoning is described as a general procedure, non-content-specific but content-sensitive, which superimposes part of the graph structure of a schema onto an unstructured set of nodes. These features have suggested a representation of knowledge calling for mental models; analogy would then be a systematic mapping between them.[6] However, the particular choice of how the two domains are represented is an *addition* to the theory of analogical reasoning, and not a part of it. A theory like Gentner's can place only very general constraints on knowledge representation—for example, it can force us to recognize that the base domain must be sorted by types, otherwise no mapping function can be correctly construed—but it cannot tell *how* such domains are internally structured. Should schemata, or models, be replaced by some other theoretical construct, the analogical theory wouldn't be touched in the least. Indeed, by representing knowledge as clusters of propositions, the required mapping can easily be defined as identity over a subclass of binary relations plus term substitution in the sentences expressing the propositions about the base domain.[7]

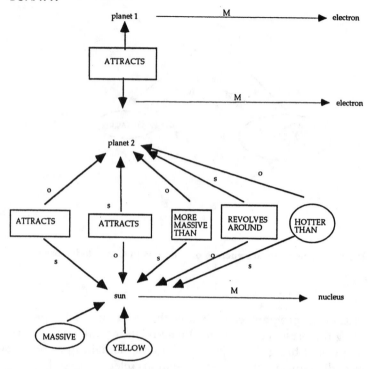

Note: Systematic relations are inside squares.

FIGURE 6.3.   How the mapping relation M works between domains (From Gentner & Gentner 1983).

Other theories of analogical reasoning exist. Notably, a pragmatic theory of analogy, though lacking the degree of development of Gentner's, has been proposed (Holyoak 1985; Holland et al. 1986, ch. 10). In this context, it is relevant only to notice that even the alternative pragmatic theory is in no better position to give information on the nature of the internal representations, by and large for the same reasons that the structural theory does not. This can be best seen in the version presented in Holland et al. (1986). The authors define analogy as a "top down mechanism for constructing mental models" (288). Schematically, the steps involved in using analogies for problem solving would be:

(1) constructing mental representations of the source and the target; (2) selecting the source as a potentially relevant analog to the target; (3) mapping the components of the source and the target [...] and (4) extending the mapping to generate rules that can be applied to the target in order to achieve a solution. (Holland et al. 1986, 292)

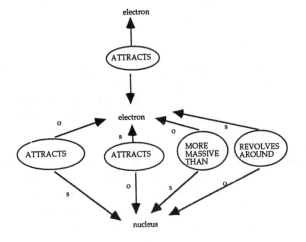

FIGURE 6.4.   New schema created as a result of analogical reasoning.

Now, again, notice that steps (1) and (2) are independent from steps (3) and (4). In particular, (1) comes *before* (3): so analogical mapping cannot place constraints on the mental representations of sources and targets. As in Gentner's solution, an analogy requires a mapping; in this case, a morphism between the two domains. And since it is also possible to define morphisms between two sets of propositions describing the supposed models, even this theory of analogy is perfectly consistent with a "nonmodelic" theory of knowledge representation.

My conclusion is that theories of analogical reasoning cannot offer any evidence for mental models, or against mental logic. If Gentner is correct, we must make room for another mental box responsible for a set of reasoning abilities, but such a box will not allow us to determine the format of the knowledge representations over which it acts.

Analog Simulations of Limited Domains of Knowledge

Another strand of studies—mostly computational studies about spatial reasoning—does suggest the existence of representations that are not just simple clusters of beliefs. The problem is that such evidence concerns only very limited domains, and not inferential abilities in general. Scholars interested in computational simulations of spatial skills hold that it would be extremely difficult, if not impossible, to replicate people's spatial abilities by explicitly representing spatial relations in propositional form. Accordingly, they have proposed to model reasoning about space by means of other kinds of representations. For example, Forbus (1983) notices that people's abilities to predict motions of objects in space hardly seem to be describable by symbolic representations:

> We do not yet know why people are so good at reasoning about space. Theorem proving and symbolic manipulation of algebraic expression do not seem to account for this ability. (...) the sheer complexity of algebraic manipulations argues against [theorem proving] as a basis for our spatial abilities (Forbus 1983, 55)[8]

More specifically, reasoning about space in terms of explicit statements and rules acting on them may involve using relational descriptions (such as meaning postulates governing patterns of implication) which "can lead to combinatorial searches" (58–59). To avoid this, Forbus proposes that spatial reasoning exploits a simple geometric representation plus motion sequences constructed as networks communicating with the space representation. Accordingly his program, FROB, constructs a simplified world of a two-dimensional scene where a bouncing ball can move and hit walls or other balls under the sole influence of gravitational force, and predicts successive positions of the ball.

FROB covers only severely limited areas of spatial reasoning. Forbus recognizes that his nonpropositional representation of spatial reasoning is "too onerous outside very small domains, and is too restrictive a style to capture all of the way people use qualitative physical knowledge" (1983, p. 70). The simple extension of the system to spatial reasoning on collisions between two moving objects would cause "an explosive increase in the connectivity of the graph" (ibid.) constructed by the program to simulate qualitative reasoning about space. So, if FROB offers arguments for nonpropositional knowledge representations, at the same time it shows how limited is the domain such representations can cover.

Other evidence, more directly psychological, also indicates that special modalities of space representation are activated in reasoning and processing spatial texts. Johnson-Laird and Byrne (1989) presented subjects with various spatial problems. The problems were identical, except for one premise in which the order of two objects was switched so as to require either one or two models. They showed that subjects respond more correctly when problems require only one model (61% of correct responses vs. 50%). Even if the results are not particularly shocking, unlike other more debatable cases, such experiments do pose a problem for possible rule-based spatial theories, because the minimal difference between the two groups of problems is hard to account for in terms of rules.

In a different context and with different paradigms, Tversky and her collaborators gathered further evidence that the cognitive base of spatial reasoning seems to be of a nonpropositional nature. Taylor and Tversky

(1992) gave different groups of subjects texts containing different kinds of "presentations" of the same spatial scene. One group received a route description—the kind of description you would give to a friend who needs to reach your house: turn left, then go three blocks ahead, and so on. Another group received a survey description—the kind of information somebody would give you if he described an area from an airplane. A third group was directly shown a map (exp. 3). It emerged that

1. Subjects were faster and more accurate in answering *nonspatial*, collateral questions about the scene (such as, for example, whether the day was sunny or not);
2. They were faster and more accurate when answering questions, both spatial and nonspatial, which were paraphrases or direct quotations from their texts; but
3. There was no group differences in ability to answer questions *inferred* from the information presented, regardless of its mode of presentation—be it a map or a text, or a survey or route description;
4. Subjects in the texts groups drew much the same maps of the environment, regardless of kind of text; *but*
5. They placed the spatial items on their maps according to the order in which the items were introduced in the texts they studied; and finally,
6. Performance in the text conditions did not significantly differ from performance in the map condition

One way to explain the sum of these results is to postulate that different representations are computed from a text. One appears to be tied to its propositional form, *but not too close* to its surface form, and is conserved even when the spatial description is unambiguous. This would explain results 1, 2, and 5: subjects use this representation to answer questions about collateral information, place the items on the maps following the order in which they find them in their mental representation of the text, and can better answer questions tied to their own texts. The second kind of representation is properly spatial. It is more costly to inspect (and this explains the direction of result 1: subjects found it more difficult to answer spatial than nonspatial questions) and is computed in the same way regardless of how spatial information is presented. This explains results 3, 4, and 6: all groups had the same performance on spatial questions; all groups drew the same maps; and all groups drew the same spatial inferences.

The way questions were answered and the relative independence from the mode of presentation suggest that such a representation for space is not an image, but something more articulated. Taylor and Tversky suggest that it is something like the structures manipulated by a three-dimensional architectural model, which can be "zoomed in" from different perspectives and maintain the relevant relational properties. They call them "spatial mental models," though they don't go beyond the intuitive suggestion that the structures are like three-dimensional objects.

In sum, evidence coming from both psychology and computer simulations may offer good reasons to appeal to nonpropositional structures in reasoning, but only for very domain-specific reasoning abilities—in fact, for a limited amount of spatial reasoning. However, the mental logic hypothesis does not deny that in special cases reasoning exploits nonlinguistic representations. In particular, their existence for space shouldn't be surprising after all. Space has a special evolutionary role, and one expects the cognitive system to adapt, at least once in a while. But even in this case, the evidence tells very little about the structure of such internal representations. We know that, roughly, they are more complex when more alternative situations can be pictured, but besides such a very gross assessment we still have to find out *how* such representations are internally structured—notably, whether they are pure or impure.

Further Evidence, Further Difficulties. General Reasoning, Mental Logic and Mental Models

Other evidence for mental models has been gathered by Johnson-Laird and his collaborators, mostly directed at assessing the role of models in general (nondomain-specific) reasoning. The number of results is impressive and is difficult to summarize in a few paragraphs. For the purpose of this article, I will concentrate only on two points relevant to my conclusion. The first is that a great deal of such evidence does not inform us about the key element of the comparison between the two structural hypotheses. The second one is that theories based on the mental model hypothesis are affected by a general problem that makes it difficult to assess how models can account for reasoning data.

Let me begin with the first point. For many domains of reasoning, model-style theories (or sketches of theories) have been proposed, but no logic-style theory exists. This in itself should count in favor of the mental model hypothesis, which seems to be more productive. Yet, it is often difficult to unambiguously interpret the evidence in its favor, because most results can be predicted on the basis of linguistic factors alone. For example, Johnson-Laird et al. (1989) proposed a theory in which models partially account for reasoning with multiply quantified statements. However, the same results could be expected on the basis of the logical form of the conclusion alone together with some response biases (see Greene 1992). Also, Johnson-Laird and Byrne (1989a) explained with mental models why problems containing "Only" are more difficult than problems containing other connectives traditionally considered to be equivalent to them, such as simple implications. Yet, according to recent independently motivated theories, the logical form of sentences containing "Only" is also more complex than the logical forms of simple implications (Bonomi & Casalegno 1994). Or again, one of the strongest results in favor of mental models is the explanation of a series of phenomena concerning syllogistic reasoning (Johnson-Laird & Bara 1984). In particular, a theory based on mental models was able to explain elegantly and generalize a long-standing puzzle in the reasoning literature, the figural effect. However, Ford (1995) showed that a more complete explanation can be framed by assuming only that subjects are sensitive to the logical form of the premises and to the order of appearance of the predicates—two factors that any logically based theory can easily account for. In short, in most cases although there is no detailed propositional-like theory, it is easy to see that any such theory would very likely predict the same phenomena currently explained by mental models.

Although this is an indirect argument, at least for the only case in which a direct comparison between models and logic can be made—the case of propositional reasoning—it does look like mental logic theories can explain all the relevant results without being troubled by the shortcomings plaguing the mental model theory. I will now summarize the state of the debate in this area, because it seems to me to have a general value.

Supporters of the mental logic view have presented various proposals for a system of natural logic (e.g., Rips 1983; Osherson 1975). The most detailed theory has been presented by Braine and his collaborators. The theory specifies the rules subjects should use, their individual difficulty, and the algorithm containing the procedures implementing natural logic. With different experimental paradigms and in different contexts, evidence has been gathered for the psychological reality of the proposed rules and of the routines implementing them. The theory can predict subject's difficulty ratings and error rates in solving abstract problems (Braine et al. 1984), and the intermediate steps subjects go through while solving a problem (Braine, O'Brien, Noveck, Samuels, Fisch, Brooke Lea & Yang, forthcoming). Brooke Lea et al. 1990 also showed that some of the mental logic procedures are used in ordinary text comprehension.

On the mental model side, Johnson-Laird, Byrne and Schaeken (1992) proposed a theory that allegedly accounts for all the known phenomena of deductive propositional reasoning, offers a general theory of conditionals, accounts for the most important aspects of Braine's theory, and predicts new phenomena that rule theories could not explain according to Johnson-Laird et al. In fact, O'Brien, Braine and Yang (1994) outlined some of the unbelievable experimental consequences of the implementation of the model theory, while Bonatti (1994a) pointed out several flaws that make most claims doubtful (but see Johnson-Laird, Byrne & Schaeken 1994). Furthermore, Bonatti (1994a) showed also that Braine's theory predicts the phenomena gathered in favor of the new model theory, whereas it is unclear how the model theory could do the same for the known data in favor of Braine's theory. Hence, even if there is no crucial experiment yet, the only direct comparison between the hypotheses seems to clearly favor the mental logic hypothesis. At a minimum, the alleged contrast between the hypotheses and the alleged support in favor of models are exaggerated.

My second point, which is more general and raises a more fundamental problem for a fruitful comparison of the hypotheses, has to do with model individuation. All else being equal, a mental model theory must claim that the difficulty of problems is a function of the number of models required. This supposes that there is a clear way to identify and count models, hopefully stable across the various domains of reasoning. However, no such criterion exists. The following is an example of what difficulties the problem of model identification poses. Braine et al. (1984) showed that an equation defined over the rules of the mental logic theory correlates very well with the degree of problem difficulty estimated by subjects (.92). Johnson-Laird et al. (1992) first presented new experiments whose results are allegedly predicted by the model theory, and then tried to show that number of models also highly correlates with subjective difficulty, thus using Braine's results as a further confirmation of their theory. Specifically, they reported a correlation of .80 between number of models and problem difficulty. In fact, Bonatti (1994a) showed that such a result *strictly depends* on how models are counted. If, as Johnson-Laird et al. did, one considers *the total sum* of the minimal amount of models needed by *all the premises* of a problem taken separately, then the correlation obtains, but at the same time, by applying the same criterion of model count to Johnson-Laird et al.'s experiments, the model theory turns out to be refuted. Alternatively, if we choose to count the minimal amount of models needed by *the integrated premises*, then models can explain the same experiments but turn out to be a totally insignificant factor for difficulty (and error) predictions. Hence it is crucial to know *which criterion* to count models is correct. The problem was that Johnson-Laird et al. had chosen one criterion to account for the data in their experiments, and another criterion to account for the data in Braine et al.'s experiments. Since the two criteria give opposite results, we cannot switch from one to the other without argument.

There are yet other ways to count models. For example, we can count the sum of models required by the interpretation of each premise *plus* the number of models required by the conclusion; or else we can count the maximal amount of models loaded in working memory at each given step of processing of new premises. Until we are given clear and principled reasons to select one criterion, we cannot even begin framing a fruitful comparison between models and logic, and we have to suspend the experimental claims in favor of the model theory.

A Short Summary of the Argument

The conclusion of my review is simple, but deceiving. I have argued that most of the evidence that would seem to speak in favor of one of the two alternatives (in fact, almost unanimously taken to prove the mental model hypothesis) is in fact mute on the real nature of the dispute because it doesn't provide evidence about the internal structure of the representations. For the case in which a comparison can be made and the structure of the representation is better specified, difficulties connected with how models are individuated seem to pose serious problems for the possibility of a fruitful comparison. Not too much to rejoice for.

FRAMING AN ANSWER TO QUESTION P

What, then, of Question P? We are in a delicate position. A naturalistic approach requires us to answer it after a thorough examination of the best theories of reasoning around. Yet browsing through a good part of the evidence showed that we know very little about reasoning.

Never mind; the little we know may be sufficient to begin addressing Question P. I propose to draw some morals on the basis of the microcase for which some data and theories based on the alternative hypotheses exist—propositional reasoning. If we had to judge the state of the debate on it, we could at least reach the following conclusions. First, there are few really possible theories, and they are all representational; second, most of the evidence is ambiguous on the crucial point separating the really possible theories; third, the existing theories are much more alike than the intuitive pictures opposing them would seem to suggest; and fourth, on the case in which a comparison can be made, the mental logic theory comes out far ahead.[9]

Let us then take Braine's theory as a psychologically real description of propositional reasoning abilities, and see what we can get out of it. The theory assigns to subjects at least a minimal amount of logical competence, described by the rules of primary reasoning. Furthermore, such rules and their algorithmic implementation are sound, although not complete. So, the first conclusion is: people's reasoning processes are truth preserving. And the first good corollary is: if being truth preserving has anything to do with rationality, then people are rational.

"So what? How could this have been otherwise? Being rational is a *condition* for interpreting and understanding human beings. Even in order to *discover* what you are telling us, we already have to be rational. You didn't communicate anything more than what sheer conceptual analysis could reveal." Many philosophers would dismiss my conclusion as trivial, on the premise that *a priori* arguments for human rationality exist. However, Stich (1990 chs. 2–4), has shown that it is not so clear that a really good argument exists. My very simple reason for thinking that humans could arbitrarily depart from acceptable standards of reasoning comes, once again, from the few empirical results we possess. Reasoning appears to engage an inferential system sensitive to the form of problems, and not only to their content. So, *contra* Quine and the holists, at least to a certain degree logical inferences can be separated from atomic, contentful beliefs. But then, since empirical beliefs and logical inferences are detachable, scientists might well find out that ordinary people have their same causal connection with the world and ordinarily come to fixate their same atomic beliefs when exposed to the same external conditions, and yet don't draw truth-preserving inferences. Humans may perfectly agree on the content of empirical beliefs, and depart on the notion of logical consequence. Perhaps in order to reach such a conclusion scientists *must* use a rational system of belief fixation, but psychology is a statistical science: there is nothing wrong in principle if scientists turn out to be many standard-deviations–away from the average fellow.

In short, the irrationality thesis is an empirical possibility. One of its formulations holds that there are no core rules of thinking common to all of humanity, hence no common system of reasoning. But if Braine's mental logic theory is empirically correct, possessing a truth-preserving system of reasoning turns out to be a property of our species. Hence, by inspecting the current theories of reasoning, it very much looks like the irrationality/relativity thesis is empirically false. Second good corollary.

"Yes, but how does all this connect with Question P?"

Deductive Organisms

Once again, natural science helps us in filling in some of the necessary blanks. Traditionally, psychologists and philosophers otherwise as diverse as Aristotle, Bacon, Hegel, Dewey, the behaviorists, and the New-Look psychologists were convinced that much of our cognitive processes are inductive. Consequently, deduction has long been considered a peripheral topic in human cognition, at most interesting to those curious about how we play chess. Induction was the key to the mind, and to science.

Such a traditional picture is now being seriously challenged. The first anti-inductivist move comes from the idea that perception is modular. According to it, perceptual systems are innate, specific hardwired detectors with strict channels of communications closed to the intervention of general knowledge; thus, no induction in perceptual processes.

But, more interestingly, the thesis that we are a mostly inductive machine vacillates also for the case of "high level" cognitive processes. In the last 15 years it has become more and more apparent that many of our cognitive abilities depend on the existence of innate theories of some specific domain of knowledge. For example, it appears that children possess an innate basis of information about other minds, whose disruption can eventuate in pathologies (Baron-Cohen, Leslie & Frith 1985, 1986; Leslie and Thaiss, 1992). This basis of innate beliefs determines children's behavior towards cospecifics.

Other domains of cognitive competence appear to depend on the existence of innate information. It seems so for our knowledge of basic properties of physical objects and of kinds of stuff (Soja, Carey and Spelke, 1991); for children's ability to exploit limited information about numbers, sets, and basic algebraic operations (Wynn, 1990 and 1992; Starkey, 1992); for adults' conception of numbers (Dehaene and Mehler 1992); for naive conceptions of the physical world (Gentner and Gentner 1983); and for our reasoning about actions and their practical consequences (Cosmides 1989, Gigerenzer and Hug 1992; Cheng and Holyoak 1986).

Now, let us imagine how a cognitive organism along the lines suggested by the new cognitive psychology would look like. Each of the relevant theories may be imagined as a box, containing a set of innate pieces of knowledge. The internal structure of these boxes need not concern us. What is relevant is that an organism endowed with them could act successfully in a friendly environment without having to learn too much from experience, but by massively engaging in deductive reasoning. Do I want to know where this stone will fall? I don't need exposure to experience, but I just consult my naive physics box. Do I want to know what the guy out there will do when I throw that stone? I don't need to try and make myself a new enemy: I just chain the output of my naive physics box to my metatheory of mind box, and I determine that since people rarely like being hit by stones, he will move and get angry at me.

So cognizing is making lots of enthymemes, whose missing premises are provided by innate beliefs. A large number of belief fixation processes once considered inductive turn out to be derivations from the main "axioms" of the relevant theory. The new cognitive science suggests a radical possibility: what Popper thought true for the logic of science is in fact true for the psychology of mind.

Question P, Finally

So. Let us begin with the connection between the first two beliefs I mentioned in presenting Question P. Often natural sciences and commonsense have been kept radically separated from mathematics, on the ground that commonsense is based on observation and mathematics isn't; or, that in commonsense and natural science there is induction, and in mathematics there is none. But if the recent cognitive science is in the right ballpark, then there is very little induction even in commonsense, because lots of natural conclusions depend on deductions from innate theories, and if the structural hypothesis as developed until now is correct—and there seem to be no alternatives—then the human processor incorporates a theorem prover acting on the forms of propositions. If we see that, we also see that the processes of belief fixation from empirical or from mathematical beliefs can be the same. Our deductive system, to a certain extent, is blind to the origin—whether empirical or not—of our beliefs, and rational fixation of beliefs is largely about proving theorems. Hence, a path of reasoning leading from quasiperceptual beliefs about how hungry tigers behave in the presence of fresh flesh (plus some information on the meaning of verbs) to the belief that tigers are dangerous can be the same path leading from some mathematical beliefs about diagonalization and self-reference to the belief that Gödel was right. Here is the first part of the answer.

We are left with the trickiest part: what's the connection between having truth preserving beliefs and taking a moral course of actions? Here I need to resort to an analogy with Hume's morals. Hume had a great idea. He asked himself where our moral feeling towards an action comes from, and he proposed to separate the answer in two parts. The first part concerns our abilities to calculate the consequences of an action. We praise an action when we see that it will have consequences useful to mankind. The second part concerns the grounds for practical evaluation. Once we are finished with the complex calculations of all the pros and cons of an action, and we finally agree that it is useful to mankind, why should we approve of it? Calculation of consequences is a theoretical operation, entirely confined in the realm of What There Is. *Doing* something, or being *moved* towards something, is *not* a result of the calculation: there is nothing in it which, in and of itself, should move us from What There Is to What There Ought To Be. What, then, allows us to give *value* to numbers and symbols? And here Hume has a disappointingly simple answer: finding that an action is useful to mankind is a sufficient reason for practical evaluation because that's the way we are wired up. We are social moral beings by nature. Thus two factors concur to explain the origin of moral judgments. There is calculation of utility, a rational process meant to assess whether a particular action/situation is useful to mankind. But once reasoning has done its part in showing that such-and-such an action is useful, no *moral* conclusion could be drawn, if there were not a *natural* power—neither rational, nor irrational: just a different kind of stuff—that stimulates a reaction of approbation for a useful action/situation. If we were not (as we would say today) *genetically determined* to be positively moved towards

actions/situations useful to others, our ability to figure out the consequences of an action wouldn't suffice to bridge the gulf between rational
determination and action.

I think that this account of the origin of moral sentiment is largely correct, except for the fact that calculation has a double duty. It is also useful to
detect contradictions. And when we attribute a right to ourselves *qua* purposive agents—to wit, the right to well being—and at the same time we deny
that right to other purposive agents, we are contradicting ourselves (Gewirth
1982). If we think for a while, we will see that we contradict ourselves.

But, even here, we can say so what? Who cares whether we make contra-
dictory statements? And here is where you just have to follow the Humean
line. Hume asked why we should care about others, and his answer was:
because. If Hume is right, there is no other level of explanation to aim for,
besides the empirical recognition that it is part of our nature to be curious
about other fellows. Likewise, we may ask why we should care about having
consistent beliefs. And the answer suggested by mental logic is: because.
We could have been organisms with no mental logic at all, or with a mental
logic implementing unsound rules. We are not. When we find a contradiction, we are naturally bothered enough to *do something*; for example, to try
and remove it. This feeling of uneasiness is the motor of many moral evalu-
ations. You don't need anything more than a natural logic plus a mechanism that tries to enforce consistency, and the same processes explaining
the commonalty between empirical belief fixation and mathematical belief
fixation will also explain the roots of practical sentiment.

Q.E.D. Well, almost. Use your natural logic to find the missing premises.

NOTES

[1]Not all connectionists are partisans of the ideology behind the nonstructural view. A
group (the dominant PDP one) has been arguing for something like a radical emergentist
view on reasoning, according to which everything "emerges" from a primordial network
if it is trained with "sufficient" data. Another group makes a firmer commitment to the existence of some degree of innate structure. My concern here is to show that the first option
is closed. The second options should deserve separate analysis. I thank Prof. Shastri for
pointing this out to me.

[2]Although the distinction does not coincide with Braine's, Rips' mental logic theory of
propositional reasoning (Rips 1983) contains two kinds of procedures, forward and backward, that have different computational demands and thus can be used to capture the previous distinction.

[3]With the possible exception of the content of the logical parts of language. There, it
may be possible that rules of reasoning also constitute the meaning of logical symbols, as
conceptual-role semantics wants it.

[4]This section is a summary of a full argument developed in Bonatti (MS), to which the interested reader is referred.

[5]See also Johnson-Laird (1983), p. 410, or Boyer (1993), pp. 21–22.

[6]See also McClelland and Rumelhart (1986), ch. 14.

[7]In fact, this is a necessary step in what SME (the Structure Mapping Engine that simulates the structure-mapping process previously described) does (see Gentner 1989). SME is given a schematic representation of the base domain, and the nodes plus some partial structure of the target domain. In inspecting the base schema and the partial structure of the target schema, SME looks for identities in relations and starts formulating local matching hypotheses, which are reinforced if the relations are higher order relations. Local matching hypotheses are expressed propositionally. They are collected in consistent groups, from which SME extrapolates global matching hypotheses, which are an expansion of the inferences in the base domain onto the target domain. This expansion consists again in a set of candidate inferences expressed propositionally. Finally, these global mapping hypotheses are ranked according to various parameters, and the analogical mapping is chosen. At the end, SME can deliver a new schema for the target domain. In all this process of translation and selection, models or other analog forms of knowledge representation have no role.

[8]Hutchins (1983) also comments on the representations of space Micronesians exploit in navigating thus: "There are no A/D or D/A converters because all of the computations are analog" (p. 223).

[9]However, presumably the points I am making in this section wouldn't change if a satisfactory theory of propositional reasoning based on the mental model hypothesis were elaborated. Also such a theory should be truth preserving, and therefore will support the same conclusions about human rationality I am suggesting here. A similar line has indeed been briefly argued for by Johnson-Laird and Byrne (1993).

REFERENCES

Bechtel, W. & Abrahamsen, A. (1991). *Connectionism and the mind.* Oxford: Basil Blackwell.

Bonatti, L. (1994). Why should we abandon the mental logic hypothesis? *Cognition, 50,* 17–39.

Bonatti, L. (1994a). Propositional reasoning by model? *Psychological Review, 101,* 725–733.

Bonatti, L. (1995). SHRUTI's ontology is representational. *Behavioral and Brain Sciences,* forthcoming.

Bonatti, L. (MS). On pure and impure representations: mental models, mental logic and the ontology of mind. Unpublished manuscript.

Bonomi, A. & Casalegno, P. (1994). 'Only' association with focus in event semantics. *Natural Language Semantics, 2,* 1–45.

Boolos, G. (1984). On 'Syllogistic inference.' *Cognition, 17,* 181–182.

Boyer, P. (1993). Cognitive aspects of religious symbolism. In Boyer, P. (Ed.), *Cognitive aspects of religious symbolism* (pp. 4–47). Cambridge: Cambridge University Press.

Braine, M.D.S. & O'Brien, D.P. (1991). A theory of if: lexical entry, reasoning program, and pragmatic principles. *Psychological Review, 98*, 182–203.

Braine, M. D. S., Reiser, B. J., & Rumain, B. (1984). Some empirical justifications for a theory of natural propositional logic. *The Psychology of Learning and Motivation, 18*, 313–371.

Braine, M. D. S., O'Brien, D. P., Noveck, I. A., Samuels, M. C., Fisch, S. M., Brooke Lea, L. B., & Yang, Y. (1995). Predicting intermediate conclusions in propositional logic inference problems: Further evidence for a mental logic. *Journal of Experimental Psychology General, 124*, 263–292.

Brooke Lea, R. B., O'Brien, D. P., Fisch, S., Noveck, I., & Braine, M. D. S. (1990). Predicting propositional logic inferences in text comprehension. *Journal of Memory and Language, 29*, 361–387.

Byrne, R. M. & Johnson-Laird, P. N. (1990). Models and deductive reasoning. In K. J. Gillholy (Ed.), *Lines of thinking* (pp. 139–151). London: Wiley & Sons.

Byrne, R. M. (1991). Can valid inferences be suppressed? *Cognition, 39*, 71–78.

Byrne, R. M. (1992). The model theory of deduction. In Y. Rogers, Rutherford, A,. & Bibby, P. A. (Eds.), *Models in the mind* (pp. 11–28). London: Academic Press.

Cheng, P. & Holyoak, K. (1986). Pragmatic reasoning schemas. *Cognitive Psychology, 17*, 391–416.

Churchland, P. M. (1990). On the nature of explanation: A PDP approach. In S. Forrest (Ed.), *Emergent computation* (pp. 281–292). Cambridge, MA: MIT Press.

Clement, J. (1983). A conceptual model discussed by Galileo and used intuitively by physics students. In D. Gentner & A. Stevens (Eds.), 325–339.

Cosmides, L. (1989). The logic of social exchange: Has natural selection shaped how humans reason? Studies with the Wason selection task. *Cognition, 31*, 187–276.

Dehaene, S. & Mehler, J. (1992). Cross-linguistic regularities in the frequency of number words. *Cognition, 43*, 1–29.

Fodor, J. A. (1975). *The language of thought.* New York, NY: Thomas Y. Crowell.

Fodor, J. D., Fodor, J. A., & Garrett, M. F . (1975). The psychological unreality of semantic representations. *Linguistic Inquiry, 4*, 515–531.

Fodor, J. A. (1983). *The modularity of mind.* Cambridge, MA: MIT Press.

Forbus, K. D. (1983). Qualitative reasoning about space and motion. In D. Gentner & A. Stevens (Eds.), 53–73.

Ford, M. (1995). Two modes of mental representation and problem solution in syllogistic reasoning. *Cognition, 54*, 1–71.

Garnham, A. (1993). Is logistic cognitive science possible? *Mind and Language, 8*, 49–71.

Gentner, D. & Gentner, D. R. (1983). Flowing waters or teeming crowds: mental models of electricity. In Gentner & Stevens (Eds.) (1983), 99–129.

Gentner, D. & Stevens, A. (Eds.). *Mental models.* Hillsdale, NJ: Erlbaum.

Gentner, D. & Toupin, C. (1986). Systematicity and surface similarity in the development of analogy. *Cognitive Science, 10*, 277–300.

Gentner, D. (1989). The mechanisms of analogical learning. In S. Vosniadu & A. Ortony (Eds.), *Similarity and analogical reasoning* (pp. 199–241). Cambridge: Cambridge University Press.

Gewirth, A. (1982). *Human rights: Essays on justification and applications.* Chicago: University of Chicago Press.

Gigerenzer, G. & Hug, K. (1992). Domain-specific reasoning: social contracts, cheating, and perspective change. *Cognition, 43,* 127–171.

Greene, S. B. (1992). Multiple explanations for multiply quantified sentences: are multiple models necessary? *Psychological Review, 99,* 184–187.

Holland, J. H., Holyoak, K., Nisbett, R. E., & Thagard, P. R. (1986). *Induction: Processes of inference, learning, and discovery.* Cambridge, MA: MIT Press.

Holyoak, K. J. (1985). The pragmatics of analogical transfer. In G.H. Bower (Ed.), *The psychology of learning and motivation* (pp. 59–87). New York: Academic Press.

Johnson-Laird, P. N. (1983). *Mental models.* Cambridge, MA: Harvard University Press.

Johnson-Laird, P. N. (1989). *Mental models.* In M. Posner (Ed.), *Foundations of cognitive science* (pp. 469–499). Cambridge, MA: MIT Press.

Johnson-Laird, P. N. & Bara, B. (1984). Syllogistic Inference. *Cognition, 16,* 1–61.

Johnson-Laird, P. N. & Bara, B. (1984a). Logical expertise as a cause of error: a reply to Boolos. *Cognition, 17,* 183–184.

Johnson-Laird, P. N. & Byrne, R. M. (1989). Spatial reasoning. *Journal of Memory and Language, 28,* 564–575.

Johnson-Laird, P. N. & Byrne, R. M. (1989a). 'Only' reasoning. *Journal of Memory and Language, 28,* 313–330.

Johnson-Laird, P. N. & Byrne, R. M. (1993). Précis of 'deduction.' *Behavioral and Brain Sciences, 16,* 323–380.

Johnson-Laird, P. N., Byrne, R. M., & Schaeken, W. (1992). Propositional reasoning by model. *Psychological Review, 99,* 418–439.

Johnson-Laird, P. N., Byrne, R. M., & Schaeken, W. (1994). Why models rather than rules give a better account of propositional reasoning: Reply to Bonatti, and to O'Brien, Braine and Yang. *Psychological Review,* 734–739.

Johnson-Laird, P. N., Byrne, R. M., & Tabossi, P. (1989). Reasoning by model: The case of multiple quantification. *Psychological Review, 96* (4), 658–673.

Leslie, A. & Thaiss, L. (1992). Domain specificity in conceptual development: Neuropsychological evidence from autism. *Cognition, 43,* 225–251.

McClelland, J. L. & Rumelhart, D. E. (Eds.) (1986). *Parallel distributed processing: Explorations in the microstructure of cognition. Vol. 2: Psychological and biological models.* Cambridge, MA: MIT Press.

McCloskey, T. (1983). Naive theories of motion. In Gentner & Stevens, 299–324.

McGinn, C. (1989). *Mental content.* Oxford: Basil Blackwell.

Norman, D. A. (1983). Some observations on mental models. In Gentner & Stevens, 7–14.

O'Brien, D .P., Braine, M. D. S., & Yang, Y. (1994). Propositional reasoning by mental models? Simple to refute in principle and in practice. *Psychological Review, 101,* 711–724.

Osherson, D. (1975). Logic and models of logical thinking. In R. J. Falmagne (Ed.), *Reasoning: Representation and process in children and adults.* Hillsdale, NJ: Erlbaum.

Partee, B. H. (1979). Semantics: mathematics or psychology? In R. Bäuerle, U. Egli & A. von Stechow (Eds.), *Semantics from different points of view.* Berlin: Springer-Verlag.

Pylyshyn, Z. W. (1980). Computation and cognition: Issues in the foundations of cognitive science. *Behavioral and Brain Sciences, 3,* 111–169.

Pylyshyn, Z. (1981). The imagery debate: analogue media versus tacit knowledge. *Psychological Review, 88* (1), 16–45.

Pylyshyn, Z. W. (1984). *Computation and cognition: Toward a foundation for cognitive science.* Cambridge, MA: MIT Press.

Rips, L. J. (1983). Cognitive processes in propositional reasoning. *Psychological Review, 90* (1), 38–71.

Rips, L. J. (1990). Reasoning. *Annual Review of Psychology, 41,* 321–353.

Rumelhart, D. E. (1980). Schemata: the building blocks of cognition. In R. Spiro, B. Bruce, & B. Brewer (Eds.), *Theoretical issues in reading comprehension* (pp. 33–58). Hillsdale, NJ: Erlbaum.

Selman, B. (1995). *Analogical representations,* this volume, chap. 5.

Shastri, L. & Ajjanagadde, V. (1993). From simple associations to systematic reasoning: a connectionist representation of rules, variables and dynamic bindings usings temporal synchrony. *Behavioral and Brain Sciences, 16,* 417–494.

Soja, N., Carey, S., & Spelke, E. (1991). Ontological categories guide young children's inductions of word meaning: object terms and substance terms. *Cognition, 38,* 179–211.

Starkey, P. (1992). The early development of numerical reasoning. *Cognition, 43,* 93–126.

Stich, S. (1983). *From folk psychology to cognitive science: The case against belief.* Cambridge, MA: MIT Press.

Stich, S. (1990). *The fragmentation of reason.* Cambridge, MA: MIT Press.

Taylor, H. & Tversky, B. (1992). Spatial mental models derived from survey and route descriptions. *Journal of Memory and Language, 31,* 261–292.

Wynn, K. (1990). Children's understanding of counting. *Cognition, 36,* 155–193.

Wynn, K. (1992). Addition and subtraction by human infants. *Nature, 358,* 749–750.

chapter 7

On the Methods of Cognitive Neuropsychology*

Clark Glymour
clark.glymour@andrew.cmu.edu
Department of Philosophy
Carnegie Mellon University

INTRODUCTION

N euronpsychology has relied on a variety of methods to obtain information about human "cognitive architecture" from the profiles of capacities and incapacities presented by normal and abnormal subjects. The 19th-century neuropsychological tradition associated with Broca, Wernicke, Meynert, and Lichtheim attempted to correlate abnormal behavior with loci of brain damage, and thus to found syndrome classification ultimately on neuroanatomy. At the same time, they aimed to use the data of abnormal cognitive incapacities to found inferences to the functional architecture of the normal human cognitive system. Contemporary work in neuropsychology involves statistical studies of the correlation of behavior with physical measures of brain activity in both normal and abnormal subjects, statistical studies of the correlations of behavioral abnormalities in groups of subjects, and studies of behavioral abnormalities in particular individuals, sometimes in conjunction with information about the locations of lesions.[1] The goal of identifying the functional structure of normal cognitive architecture remains as it was in the 19th century.

The fundamental methodological issues about the enterprise of cognitive neuropsychology concern the characterization of methods by which

*Research for this chapter was made possible by a fellowship from the John Simon Guggenheim Memorial Foundation. I thank Martha Farah for teaching me what little I know of cognitive neuropsychology. Jeffrey Bub for stimulating me to think about these issues and for commenting on a draft of this paper and Peter Slezak for additional comments. Alfonso Caramazza provided very helpful comments on a second draft.

Originally appeared in British Journal for the Philosophy of Science Vol 45 No. 3 1994. Reprinted here by permission of Oxford University Press.

features of normal cognitive architecture can be identified from any of the kinds of data just mentioned, the assumptions upon which the reliability of such methods are premised, and the limits of such methods—even granting their assumptions—in resolving uncertainties about that architecture. These questions have recently been the subject of intense debate occasioned by a series of articles by Caramazza and his collaborators; these articles have prompted a number of responses, including at least one book. As the issues have been framed in these exchanges, they concern:

1. whether studies of the statistical distribution of abnormalities in groups of subjects selected by syndrome, by the character of brain lesions, or by other means, are relevant evidence for determining cognitive architecture;
2. whether the proper form of argument in cognitive neuropsychology is "hypothetico-deductive"—in which a theory is tested by deducing from it consequences whose truth or falsity can be determined more or less directly—or "bootstrap testing"—in which theories are tested by assuming parts of them and using those parts to deduce (non-circularly) from the data instances of other parts of the theory;
3. whether associations, dissociations or double dissociations are the "more important" form of evidence about normal cognitive architecture.

Bub and Bub object that Caramazza's arguments against group studies assume a "hypothetico-deductive" picture of theory testing in which a hypothesis is confirmed by a body of data if from the hypothesis (and perhaps auxiliary assumptions) a description of the data can be deduced. They suggest that inference to cognitive architecture from neuropsychological data follows instead a "bootstrap" pattern much like that described by Glymour.[2] They, and also Shallice, reassert that double dissociation data provide especially important evidence for cognitive architecture. Shallice argues that if a functional module underlying two capacities is a connectionist computational system of which one capacities requires more computational resources than another, then injuries to the module that remove one of these capacities may leave the other intact. The occurrence of subjects having one of these capacities and lacking the other (dissociation) therefore will not permit a decision as to whether or not there is a functional module required for the first capacity but not required for the second. Double dissociations, Shallice claims, do permit this decision.

The main issue in these disputes is this: By what methods, and from what sorts of data, can the truth about various questions of cognitive architecture be found, whatever the truth may be? There is a tradition in computer science and in mathematical psychology that provides a means for resolving such questions. Work in this tradition characterizes mathematically whether or not specific questions can be settled in principle from specific kinds of evidence. Positive results are proved by exhibiting some method and demonstrating that it can reliably reach the truth; negative results are proved by showing that *no possible* method can do so. There are results of these kinds about the impossibility of predicting the behavior of a "black box" with an unknown Turing machine inside; about the possibility of such predictions when the black box is known to contain a finite automaton rather than a Turing machine (Gold p. 65); about the indistinguishability of parallel and serial procedures for short term memory phenomena (Luce); about which classes of mathematically possible languages could and could not be learned by humans (Osherson and Weinstein); about whether a computationally bounded system can be distinguished from an uncomputable system by any behavioral evidence (Kelly and Glymour); about the logical limits of the propositions that can be resolved by any learner (Kelly) and much more. However abstract and remote from practice such results may seem, they address the logical essence of questions about discovery and relevant evidence. From this point of view disputes in cognitive neuropsychology about one or another specific form of argument are well motivated but ill directed: they are focused on the wrong questions.

From what sorts of evidence, and with what sorts of background assumptions, can questions of interest in cognitive psychology be resolved—no matter what the answer to them may be—by some possible method; and from what sorts of evidence and background assumptions can they *not* be *resolved* by any possible method? With some idealization, the question of the capacities of various experimental designs in cognitive neuropsychology to uncover cognitive architecture can be reduced to comparatively simple questions about the prior assumptions investigators are willing to make. The point of this paper is to present some of the simplest of those reductions.

THEORIES AS FUNCTIONAL DIAGRAMS AND GRAPHS

Neuropsychological theories typically assume that the brain instantiates "functional modules" that have specific roles in producing cognitive behavior. In the processes that produce cognitive behavior, some of the output of some modules is sent as input to other modules until eventually the task behavior is produced. Various hypothetical functional modules have standard names, e.g., the "phonemic buffer" and accounts of what the modules are supposed to do. Such theories or "models" are often presented by diagrams. For example, Ellis and Young consider the following "functional model" for object recognition:

What do the arrows in Figure 7.1 mean, and what does it mean if one or more of them is missing because of injury?

In explaining profiles of normal capacities and abnormal incapacities with the aid of such a diagram, the modules and their connections are understood to be embedded in a larger structure that serves as a kind of *deus ex machina* in producing particular inputs or particular outputs. For example, a subject's capacity to name familiar objects in experimental trials is explained by assuming the objects are supplied as input to this diagram, and that the subject has somehow correctly processed the instruction "name the object before you" and this processing has adjusted

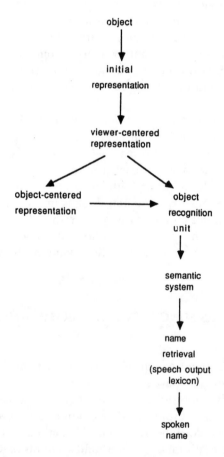

FIGURE 7.1.   Functional model for object recognition.

the parameters of the functional modules and their connections so that the subject will indeed attempt to name the object. None of the instructional processing is represented in the diagram. Further, it is understood that the modules represented in such diagrams are connected to other possible outputs that are not represented, and with different instructional processing the very same stimulus would activate a different collection of paths that would result in a different output. For example, if the subject were instructed "copy the object before you" and processed this information normally, then the presentation of the object would not bring about an attempt to speak the name of the object but instead to draw it.

In effect, most parts of theories of cognitive architecture are tacit, and the normal behavior to be expected from a set of instructions and a stimulus can only be inferred from the descriptions given of the internal modules. For example, when Ellis and Young describe an internal module as the "speech output lexicon" we assume that it must be activated in any process producing coherent speech, but not in processes producing coherent writing or in the processes of understanding speech, writing or gestures. Evidently leaving much of the theory tacit and indicated only by descriptions of internal modules is a great convenience and a practical necessity, although it may sometimes occasion misunderstanding, equivocation and unprofitable disputes.

The practice of cognitive neuroscience makes a great deal of use of scientist's capacities to exploit descriptions of hypothetical internal modules in order to contrive experiments that test a particular theory. Equally, the skills of practitioners are required to distinguish various kinds or features of stimuli as belonging properly to different inputs, meaning that these features are processed differently under one and the same set of instructions. To address the questions at issue I propose to leave these features of the enterprise to one side, and assume for the moment that everyone agrees as to what stimulus conditions should be treated as inputs to a common input channel in the normal cognitive architecture, and that everyone agrees as to what behaviors should be treated as outputs from a common output channel.

It is also clear that in practice there are often serious ambiguities about the range of performance that constitutes normal, or respectively abnormal, behavior and that much of the important work in cognitive neuropsychology consists in resolving such ambiguities. I will also put these matters to one side and assume that all such issues are settled, and there is agreement as to which behaviors count as abnormal in a setting, and which normal.

With these rather radical idealizations, what can investigation of the patterns of capacities and incapacities in normal and abnormal subjects tell us about the normal architecture?

FORMALITIES

Figure 7.2 is another diagram given by the same authors: The idea is that a signal, auditory or visual, enters the system, and various things are done to it; the double arrows indicate that the signal is passed back and forth, the single arrows indicate that it is passed in only one direction. The intended reading of the diagram is that if it is intact then spoken and written words will be understood and can produce speech in response that indicates understanding. If, however, any path through the semantic system from the input channel is disrupted while the rest of the system remains intact, then the remaining paths to the phoneme level will enable the subject to repeat a spoken word or pronounce a written word, but not to understand it.

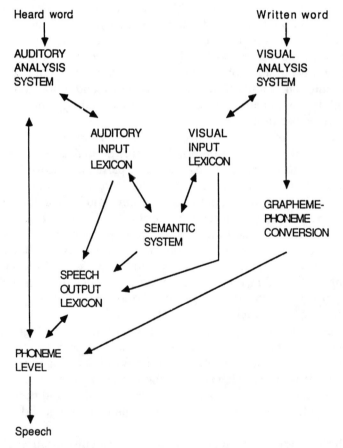

FIGURE 7.2.   Functional model for the recognition, comprehension and naming of written words in reading.

The evidence offered for a diagram consists of profiles of capacities that are found among people with brain injuries. There are people who can repeat spoken words but cannot recognize them; people who can recognize spoken words but can't understand them; people who show parallel incapacities for written words; people who can repeat, or recognize or understand spoken words but not written, and people with the reverse capacities. What is the logic of inferences from profiles of this kind to graphs or diagrams? To investigate that question I want to consider diagrams that are slightly different from those illustrated.

First, I want the performances whose appearance or failure (under appropriate inputs) is used in evidence to be explicitly represented as vertices in the graphs, and I want the corresponding stimuli or inputs to be likewise distinguished. So where Ellis and Young have an output channel labeled simply "speech" I want output nodes labeled "repeats," "repeats with recognition," "repeats with understanding." Anyplace that a psychologist would identify a normal capacity I want a corresponding set of input nodes and an output nodes. This convention in no way falsifies the problem for such relations are certainly implicit in the theory that goes with the conventional diagram; I am only making things a bit more explicit. Second, I want to consider only the identification of pathways that are *essential* for a normal capacity. So if we were considering only the structure associated with the capacity to repeat a spoken word with understanding, the existence of pathways from the heard world to speech that do not pass through the "semantic system" would be irrelevant. There are certainly examples in the literature of capacities that have alternative pathways, either of which will produce the appropriate outputs. I will ignore this complication. The justification for this second assumption is that I want to explore limitations on any possible strategy for identifying cognitive structure from normal and abnormal profiles of capacities. Restricting ourselves to identifying essential pathways and ignoring the possibility of alternative pathways that are sufficient for a capacity makes the problem of distinguishing one graph from others easier rather than harder. Limitations that hold for easier problems will hold as well for more difficult problems.

The system of hypothetical modules and their connections form a **directed graph**, that is, a set V of vertices or nodes and a set E of ordered pairs of vertices, each ordered pair representing a **directed edge** from the first member of the pair to the second. Some of the vertices represent input that can be given to a subject in an experimental task, and some of the vertices represent measures of behavioral response. (We count instructions to subjects as part of the input.) Everything in between, which is to say most of the directed graph that represents the cognitive architecture, is unobserved. Each vertex in between input and behavioral response can represent a very complicated structure which may be localized in the brain or may somehow be distributed: each directed edge represents a pathway by which information is communicated.

Such a directed graph may be a theory of the cognitive architecture of normals; the architecture of abnormals is obtained by supposing that one or more of the vertices or directed edges of the normal graph has been removed. Any individual subject is assumed to instantiate some such graph. In the simplest case, we can think of the output nodes of such a directed graph as taking values 0 and 1, where the value 1 obtains when the subject exhibits the behavior expected of normal subjects for appropriate inputs and instructions, and the value of 0 obtains for abnormal behavior in those circumstances.

One of the ideas of cognitive neuropsychology is that one and the same module can be involved in the processing of quite different inputs related to quite different outputs. For example, a general "semantic system" may be involved in using knowledge in speech processing, but it may also be involved in using knowledge in writing or in non-verbal tasks. Some of the input channels that are relevant to a non-verbal task that accesses the "semantic system" may not be input channels for a verbal task that accesses the "semantic system." Although there is in the diagram or graph a directed path from inputs channels particular to non-verbal tasks to the output channels of verbal tasks, those inputs are nonetheless irrelevant to the verbal task. Formally, the idea is that in addition to the directed graph structure there is what I shall call a **relevance** structure that determines for a given output variable that it depends on some of the input variables to which it is connected in the directed graph but not on other input variables to which it is so connected. The relevance structure is simply part of theory the cognitive scientist provides. One and the same output variable can have several distinct relevant input sets. I will call a **capacity** any pair <I,U>, where U is an output variable (or vertex) and I is a set of input vertices, such that in normals the set I of inputs is relevant to output U.

Between input and output a vast number of alternative graphs of hypothetical cognitive architecture are possible *a priori*. The fundamental inductive task of cognitive psychology, including cognitive neuropsychology, is to correctly describe the intervening structure that is common to normal humans.

To begin with I make some simplifying assumptions about the directed graph that represents normal human cognitive architecture. I will later consider how some of them can be altered.

A1.   Assume the graph is **acyclic**. That is, the internal process that results in a subject's exhibiting a normal cognitive competence on any particular occasion in response to any particular set of inputs is such that for each functional module X activated in the process, there is no sequence of modules X1, X2, . . . Xn, such that some output of X goes to X1, some output of X1 goes to X2, . . . , and some output of Xn goes to X.

A2. Assume that the behavioral response variables take only 0 or 1 as values, where the value 1 means, roughly, that the subject exhibits the normal competence, and the value 0 means that the subject does not exhibit normal competence.

A3. Assume that all normal subjects have the same graph, i.e., the same cognitive architecture.

A4. Assume that the graph of the cognitive architecture of any abnormal subject is a **subgraph** of the normal graph—i.e., is a graph obtained by deleting either edges or vertices (and of course all edges containing any deleted vertex) or both in the normal graph.

A5. The default value of all output nodes—the value they exhibit when they have not been activated by a cognitive process—is zero.

A6. If any path from a relevant input variable to an output variable that occurs in the normal graph is missing in an abnormal graph, the abnormal subject will output the value 0 for that output variable on inputs for which the normal subject outputs 1 for that variable.

A7. Every subgraph of the normal graph will eventually occur among abnormal subjects.

These assumptions are in some respects unrealistic; input and output are not clear 0, 1 valued functions, for example, and undoubtedly there is feedback among modules. These complications do not affect negative results below, but they make suspect the application to practice of positive formal results. Further one might object to the assumption that all pathways in a graph between input and output must be intact for the normal capacity. An alternative explored by Bub and Bub is that just one pathway need be intact. It turns out, however, that this interpretation only makes identification of structure more difficult, but does not change the essential results. I have assumed, in keeping with what seems to be theoretical practice, that the architectural diagrams do not include directed edges representing connections that *inhibit* an effect. If such edges were allowed injuries could present new capacities not present in normals; from a formal point of view the possibility is interesting and should be investigated.

DISCOVERY PROBLEMS AND SUCCESS

We want to know when, subject to these assumptions, features of normal cognitive architecture can be identified from the profiles of the behavioral capacities and incapacities of normals and abnormals. It is useful to be a little more precise about what we wish to know, so as to avoid some likely confusions.

I will say that a **discovery problem** consists of a collection of alternative conceivable graphs of normal cognitive architecture. So far as we know *a priori*, any graph in the collection may be the true normal cognitive architecture. We want our methods to be able to identify the true structure, no matter which graph in the collection it is, or we want our methods to be able to answer some question about the true structure, no matter which graph in the collection it is. Whichever graph may actually describe normal architecture, the scientist receives examples—subjects—who instantiate the normal graph and who instantiate various subgraphs of the normal graph. For each subject the scientist obtains a **profile** of that subject's capacities and incapacities. So, abstractly, we can think of the scientist as obtaining a sequence of capacity profiles, where the maximal profiles (those with the most capacities) are all from the true but unknown normal graph, and other profiles are from subgraphs of that normal graph.

Because of A7 eventually the scientist will see every profile of capacities associated with any subgraph of the normal graph. Let us suppose, as is roughly realistic, that the profiles are obtained in a sequence, with some (perhaps all) profiles being repeated. After each stage in the sequence let the scientist (or a method) conjecture the answer to a question about the cognitive architecture. No matter how many distinct profiles have been observed at any stage of inquiry, the scientist cannot be sure that further distinct profiles are not possible. We cannot (save in special cases) be sure at any particular time that circumstance has provided us with every possible combination of injuries, separating all of the capacities that could possibly be separated. Hence, if by success in discovering the normal cognitive architecture we mean that after some finite stage of inquiry the scientist will be able to specify that architecture and know that the specification will not be refuted by any further evidence, success is generally impossible. We should instead require something weaker for success: the scientist should eventually reach the right answer by a method that disposes her to stick with the right answer ever after, even though she may not know when that point has been reached. (See Osherson and Weinstein, 1989).

I will say that a method of conjecturing the cognitive architecture (or conjecturing an answer to a question about that architecture) **succeeds** on a discovery problem provided that for each possible architecture, and for each possible ordering (into an unbounded sequence) of the profiles of normals and abnormals associated with that architecture, there is a point after which the method always conjectures tho true architecture or always answers the question correctly. If no method can succeed on a discovery problem, I will say the problem is **unsolvable**.

SOME EXAMPLES

Consider the graphs in Figure 7.3:

The discovery problem posed by this collection of alternative graphs can be solved: whichever graph should describe the true cognitive architecture, one can eventually conjecture the correct graph from a sequence of profiles of normal and abnormal capacities and stick with that conjecture. All of these graphs allow the same normal profile: N = {<I1, U1>, <I1, U2>, <I2,U1>, <I2, U2>}. With each of these graphs there is associated the subgraphs that can be formed by deleting one or more edges or vertices. Each normal graph entails constraints on the profiles that can occur in abnormals. Graph (1), for example, entails the empty set of constraints; every

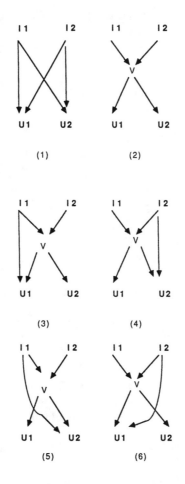

FIGURE 7.3.

subset of N is allowable as an abnormal profile if (1) represents the normal architecture. Graph (2) imposes strong constraints: If an abnormal has two intact capacities that together involve both inputs and both outputs, then he must have all of the normal capacities. Graph (3) permits that an abnormal may be missing <I1, U1> while all other capacities are intact. Graph (4) allows that an abnormal may be missing the capacity <I2, U2> while all other capacities are intact. We have the following inclusion relations among the sets of allowable (normal and abnormal profiles) associated with each graph: The set of profiles allowed by graph (1) includes those allowed by (3) and (4). The set of profiles allowed by (4) is not included in and does not include the set of profiles allowed by (3). The sets of profiles allowed by (3) and (4) both include the set of profiles allowed by (2). And so on.

To make matters as clear as possible, I give a list of the profiles that the six graphs permit, where a profile is a subset of the four capacities, and the capacities (Ii,Uj) are identified as ordered pairs i,j. The set of all possible profiles is as follows:

N:	1,1	1,2	2,1	2,2
P1:	1,1	1,2	2,1	
P2:	1,2	1,2		2,2
P3:	1,1		2,1	2,2
P4:		1,2	2,1	2,2
P5:	1,1	1,2		
P6:	1,1		2,1	
P7:		1,2	2,1	
P8:	1,1			2,2
P9:		1.2		2.2
P10:			2,1	2,2
P11:	1,1			
P12:		1,2		
P13:			2,1	
P14:				2.2
P15:				

Graph 1:   Abnormals with every profile occur.

Graph 2:   Abnormals with P5, P6 and P9-P15 occur.

Graph 3:   Abnormals with P4, P5, P6 and P9-P15 occur.

Graph 4: Abnormals with P1, P5, P6 and P9-P15 occur.

Graph 5: Abnormals with P3, P5, P6 and P9-P15 occur.

Graph 6: Abnormals with P2, P5, P6 and P9-P15 occur.

The following procedure solves the discovery problem: *conjecture any normal graph whose set of normal and abnormal profiles includes all of the profiles seen in the data and having no proper subset of profiles (associated with one of the graphs) that also includes all of the profiles seen in the data.*

One can think of the inference procedure in this case as embodying a kind of simplicity principle. This doesn't mean that every discovery problem posed by a collection of possible cognitive architectures and assumptions A1 through A7 is solvable. There are at least three ways in which indistinguishable structures can occur: The edges coming into a vertex v can be pinched together at a new vertex v′ and a directed edge from v′ to v introduced; the edges coming out of a vertex v can be moved so that they are out of a new vertex v′ and an edge from v to v′ introduced; and, finally, a vertex v can be replaced by a subgraph G such that every edge in v is replaced by an edge into G, every edge out of v is replaced by an edge out of G, and every input to G has a path in G to every output of G. Each of these operations results in a graph that is indistinguishable from the original graph in the normal and abnormal profiles it allows. The first two operations are really only special ways of thinking about the third.

For example, Figure 7.4 is indistinguishable from graphs (3). If it is added to the preceding set of six graphs, the corresponding discovery problem cannot be solved.

Whenever two capacities have the same output variable, we can "pinch" any subset of their paths and obtain an indistinguishable graph, Figure 7.5:

Of course the possibilities are not restricted to a single pinch. There can be any grouping of lines, and there can be hierarchies of intermediate nodes. The space of possibilities is *very* large. The number of ways of introducing extra vertices that are immediately between the inputs and a single

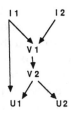

FIGURE 7.4.

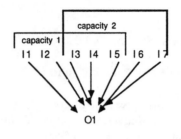

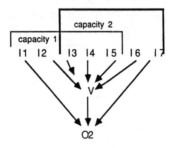

FIGURE 7.5.

output is an exponential function of size of that set. And, of course, directed edges between intermediate vertices at the same level can be introduced. One possible view about such indeterminacies is of course that they represent sub-structure that is not to be resolved by cognitive neuropsychology. Bub and Bub have suggested that if there is for each internal module an input/ouput pair specific to that module then the entire graph structure can be identified, and that seems correct if extraordinarily optimistic.

The conclusion seems to be that under the assumptions A1 through A7 a good many features of cognitive architecture can be distinguished from studies of individuals and the profiles of their capacities, although a graph cannot be distinguished from an alternative that has functionally redundant structure. Under assumptions At through A7, several of Caramazza's claims are essentially correct: he is correct that the essential question is not whether the data are associations, dissociations or double dissociations; the essential question is what profiles occur in the data. He is correct that from data on individuals one can solve some discovery problems. In any particular issue framed by assumptions of this kind, an explicit characterization of the alternatives held to be possible *a priori*, and clear formulation in graph theoretic terms of the question at issue would permit a definite decision as to whether the question can be answered in the limit, and by what procedures.

Unfortunately, when the framework is modified to include other, plausible theoretical assumptions that seem to have a hold in cognitive neuropsychology, the prospects are less bright. The assumptions made by Shallice, in particular, while substantively plausible, reduce the possibility of using abnormal data to identify properties of normal cognitive architecture.

RESOURCE/PDP MODELS

A picture of the brain that has some currency supposes that regions of the brain function as parallel distributed processors, and receive inputs and pass outputs to modules in other regions. Thus the vertices of the graphs of cognitive architecture that we have thus far considered would be interpreted as something like parallel distributed processing networks (McClelland et al.). These "semi-PDP" models suggest a different connection between brain damage and behavioral incapacities than is given in A1 through A7. A familiar fact about PDP networks is that a network trained to identify a collection of concepts may suffer differential degradation when some of its vertices are removed. With such damage, the network may continue to be able to make some inferences correctly but be unable to perform others. Thus a "semi-PDP" picture of mental functioning argues that damage to a vertex in a graph of cognitive architecture is damage to some of the neurons of a network and may result in the elimination of some capacities that involve that vertex, but not others. Shallice, for example, has endorsed such a picture, and uses it to argue for the special importance of double dissociation phenomena in cognitive neuropsychology. He suggests that some capacities may be more difficult or computationally demanding than others, and hence more easily disrupted. Double dissociations, he argues, show that of two capacities, at least one of them uses some module not involved in the other capacity.

On reflection, it seems clear that Shallice's point could be made about connections between the PDP modules; some capacities may place greater demands on an information channel than do other capacities that use that same channel. Further, of two capacities that use in common two PDP modules (or channels), one capacity may be the more demanding of one of the modules, and the other the more demanding of the other module. If, in fact, two capacities use exactly the same channels and internal modules, and involve at least two distinct internal modules, then double dissociation may occur provided one capacity uses more of the resources of one of the internal modules while the other capacity uses more of the resources of another, distinct, internal module. Consider the following contrived example, Figure 7.6:

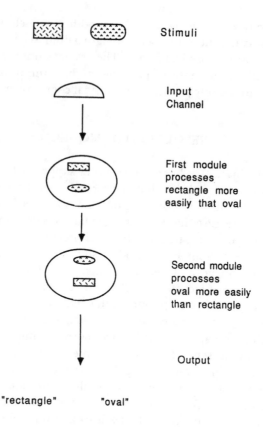

FIGURE 7.6.

Suppose the first module is injured, but only enough to prevent processing the oval (Figure 7.7):

Suppose, now, that the second module is damaged, but only enough to prevent processing the rectangle (Figure 7.8).

With semi-PDP models, double dissociations thus support the inference that there exists a module m(A) involved in capacity A and there exists a distinct module m(B) involved in capacity B, but double dissociations *do not* support any inference to the conclusion that module m(A) is unnecessary for capacity B or that module m(B) is unnecessary for capacity A.

Consider next whether under the same hypothesis information about profiles of capacities and incapacities permits us to discover anything at all about cognitive architecture. Shallice's assumptions amount to replacing A6 with a more complicated condition, and altering slightly the character of discovery problems.

With each vertex or edge of the normal graph we should imagine a **partial ordering** of the capacities that involve that edge or vertex. That capac-

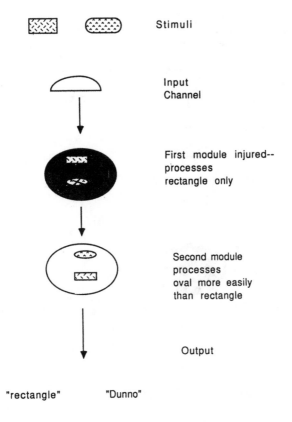

Stimuli

Input
Channel

First module injured--
processes
rectangle only

Second module
processes
oval more easily
than rectangle

Output

"rectangle"   "Dunno"

FIGURE 7.7.

ity 1 is less or equal to capacity 2 in the partial ordering indicates that any damage to that edge or vertex that removes capacity 1 also removes capacity 1. If capacity 1 is less than or equal to capacity 2 and capacity 2 is less than or equal to capacity 1, then any injury to the module that removes one capacity will remove the other. If capacity 1 is less than or equal to capacity 2 for some edge or vertex, but capacity 2 is not less than or equal to capacity 1 for that edge or vertex, then capacity 1 is **less than** capacity 2 for that edge or vertex, meaning that capacity 2 can be removed by damage to that element without removing capacity 1. If capacity 1 is not less than or equal to capacity 2 for some edge or vertex, and capacity 2 is also not less than or equal to capacity 1 for that edge or vertex, then they are **unordered** for that graph element, meaning that some injury to that graph element can remove capacity 1 without removing capacity 2, and some injury to that graph element can remove capacity 2 without removing capacity 1. A degenerate case of a partial ordering leaves all capacities unordered. I will

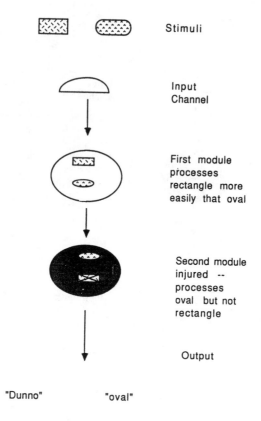

Stimuli

Input
Channel

First module
processes
rectangle more
easily that oval

Second module
injured --
processes
oval but not
rectangle

Output

"Dunno"   "oval"

FIGURE 7.8.

call a graph in which there is attached to each vertex and directed edge a partial ordering (including possibly the degenerate ordering) of the capacities involving that graph element a **partially ordered graph**.

The set of objects in a discovery problem are now not simply directed graphs representing alternative possible normal cognitive architectures. The objects are instead partially ordered graphs, where one and the same graph may appear in the problem with many different orderings of capacities attached to its edges and vertices. The presence of such alternatives indicates an absence of background knowledge as to which capacities are more computationally demanding than others. I will assume that the goal of inference remains, however, to identify the true graph structure.

Rather than forming abnormal structures by simply deleting edges or vertices, an injury is implicitly represented by **labeling** a directed edge or vertex with the set of capacities involving that edge or vertex that are assumed to be damaged. The profile of capacities associated with such a

FIGURE 7.9.   If (I1,U1) is more demanding than all other capacities, profile P4 is added.
If (I1,U2) is more demanding than all other capacities, profile P3 is added.
If (I2, U1) is more demanding than all other capacities, profile P2 is added.
If (I2, U2) is more demanding than all other capacities, profile P1 is

damaged, labeled graph excludes the labeled capacities. Depending on whether or not there is a partial ordering of capacities or outputs attached to graph elements, there are restrictions on the possible labelings. When partial orderings are assumed a discovery problem is posed by a collection of labelled graphs.

On these assumptions alone the enterprise of identifying modular structure from patterns of deficits is hopeless, as a little reflection should make evident. Even the simplest graph structures become indistinguishable. An easy illustration is given by six graphs in the discovery problem of the previous section. Consider what happens when the discovery problem is expanded by adding to graph 2 some possible orderings of the computational demands placed on the internal module v by the four capacities considered in this example (Figure 7.9):

Thus in addition to the profiles allowed by graph (2) previously, and one of the four profiles characteristic of graphs 3–6 may appear, depending on which capacity places the greatest computational demands on the internal module. If all capacities are equally fragile, the set of profiles originally associated with graph 2 is obtained; still other profiles can be obtained if orderings of the internal module of graph 2 are combined with orderings of the directed edges in that graph. Similar things are true of graphs 3–6. Thus unless one has strong prior knowledge as to which capacities are the most computationally demanding (for every module), even simple discovery problems appear hopeless.

CONCLUSION

The conclusion I draw is not that cognitive neuropsychology is in vain; quite the contrary. My conclusion is that even the littlest formal analysis makes clear some weak points in the project, and emphasizes where argument and inquiry ought to be focused. I regard computational neuropsychological models as interesting and even plausible in many respects, but it should be apparent that any attempts to identify modular functional structure on the assumptions such theories incorporate will depend almost entirely on making good cases about the comparative processing demands of different capacities.

NOTES

[1]Neuropsychology has generally made comparatively little use of response times, and I will ignore them here. But see the excellent study by Luce for a discussion of response time problems related to those considered in this paper.

[2]Professor Caramazza informs me that he regards inference in cognitive neuropsychology as having a bootstrap structure, and intended as much in his articles.

REFERENCES

Bub, J. & Bub, D. (1988). On the methodology of single-case studies in cognitive neuropsychology. *Cognitive Neuropsychology*, 5, 565–582.

Bub, J. & Bub, D. (1991). On testing models of cognition through the analysis of brain-damaged performance. *Cognitive Neuropsychology*.

Caramazza, A. (1984). The logic of neuropsychological research and the problem of patient classification in aphasia. *Brain and Language, 21*, 9–20.

Caramazza, A. (1986). On drawing inferences about the structure of normal cognitive systems from the analysis of patterns of impaired performance: The case for single-patient studies. *Brain and Cognition, 5*, 41–66.

Ellis, A., & Young, A. (1988). *Human cognitive neuropsychology.* New Jersey: Erlbaum.

Glymour, C., & Kelly, K. (in press). Why you'll never know if Roger Penrose is a computer. *Behavioral and Brain Sciences.*

Gold, E. Mark. (1965). Limiting recursion. *Journal of Symbolic Logic, 30*, 28–48.

Kelly, K. (in preparation). General characterizations of inductive inference over arbitrary sets of data presentations. *Journal of Symbolic Logic.*

Luce, R. D. (1986). *Response times.* Oxford: Oxford University Press.

McClelland, J. & Rumelhart, D. et al. (1986). *Parallel distributed processing.* Cambridge: M.I.T Press.

McCloskey, M. & Caramazza, A. (1988). Theory and methodology in cognitive neuropsychology: A response to our critics. *Cognitive Neuropsychology*, 5, 583–623.

Osherson, D., Stob, M., & Weinstein, S. (1985). *Systems that learn.* Cambridge: M.I.T. Press.

Osherson, D. & Weinstein, S. (1989). Paradigms of truth detection. *Journal of Philosophical Logic.*

Shallice T. (1988). *From neuropsychology to mental structure.* Cambridge: Cambridge University Press.

chapter 8

Architectural Influences on Language Comprehension*

Jill Fain Lehman
jef@cs.cmu.edu
Computer Science Department
Carnegie Mellon University

Richard L. Lewis
rick@cis.ohio-state.edu
Department of Computer and Information Science
Ohio State University

Alan Newell

A candidate unified architecture for cognition must support a wide range of cognitive tasks, from the highly reactive to those that require deliberation over extended time. The diversity of this range constrains the design of the architecture; a candidate is clearly inadmissible if it can be shown to be inadequate for a particular task or class of tasks. Language comprehension has always been considered a key cognitive capability. It can be broadly characterized by a set of constraints that must be met by any system claiming to have that capability. As such, comprehension constrains the architecture; an architecture that cannot support comprehension per se, or that results in a comprehension capability with significantly different characteristics than those observed in humans, would be inadmissible.

Although the role of language comprehension as a constraint on the architecture seems uncontroversial,[1] we contend that there is symmetrical constraint from the architecture onto comprehension as well. In particu-

*The model presented in this chapter has evolved considerably since 1991. Although still responsive to the constraints enumerated in Section 1, the theory has grown significantly in its ability to account for detailed psycholinquistic data (see Lewis, 1983a; 1983b; Lewis & Lehman, 1996). Further exploration of real-time issues and the interaction between language and task can be found in Green and Lehman (1996), Lehman, Van Dyke, and Rubinoff (1995), and Nelson, Lehman, and John (1994). The extension of NL-Soar to include language generation is described in Lehman, Van Dyke, and Rubinoff (1995).

lar, the architecture influences the realization of the comprehension capability in two important ways: first, by providing mechanisms that shape that realization, and second, by providing mechanisms that afford it. Shaping captures the idea of satisfying a constraint *with* or *by* the architecture or a particular architectural mechanism. In contrast, affording captures the idea of merely satisfying a constraint *in* the architecture. To make the distinction as clear as possible we will say that the system has been shaped by the architecture only when a constraint *must* be satisfied using an architectural mechanism.[2]

To support our contention, we take a concrete approach, considering a particular architecture and a particular system. Soar is a candidate unified architecture for cognition in which a broad range of cognitive tasks has been implemented (Lewis, Huffmen, John, Laird, Lehman, Newell, Rosenbloom, Simon, & Tessler, 1990; Newell, 1990) NL-Soar is the realization of the comprehension capability in Soar. To pinpoint the role of the Soar architecture in the design and implementation of NL-Soar, we will examine two questions: "What are the constraints that define the comprehension task?" and "What are the influences of the architecture on meeting those constraints, in terms of both shaping and affordance?" The answers to these questions will uncover features of language comprehension that may well be necessary targets of architectural influence.

BASIC CONSTRAINTS ON COMPREHENSION

Our first task is to identify the cognitive desiderata for a comprehension system. The constraints we present are neither fine-grained nor exhaustive. They emerge from the characteristic situation in which language use is immersed. Specifically, they proceed from the fact that there is a speaker and a listener between whom meaning must be conveyed through elements that occur sequentially, in real-time. The nine constraints that we consider to be the first-order implications of this situation are listed in Figure 8.1 and are discussed, in order, in the following.

C1: Real-time processing
C2: Deliberation for novelty
C3: Transition from deliberate to real-time
C4: Multiple knowledge sources
C5: Constant-time access to a large lexicon
C6: Task integration
C7: Sequentiality in time
C8: Limited interpretations
C9: Incremental construction of meaning

FIGURE 8.1.   Nine constraints on comprehension.

1. **C1: Real-time processing**. In general, comprehension can require only time that is linear in the number of words uttered, and is usually considered to proceed at an average rate of about 200 to 300 milliseconds per word during reading, somewhat more slowly for speech. The critical point is that the amount of processing available for comprehension is quite limited, precluding extensive search. Expressed qualitatively, this constraint means that a comprehension system must behave essentially as if it knows the right meaning for each word in context as it is encountered. We call this type of behavior *recognitional* comprehension.

2. **C2: Deliberation for novelty**. Seemingly at odds with C1 is the observation that people routinely understand language they have never encountered before. Thus, it must be possible to deliberate in novel contexts. This is not to say that all novel utterances require deliberation, just that the possibility of deliberation must be available in a comprehension system. Circumstances in which a large amount of deliberation is required for comprehension may, in fact, require additional processes (e.g., rereading) as well, or may simply result in a lack of comprehension. What is important here is that when *some* deliberation is needed, the capability is available.

3. **C3: Transition from deliberate to real-time**. Novelty is, by definition, a short-lived phenomenon. As the once-novel context is repeatedly encountered, behavior with respect to that context must become routine. Thus, it must be possible for deliberate comprehension to become recognitional. As long as the system acts to make what was deliberate recognitional, C2 is not at odds with C1—C1 reflects the asymptotic behavior of the system.

4. **C4: Multiple knowledge sources**. Comprehension, the act of assigning meaning (rather than simply structure), involves multiple knowledge sources. A typical decomposition of sources includes at least the lexicon, syntax, semantics, and pragmatics, any or all of which may be necessary for establishing the correct meaning.

5. **C5: Constant-time access to a large lexicon**. Since processing time does not grow as the lexicon grows, the system must be able to access the elements of a potentially very large lexicon in essentially constant time. This constraint is related to C1. Consider, for example, a system with access linear in the size of the lexicon. As the lexicon grows over time, so would the time for lexical access. Yet, for any given utterance, performance would still appear linear in the number of words, with the size of the lexicon acting as a constant term for the single example. C1 precludes this scenario by putting an absolute bound on lexical access—the size of the constant term cannot grow beyond the total average time per word.

6. **C6: Task integration**. Comprehension does not proceed in a vacuum, but as part of task-related problem-solving behavior that occurs within the same cognitive architecture. The task knowledge source is distinct from the knowledge sources outlined in C5 in that its content is independent of the use of language in performing the task. In other words, we conceive of syntax, semantics, etc., as knowledge sources whose knowledge exists in a form that is immediately useful to language processes. Task knowledge, on the other hand, exists in a form that is useful to task processes, and may or may not be immediately available to language processes. Nevertheless, it must be possible for the content and goals of the task to exert an influence on our interpretation of language (Lehman, Newell, Polk, & Lewis, 1993).

7. **C7: Sequentiality in time**. The system must be able to process words, recognitionally or deliberately, as they naturally occur, sequentially in time. Note that C7 is also orthogonal to C1: a "single-path" chart parser, for example, could take time linear in the number of words while using an island-growing technique that violated sequentiality.

8. **C8: Limited interpretations**. Since both polysomy and local syntactic ambiguity are pervasive in natural languages, a comprehension process that constructs all partial interpretations could perform exponential work in arriving at the meanings. Thus, a comprehension system must control the number of interpretations in a way that preserves its linear, real-time character. Additional evidence for this constraint comes from psycholinguistic research on garden-path phenomena that demonstrates empirically that people do not maintain all partial interpretations during comprehension (Crain & Steedman, 1985 and Warner & Glass, 1987).

9. **C9: Incremental construction of meaning**. By this constraint we mean that each word contributes to the total meaning in such a way that at each point in the utterance the meaning is as complete as the content to that point can determine it. There are a number of informal arguments that support the construction of meaning on a word-by-word basis: for example, the regularity with which meaning is conveyed in natural conversation by utterances that are incomplete at the phrasal, clausal, or sentential level, or the need to limit interpretations by committing to a single meaning for a polysemous word.[3] As in C8, however, strong empirical support for incremental construction comes from the psycholinguistic community, in the form of speech shadowing, eye movement, and priming studies (Carpenter & Just, 1983; Dell, McKoon, & Ratcliffe, 1983; Marslen-Wilson, 1973).

Clearly some of these constraints are interrelated. Although we normally think of comprehension as the process of assigning meaning to an utterance, when viewed together, constraints C1-C3 imply the existence of another, concurrent process during comprehension. This second process is the continual transformation of deliberation into recognition. Such a process must exist if comprehension is to be flexible enough to both function in real-time and overcome novelty.[4] C5 and C8 derive, at least in part, from the real-time constraint in C1. C9 is a further specification of what we mean by *process* in C7. Still, interrelationship is not identity; we tease the constraints apart, establishing each as an individual desideratum, because to solve one is not necessarily to guarantee a solution to the others. Moreover, there exists the potential for separate architectural influences on each solution. Indeed, it will turn out that, for Soar and NL-Soar at least, the first five constraints lead to architectural shaping of the system's design, but the last four can be met by affordance alone.

OVERVIEW OF THE SOAR ARCHITECTURE

In the previous section we answered the question "What are the constraints that define the comprehension task?" In preparation for answering our second question, "What are the influences of the architecture on meeting those constraints, in terms of both shaping and affordance?" we briefly review the Soar architecture.

Figure 8.2 gives a schematic overview of the architecture, showing the basic mechanisms and processes. Critical to our analysis is the way that many of these architectural elements can be tied to the time-course of human cognition (a full description of the architecture and its relationship to cognitive behavior can be found in Newell (1990). Still, it is important to realize that no claim is being made in the following discussion about Soar's execution speed as an implemented computer system. Rather, a relation is being forged between human cognitive operations that occur at the stated response times and the architectural mechanisms that perform those cognitive functions. Our description follows the numbers in parentheses in the figure.

At the bottom of the cognitive band is the level of distal access, with access operations taking on the order of ten milliseconds. The function of distal access is accomplished in the architecture by matching the contents of *working memory* (1) against *patterns* in the long-term *recognition memory* (2) and delivering the matched patterns' associations back to working memory.[5] Knowledge flows from long-term memory into working memory in a chain of parallel distal accesses until no more knowledge is evoked. This point of quiescence marks the end of the *elaboration phase* (3) of Soar's *decision cycle* (4).

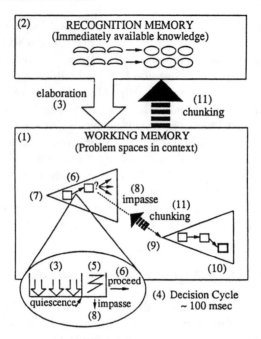

FIGURE 8.2. Overview of the Soar architecture.

The decision cycle is the architecture's elementary act of deliberation, placing it at the second level of the cognitive band and in the 100 millisecond range. The knowledge that flows into working memory during elaboration includes preferences for new problem spaces, operators, or states. Once all patterns have delivered their associations, a fixed decision procedure is invoked (5) to reason about the accumulated preferences. If, at the end of the decision procedure, there is an unequivocal next step, it is taken (6), and the outcome of deliberation is a transition in the problem-solving context defined by the current working memory. The transition occurs via the application of an *operator*, one operator per decision cycle. Thus, problem solving (behavior at one second and beyond) occurs in *problem spaces* shown as triangles (7), by the successive application of operators over multiple decision cycles to produce state-to-state transitions from an initial state to a desired state.

If, at the end of the decision procedure, there is no unequivocal next step, the architecture *impasses* (8) and a new *goal* is established to overcome the lack of recognitional knowledge that caused the impasse. The new goal gives rise to a new problem space (9), and problem solving continues. Once the impasse is resolved by reaching a desired state in the subspace (10), Soar's learning mechanism forms associations between the conditions that led to the impasse and the results of problem solving available in the desired state. These associations, or *chunks*, are added to long-term memory (11), making available knowledge that avoids the impasse in future, similar contexts.

Critical to our analysis of architectural influence is Soar's commitment to the correspondence between the decision cycle and the elementary act of deliberation in human behavior. Given this correspondence, observe that if an elementary act of deliberation takes about 100 milliseconds in humans, and the application of an operator in Soar takes a single deliberate act (i.e., one decision cycle), then there is time for only a small number of operators to be applied in the 200 to 300 milliseconds per word that characterizes recognitional comprehension.

ARCHITECTURAL SHAPING

We now have both a set of architecture-independent constraints on comprehension and an architecture in which to construct a comprehension system. Let us proceed to design a comprehension system that meets those constraints within that architecture. In designing our system we will look first to those constraints we can satisfy with the architecture; that is, we will look first to how the architecture shapes our design. By examining each of C1–C5 in turn, we slowly will build the basic capability for comprehension that is NL-Soar.

Real-Time Processing (C1)

Since Soar is a problem space architecture, we must begin by casting the comprehension process as sets of operators that define problem spaces. We are, therefore, constructing comprehension within the problem solving architecture itself (as opposed to constructing a language module separate from cognition).[6] As shown in Figure 8.3, we need, at the very least, a problem space (call it Comprehension) whose operators attend to each word and assign it a meaning in context. In this as in all figures, problem spaces are represented by triangles, states by squares, and operators by arrows.

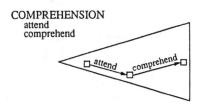

COMPREHENSION
attend
comprehend

FIGURE 8.3. The effect of the real-time constraint on the shape of NL-Soar.

The problem space name and the names of operators that define that space are given at the left.

How does the real-time constraint of 200 to 300 milliseconds per word affect Comprehension's operators? As we noted in the previous section, since Soar ties the application of an operator to the 100 millisecond decision cycle, there is only enough time for a few operators per word, on average. Thus, in NL-Soar, the **attend** operator focuses attention on the next word and the remaining work is done by **comprehend**. If the comprehension operator is adequate to assign the right representation to each word in context, then no impasses will occur in this problem space and comprehension will proceed truly recognitionally. Here, shaping comes from the decision of what constitutes the architectural act of deliberation in Soar, a decision that exists independent of NL-Soar and the realization of a language capability in the architecture.

Deliberation for Novelty (C2)

The operators in the Comprehension space achieve recognitional comprehension just as long as the system has adequate knowledge of the meaning of each word in context. Since this cannot always be the case, it must be possible to comprehend nonrecognitionally as well. In Soar terms, this means we must also have a problem space, call it Construct, in which to problem solve or search for the meaning (and, of course, we must also have a bit of time left over to do a small amount of problem solving when it's necessary). As shown in Figure 8.4, we can meet this constraint *in* the architecture because Soar supports multiple problem spaces. Moreover, the architectural notion of impasse defines exactly the needed relationship

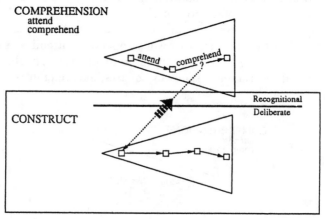

FIGURE 8.4. The effect of the deliberation and transition constraints on the shape of NL-Soar.

between Comprehension and Construct: search in the deliberate problem space occurs because of a lack of recognitional knowledge. The hierarchical relationship among problem spaces is indicated downward by thin impasse arrows and upward by thicker chunking arrows.

How do we know that we need another problem space? Might it not be the case that deliberation simply corresponds to a different set of operators in the Comprehension space? If so, then multiple problem spaces and Soar's impasse mechanism merely afford the mapping in Figure 8.4 rather than shaping it. Considering the transition constraint will decide the question.

Transition from Deliberate to Real-Time (C3)

Novelty is relative; novel contexts become mundane. What once required deliberation must eventually become recognitional or there is no hope that comprehension as a whole can have a recognitional character. The transition from deliberate to recognitional comprehension is achieved in NL-Soar by the architecture's continuous learning mechanism, chunking (see Figure 8.4).

The chunking process is automatic but it is invoked only at the resolution of an impasse, when the system has found the knowledge in a lower problem space that will allow it to proceed in the higher space. Thus, we cannot, in fact, consider our solution to the deliberation constraint (C2) a mere affordance. The knowledge provided by a set of deliberative operators in the Comprehension space would always remain deliberative in that space; knowledge can be transformed only across problem spaces. Architectural shaping for C2 and C3 comes from the fact that no new knowledge can be added to long-term memory without an impasse and its resolution.

The Soar architecture and the first three constraints have shaped the basic structure of NL-Soar as a system that comprehends recognitionally when the knowledge is available, deliberately when it is not, but is always moving toward fully recognitional behavior. Recognitional comprehension takes the form of a comprehension operator that brings to bear all the knowledge required to understand a word in context. When the comprehension operator is inadequate for the current context, an impasse arises and the architecture sets the goal of overcoming the lack of recognitional knowledge. As a result, NL-Soar continues processing deliberately in a different problem space.

Is such a scheme likely to meet the real-time constraint in practice? Figure 8.5 shows how the system behaves over time as it processes 61 sentences.[7] Each point represents the percentage of words comprehended recognitionally in a 24-word sliding window. Small dips in the graph tend to indicate new lexemes, larger dips tend to indicate new syntactic con-

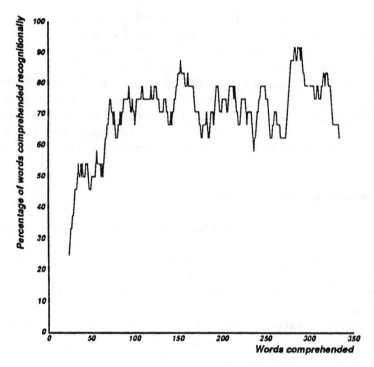

FIGURE 8.5.   Mixed recognitional and deliberate comprehension in NL-Soar.

structions. At the first data point of 24 words, for example, about one fourth were processed by comprehension operator (i.e., there was transfer from the earlier part of the twenty-four to the later portion). At a 24-word window around the 280th word in the corpus, recognitional comprehension occurs for about 95% of the words. Overall, the system runs about 70% recognitionally.

Of course, this empirical evidence is only suggestive. To meet the real-time constraint in practice, we believe that the system must run closer to 90% recognitionally, on the average. The percentage of time during which the system operates recognitionally depends in great part on the generality of the comprehension operator chunks (and to a lesser degree on the total time spent in deliberation each time an impasse in Comprehension arises). Although the chunking process itself cannot be changed, chunk generality can, nevertheless, be indirectly manipulated by choices in the way knowledge is represented and in the kinds of relations that hold between problem spaces. Although it is possible to increase (or decrease) chunk transfer in NL-Soar, many of the key design decisions affecting transfer are underconstrained by considering comprehension alone. Thus, a definitive answer to the question of whether this organization can meet the real-time constraint in practice must wait until we have generation and acquisition theories that remove many of the degrees of freedom.

Multiple Knowledge Sources (C4)

As we examine the remainder of our shaping constraints we must explore their effects with respect to both recognitional and deliberate comprehension. For example, all of the linguistic knowledge sources must be brought to bear simultaneously in the application of a single comprehension operator during recognitional comprehension. On the other hand, those same knowledge sources may be used in a sequential fashion during deliberate comprehension. The integration of knowledge sources in the comprehension operator arises via chunking (we will see an example later). Indeed, the comprehension operator *is* the integration of those knowledge sources that define the meaning of a word in context.

The architecture affords three ways to bring the individual knowledge sources to bear sequentially: a single problem space with operators representing each knowledge source, sibling problem spaces each of which represents a single source, or a hierarchy of problem spaces with the knowledge sources spread among them. Yet, our design is shaped by the need to minimize the amount of processing done during deliberate com-

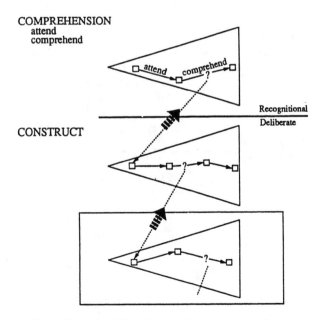

FIGURE 8.6.   The effect of multiple knowledge sources on the shape of NL-Soar.

prehension. Thus, we organize the knowledge sources in such a way that our problem solving goes on in multiple problem spaces defined hierarchically by impasses (see Figure 8.6). Since chunking occurs at the resolution of any impasse, this arrangement is the only one that allows processing to speed up during deliberation as well.

Constant-time Access to a Large Lexicon (C5)

The integration of knowledge sources found in the Comprehension space arises out of the sequential application of knowledge sources during deliberation. Once lexical knowledge has been integrated with the other sources into a piece of the comprehension operator, we know it will be brought to bear with the other sources in a single operator application; that is, in constant time. When lexical access is only one step of a deliberate process, however, we must be careful that it takes time independent of the size of the lexicon. We can achieve this by relying on our long-term parallel recognition memory to achieve lexical access in a single operator application in the Construct space as well (see Figure 8.7).

The system as it stands thus far has many of the properties we desire. Each of the first five desideratum has been met by tying some functional characteristic of comprehension to one or more of the architectural mech-

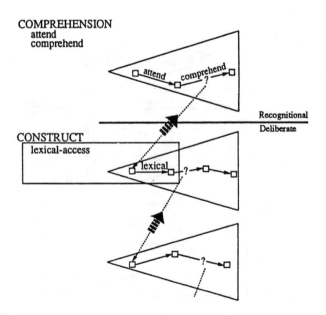

FIGURE 8.7.   The effect of the lexical constraint on the shape of NL-Soar.

anisms in Soar. Within this framework, we now turn to the remaining four constraints.

ARCHITECTURAL AFFORDANCES

Of our original list, task integration, sequentiality, limited interpretation, and incremental construction of meaning remain. Missing, however, is a specification of the knowledge in and organization of the multiple knowledge sources that, together with the Construct space, contribute to the deliberate part of the system. Figure 8.8 fills in the missing details. As in previous figures, the problem space names are listed along with their oper-

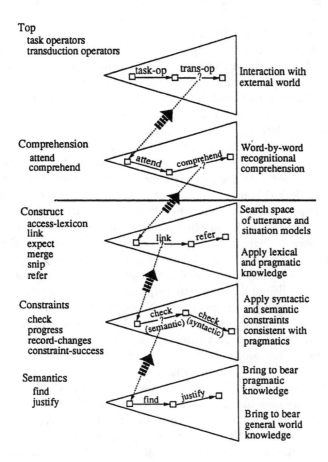

FIGURE 8.8.   NL-Soar complete.

ators at the left. A brief description of the problem space's behavior is given at the right.

Comprehension does not exist in a vacuum. Indeed, it is a normal adjunct to the problem space view to treat comprehension as a skill or black-box to be deployed by the task space when the need arises for language capabilities (Lehman, Newell, Polk, & Lewis, 1993 and Polk, 1992). Language processes act to transduce part of the task state into a form that task operators can recognize and manipulate. For language to play the role of transducer, there must be both appropriate operators in Soar's Top problem space (the space through which all interaction with the external world is conducted) and a part of the task state that is available to comprehension. Two configurations are afforded by the architecture: a hierarchical arrangement such as the one shown in Figure 8.8, and an alternative in which the **attend** and **comprehend** operators are located in the Top problem space also.[8]

At the top of the hierarchy of language spaces is Comprehension. Here sequentiality is afforded by simple control knowledge that governs the behavior of the **attend** and **comprehend** operators. Attention proceeds left to right through the sentence, each word being comprehended in turn, its meaning established by a single operator application that brings all the relevant knowledge to bear simultaneously.

When comprehension cannot proceed recognitionally, an impasse arises that leads to deliberate behavior in the Construct space. Here incremental construction of meaning is afforded by **lexical-access** and the structure building operators **link, expect, merge,** and **refer.** The first three structure builders construct the *utterance model,* a dependency graph of words and expectations and their functional roles that reflects the structure of the utterance. The utterance model and the **refer** operator are used in constructing the system's meaning structure, the *situation model.* The situation model reflects the structure of the situation described by the utterance. The remaining operator in Construct, **snip,** is a deconstructor, severing an established link to create disjoint pieces of the graph that may be recombined through link operators. NL-Soar's limited path behavior is afforded by control knowledge associated with the constructor and deconstructor operators. Specifically, although there may be many possible links suggested by a new word for the existing utterance model, links are explored only until one is found that results in a single graph structure. Further, if no link results in a coherent structure, then only a subset of links in the utterance model may be **snipped,** with the ensuing relinking explored only until a sequence is found that produces a single graph. We will see an example of NL-Soar's limited path behavior shortly. For the moment, note simply that deliberate comprehension can be viewed as a search among the various possible sequences of these operators in order to find a way of attaching the new word and its meaning to the current utterance and situation models. The chunks that result from this deliberation avoid this search for an attachment in the future.

The Constraints space is the source of the syntactic, semantic, and pragmatic knowledge that permits or vetos the implementation of a **link, expect, merge,** or **snip** operator proposed in the Construct space. In simplest terms, we can consider the Constraints space as a kind of oracle. Via an impasse, Construct asks the question, *Is this attachment syntactically, semantically, and pragmatically consistent?* and Constraints resolves the impasse by answering *yes* or *no* after bringing all the pertinent constraints to bear via **check** and **progress** operators (we will see examples of this in the next section).

The problem space at the bottom of the hierarchy shown in Figure 8.8 is Semantics. When the Constraints space does not have the knowledge needed to verify an attachment's semantic consistency, a search for that knowledge occurs here. The Semantics space has two ways of validating an attachment: pragmatic justification and inference. In the former, the **find** operator looks at the current situation model for instances of the proposed attachment. If an instance of the relation is already present, it must be semantically correct. If, for example, there is already a blue block in the situation, then blue must be a legitimate modifier for block. If no evidence is found in the situation model, the justify operator uses NL-Soar's general world knowledge to infer a validating relation.

Within this system, integration with the task, sequentiality, limited interpretation, and incremental construction of meaning are all accomplished by knowledge about the proposal and implementation of operators. This knowledge defines a set of mechanisms in NL-Soar that realize the four constraints but which are not themselves part of the Soar architecture. Other architectures may well afford these same solutions. That is the inherent difference between shaping and affordance.

EXAMPLES OF COMPREHENSION IN NL-SOAR

Having constructed a system that we believe meets our cognitive desiderata, let us now examine the behavior of the system during processing as a check that no unexpected consequences are in the design. For expository purposes we have chosen two simple sentences: *John knows Sharyn* and *John knows Sharyn knows a chemist.* To reflect a typical situation for NL-Soar, we assume that the comprehension operator is adequate for some of the words (i.e., *John* and *Sharyn*) in the context in which they appear. We also assume that the second sentence occurs after the first sentence in time—in

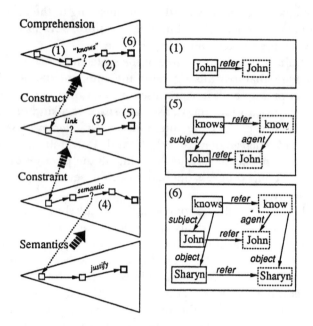

FIGURE 8.9.   Processing John knows Sharyn

other words, that the chunks from the first sentence are available when the second sentence is encountered.

Figure 8.9 highlights the system's performance in comprehending *John knows Sharyn*. We trace the processing steps sequentially by the numbers in the problem space hierarchy, some of which also refer to the utterance models (solid border) and situation models (dashed border) shown at various points to the right. Due to space, only some of the operators and states are shown.

Since we assume that the comprehension of *John* is recognitional, (1) shows the utterance and situation models that result after an **attend** and **comprehend** operator are applied to that word. Next, *knows* is attended to, but an impasse occurs on the comprehension operator.

Processing continues in the Construct space where lexical access for *knows* suggests possible meanings. This lexical information results in the proposal of a subject link between a particular meaning of *knows* and *John*. Before this link can be made in the utterance model however, it must be shown to be meaningful and to leave the models cohesive. That knowledge is available via an impasse (3) into the Constraints space where *check* operators are applied to test word order, number agreement, and semantic consistency. The latter test requires knowledge from the Semantics space that is brought to bear via another impasse (4). Proving semantic consistency in the Semantics space resolves impasse (4) and makes that knowledge immediately available in the future in Constraint. The progress constraint then ensures that the models created by the proposed link remain a single graph. With all constraints passed, impasse (3) is resolved, and the link in the utterance model is made, terminating any further search for interpretations. At the same time, chunking adds knowledge to Construct that will recognize appropriate conditions for making this link in the future, without the impasse and sequential operator application in Constraint. The **refer** operator is then applied to construct the relevant increment to the situation model, bringing deliberate comprehension to a close (5), and resolving the comprehension operator impasse (2).

The resolution of impasse (2) results in associations being added to long-term memory that extend the contexts in which the system can behave recognitionally. Simplified for explanatory purposes, these associations can be paraphrased as:

IF comprehending *knows*, and	lexical/Construct
there's a preceding word, and	syntactic/Constraint
that word can receive the subject role, and	syntactic/Constraint
the word refers to a person, and	semantic/Semantics
the word is third person singular,	syntactic/Constraint
THEN use sense1[9] of *knows*	lexical/Construct
assign the word as the subject of *knows*,	syntactic/Constraint
establish a referent for the act of knowing,	pragmatic/Construct
with the subject's referent as the agent.	pragmatic/Construct

Each line is tagged by the knowledge source and problem space that contributed it (because of chunking the problem space that contributes a piece of knowledge may change over time, but the knowledge source will not). Clearly if we gave NL-Soar this example sentence again, comprehension of *knows* would require only the single operator application of **comprehend** rather than the elaborate problem-solving we have just seen. Note, however, that the word *John* is not in the IF-portion of the rules. Neither are any number of attributes about John that we may know, over and above that he is a person. Thus, this association has made many other contexts recognitional as well.

How does the system's performance on this example relate to our set of constraints? The system was able to act both recognitionally and deliberately and to smoothly change some of its deliberate knowledge into recognitional knowledge. It used multiple knowledge sources and had constant-time access to the lexicon. It processed the utterance sequentially, pursued only a single interpretation and constructed its meaning structure incrementally. To concentrate on the performance of NL-Soar per se, the example did not show integration with a task (but see Huffman & Laird, 1992).

So it would seem that we have achieved what we set out to do. On the other hand, perhaps the system appears to work only because the single interpretation it pursued was the correct one. The next example, *John knows Sharyn knows a chemist*, shows how the system recovers from an incorrect interpretation. Because of space, only the utterance model is shown in this example.

As previously mentioned, we assume that the chunks built during processing of the last sentence are now available. Thus, with three instances of **attend/comprehend** we must find ourselves in the same situation as before (compare the utterance models at (1) in Figure 8.10 and at (5) in Figure 8.9). The incorrect assignment of *Sharyn* as object cannot be detected until the next word is encountered (the second *knows*), after the object link between *knows* and *Sharyn* has already been made.

NL-Soar undoes this incorrect interpretation as part of processing the second instance of *knows*. Although the verb is familiar, the current comprehension operator is inadequate for this context, so an impasse arises (2). After lexical access, a link is proposed to treat the main verb as the clausal object of the embedded verb. This link fails in the Constraints

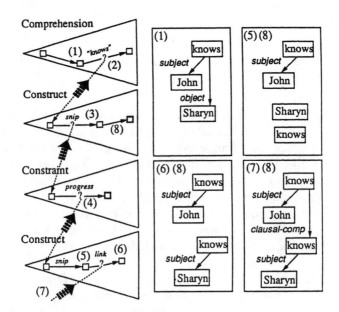

FIGURE 8.10. Processing *John knows Sharyn knows a chemist.*

space due to a word order violation (not shown). Since no other link is proposed, the **expect** operator is proposed next. Again, deliberation resulting from this choice will fail to produce cohesive models. As a last resort, the *snip* operator is proposed to remove the object link that exists between *Sharyn* and the first instance of *knows*.[10]

The snip operator itself contains no special knowledge; it acts only to remove an existing link. The actual repair of the models must be performed by Construct's other operators. Thus, the only constraint the proposed **snip** must pass is the progress constraint that ensures the models can be made cohesive if the *snip* is implemented (4). That knowledge becomes available by a look-ahead search through the space of possible reconstructions. The look-ahead is implemented by impassing into a new version of the Construct space where we act as if the snip has been made (5) and see if we can relink the pieces of the models. Using impasses between alternating Constraint and Construct spaces, the look-ahead search will find that *snip* makes progress if the second instance of *knows* is linked to *Sharyn* as subject (6), which in turn makes progress if the second *knows* is linked to the first *knows* as a clausal complement (7). Note that as each of these impasses resolves (e.g., (7)), chunks are built that recognize the contexts under which the actual links should be made. Thus, when impasse (3) resolves, those chunks will transfer, making real the **snip-link-link** sequence we found during look-ahead (8). Once the situation model has been augmented and referential links have been added, deliberation comes to an end, resolving impasse (2).[11]

Our purpose in looking at this second example was to understand whether NL-Soar would behave differently with respect to our cognitive constraints when its single interpretation proved to be wrong. What the system learns upon resolution of the impasse on the comprehension operator in this example is two kinds of chunks that together perform *recognitional repair*. The first kind of chunk recognizes when to remove a link between two nodes in the utterance model:

> IF comprehending *knows*, and
>   there's a preceding word, and
>   the word can assign a clausal complement, and
>   the word assigns an object role, and
>   the object refers to a person, and
>   the object can receive the subject role, and
>   the object is third person singular,
> THEN remove the object role from the word.

Once the old link has been severed, chunks of the second kind link up the unconnected pieces of the model. This second type of chunk is the same as we saw in the previous example. What is important to note is that recognitional repair is a mechanism in NL-Soar that allows the system to make wrong choices in limiting its interpretation without changing the character of the system overall.

THE ROLES OF THE ARCHITECTURE

We have been examining the roles that a particular architecture, Soar, played in the design of a particular comprehension system, NL-Soar. By defining a set of constraints that any comprehension system must meet irrespective of the architecture in which it is embedded, we have uncovered a distinction between architectural shaping and affordance. We believe that the architecture shaped our solutions to the real-time, deliberation, transition, multiple knowledge source, and constant-time lexical access constraints, but afforded solutions to task integration, sequentiality, limited interpretations, and incremental construction of meaning.

Why is there shaping? Isn't affordance all we can reasonably expect from a general architecture? Shaping occurs, by our definition, only when a constraint *must* be satisfied using an architectural mechanism. Thus, for shaping to be possible there must be an interaction between architecture specification and constraint specification such that the architecture admits only solutions to the constraint that rely on architectural mechanisms. Consider the real-time constraint. The interaction for this constraint is between the mapping of the decision cycle to the elementary act of deliberation and the 200 to 300 millisecond bound. Given that interaction, there is no other role for the architecture to play in meeting the real-time constraint because there is no time to build up the layer of mechanism on top of the architecture that would convert shaping to affordance.

Why is there affordance? Since the architecture underlies everything, isn't shaping all? Affordance occurs, by our definition (albeit implicitly), when the interaction between architecture specification and constraint specification admits solutions built atop architectural mechanisms. Consider the incremental construction of meaning. This constraint is met, in part, by operators that create a dependency graph augmented with expectations. Nothing in the constraint per se forces that solution—we might just as well have used operators that implemented a purely bottom-up scheme, or ones that derived LFG or GB structures (Sells, 1987).

Why is the distinction between shaping and affordance a useful one? An architecture contributes theoretical power when it provides a solution whose character would be substantively different in another architecture, measured along some architecturally-independent dimension (e.g., time, space, cost, fit to data, etc.). This is as true for cognitive architectures as it is for software architectures and hardware architectures. No one would deny that the ability to support a wide variety of cognitive tasks is an acid-test for a candidate unified architecture for cognition. Over and above whether candidate X supports capability Y, however, is the question of how candidate X contributes to the theory of Y. Delineating shaping from affordance is the first step in answering that question. Of course, not all the constraints defining a capability have or need architectural solutions. Similarly, not every architecture will shape the solutions to the same subset of constraints.[12] Still, by distinguishing the two classes, the shaping influence of an architecture provides a space of partial solutions into which the other constraints can be fit, and makes it easy to see where that architecture shines through.

NOTES

[1]For example, language is a central concern for modular theories of mental architecture (Fodor, 1983) as well as nonmodular theories such as ours.

[2]Note that shaping implies that satisfying the constraint in a significantly different architecture would require a substantively different solution, whereas affording allows that the same solution might be realizable in any other flexible architecture as well.

[3]Despite the appeal to limited interpretations in support of the incremental construction of meaning, C8 and C9 should be considered as independent constraints. It is possible to imagine a system that limits its interpretations but only at phrasal or clausal boundaries. Similarly, it is possible to imagine a system that incrementally constructs all possible interpretations.

[4]Consider what it would mean for a comprehension system to exist without such a process: the system could fail to deliberate or to recognize (obviating the need for the transformation from one form into the other), or it could act both deliberately and recognitionally but fail to transform its knowledge from one form to the other. To have a system without the ability to deliberate is implausible if we examine the character of comprehension in the young child, whereas to have a purely deliberative system ignores the fundamental character of adult comprehension. Finally, to bifurcate the comprehension process into unchanging deliberate and recognitional portions ignores the fact that it is essentially the same content that appears to require deliberation in the child that is recognitional in the adult.

[5]These patterns-with-associations are usually described as *productions* in the Soar literature. This is technically correct, but has proven confusing because productions are often taken in the sense used within the expert systems literature. Productions in Soar form a type of associative memory. Productions in expert systems correspond to the operators of problem spaces in Soar.

[6]But the relationship of NL-Soar and modularity is an interesting one (see [ ]).

[7]The 61 sentences were developed to test all the lexical and syntactic knowledge in the system at the time (Spring 1991), not to optimize transfer in the comprehension operator.

[8]The configuration in Figure 8.8 was implemented first and is shown here for historical purposes. More recently, however, we have moved to the second alternative, in keeping

with the model suggested by the discussion of immediate interaction in [ ].

[9]This is simply a shorthand way of designating the particular sense that led to a desired state during deliberate comprehension.

[10]Why is the object link snipped? How does the system know some other link in the utterance model is not the source of the error? It doesn't. At any point in time, only a subset of the links are available for snipping. The particular set of features that determines which links are available in the version of NL-Soar being described (Spring 1991) represents only one of the possible ways of limiting the system's repair capability. For an exploration of the space of such sets of features, see [ ].

[11]A detailed, step-by-step explanation of what goes on in the look-ahead search and in processing the remainder of the example sentence can be found in Lehman, Lewis, & Newell (1991).

[12]For example, the architecture for reading put forward by Carpenter and Just shapes the solution to the limited interpretations constraint that is solved by affordance in NL-Soar (Just & Carpenter, 1992).

REFERENCES

Carpenter, P. A. & Just, M. A. (1983). What your eyes do while your mind is reading. In *Eye movements in reading: Perceptual and language processes*. Rayner, K. (ed). New York: Academic Press.

Crain, S., & Steedman, M. (1985). On not being led up the garden path: The use of context by the psychological syntax processor. In D. R. Dowty, L. Karttunen, & A. M. Zwicky (Eds.), *Natural language parsing*. Cambridge, U.K.: Cambridge University Press.

Dell, G. S., McKoon, G., & Ratcliffe, R. (1983). The activation of antecedent information during the processing of anaphoric reference in reading. *Journal of Verbal Learning and Verbal Behavior, 22,* 121–132.

Fodor, J. A. (1983). *Modularity of mind: An essay on faculty psychology.* Cambridge, MA: MIT Press.

Green, N. & Lehman, J. F. (1996). Comparing agent modeling for language and action, Proceeding of the 1996 AAAI Workshop on Agent Modeling, to appear.

Huffman, S. B. & Laird, J. E. (1992). Dimensions of complexity in learning from interactive instruction. *Cooperative Intelligent Robotics in Space III, SPIE, vol. 1829.* November 1992. Jon Erikson, (Ed.), Boston, MA.

Just, M. A. & Carpenter, P. A. (1992). A capacity theory of comprehension: Individual differences in working memory. *Psychological Review, 99* (1), 122–149.

Lehman, J. F., Lewis, R., & Newell, A. (1991). Natural language comprehension in Soar. Tech. report, Carnegie Mellon University CMU-CS-91–117.

Lehman, J. F., Newell, A. N., Polk, T., & Lewis, R. L. (1993). The Role of language in cognition. In G. Harman (Ed.), *Conceptions of the human mind*. Hillsdale, NJ: Erlbaum .

Lehman, J. F., Van Dyke, J., & Rubinoff, R. (1995). Natural language processing for IFORS: Comprehension and generation in the air combat domain. Proceedings of the Fifth Conference on Computer Generated Forces and Behavioral Representation, pp. 115–123.

Lewis, R. L. (1992). Recent developments in the NL-Soar garden path theory. Tech. report CMU-CS-92–141, School of Computer Science, Carnegie Mellon University.

Lewis, R. L. (1996). Modularity matters: What Soar has to say about modularity. In D. Steier & T. Mitchell (Eds.), *Mind matters: A tribute to Allen Newell*. Hillsdale NJ: Erlbaum.

Lewis, R. L., Huffman, S. B., John, B. E., Laird, J. E., Lehman, J. F., Newell, A., Rosenbloom, P. S., Simon, T., & Tessler, S. G. (1990). Soar as a unified theory of cognition: Spring. *Twelfth Annual Conference of the Cognitive Science Society*, pp. 1035–1042.

Lewis, R. L. (1993a). An architectutally-based theory of human sentence comprehension. Doctoral dissertation, Carnegie Mellon University, School of Computer Science, December, Available as Technical Report CMU-CS-93-226 from reports@cs.cmu.edu.

Lewis, R. L. (1993b). An architecturally-based theory of human sentence comprehension. Proceedings of the Fifteenth Annual Conference of the Cognitive Science Society, pp. 108–113.

Lewis, R. L. & Lehman, J. F. (1996). A theory of the computational architecture of sentence comprehension. Unpublished manuscript.

Marslen-Wilson, W. (1973). Linguistic structure and speech shadowing at very short latencies. *Nature, 244,* 522–523.

Newell, A. (1990). *Unified theories of cognition.* Cambridge, MA: Harvard University Press.

Nelson, G., Lehman, J. F., & John, B. (1994). Integrating cognitive capabilities in a real-time task. Proceedings of the Sixteenth Annual Conference of the Cognitive Science Society, pp. 658–663.

Polk, T. A. (1992). Verbal reasoning. Doctoral dissertation, Carnegie Mellon University, School of Computer Science, August.

Sells, P. (1987). *Lectures on contemporary syntactic theories: An introduction to government-binding theory, generalized phrase structure grammar, and lexical-functional grammar.* Center for the Study of Language and Information; Stanford, CA.

Warner, J. & Glass, A. L. (1987). Context and distance-to-disambiguation effects in ambiguity resolution: Evidence from grammaticality judgments of garden path sentences. *Journal of Memory and Language, 26,* 714–738.

chapter 9

Interactive Coordination Processes: How the Brain Accomplishes What We Take for Granted in Computer Languages—And Then Does It Better

William J. Clancey
bill_clancey@irl.org
Institute for Research on Learning

...it was a long time before I fully realized the importance, for many psychological experiments, of putting the situations which are used to produce response into sequential form.
—Sir Frederic Bartlett, *Thinking*, 1958, p. 141

BACKGROUND

By the mid1980s, many AI researchers began to realize that the mainstream approaches to developing intelligent machines were fruitful, but incomplete. For example, knowledge engineering—the process of codifying human knowledge in expert systems—makes a solid contribution to computer modeling, but such programs neither replicate in all important aspects, nor explain the full capability of human intelligence (Clancy, 1997). A means–end approach to engineering an artificial intelligence machine now suggests that we focus on the differences between human capabilities and the best computer programs. These differences suggest two basic limitations in the "symbolic" approach of gameplaying programs, expert systems, natural language processing, planning, etc. First, human memory is much more than a storehouse where structures are put away, indexed, and rotely retrieved. Second, human reasoning involves more than searching, matching, and recombining previously stored descriptions of situations and action plans. Indeed, these hypotheses are related: Remembering and reasoning both involve *reconceptualization*. That is, human learning occurs with every thought; learning is not just a reflective process of formalizing knowledge after deeds are done.

For many computer scientists the phenomenon to be replicated—human intelligence—and knowledge are placed in new relation. Previously, we explained intelligent behavior in terms of knowledge stored in memory: word definitions, facts and rules modeling complex causal processes in the world, plans and procedures for doing things. Now, we view these descriptions as *descriptive models*—which people use like maps, handbooks, and standards for guiding their actions. These descriptions, like the rules in an expert system, are not knowledge itself, but *representations of knowledge*—a step removed from what is occurring in the brain. Like an article in an encyclopedia, such descriptions require interpretation in the context of use, which, in people, involves not only generating additional descriptions, but conceptualizing in nonverbal modes. As Newell (1982) put it, "Knowledge is never actually in hand . . . Knowledge can only be created dynamically in time."

The change in perspective can be bewildering: no longer are symbols, representations, text, concepts, knowledge, and formal models equated. Symbols in the brain are not immutable patterns, but structural couplings between modular systems, continuously adapted in use by a generalization process that dynamically recategorizes and sequences different modalities of sensation, conception, and motion (Merzenich, 1983). Representations are not just coded artifacts such as diagrams and text, but in the brain are active processes that categorize and sequence behavior in time (Edelman, 1992; Rosenfield, 1992; Bickhard, 1995). Conceptualization is not just verbal, but may be rhythmic, visual, gestural—ways in which the neural system categorizes sequences of multimodal categorizations in time. In the view of Gardner (1985), people have multiple intelligences, with different ways of making sense and coordinating action. The neuropsychological studies of Sacks (1987) reveal how people that cannot verbally abstract their experience may nevertheless dance and speak poetically; and people that speak in the particulars of geometric forms and rules may be unable to see the forest for the trees.   Indeed, our textually rooted robots, like these patients, once loaded with a knowledge base and shoved out into the world of shopping malls, doctors' offices, and national parks, may appear to be dysfunctional morons or *idiot savants*.

With these observations in mind, we seek to invent a new kind of machine with the modularity and temporal dependence of neural coordination. Some connectionists are exploring computational recognition systems based on dynamic coupling, in which subsystems only exist in mutual reinforcement (Freeman, 1991). Structures in the brain form during action itself, like a car whose engine's parts and causal linkages change under the load of a steeper hill or colder wind. Such mechanisms are situated because the repertoire of actions becomes organized by what is perceived.

In retrospect, we view symbolic models (e.g., natural language grammars) as descriptions of gross patterns that subsymbolic systems produce in the agent's interactive behavior. The symbolic AI of the 1950s through the early 1980s is not wrong, but it may be a bit inside out. People do articulate rules, scripts, and definitions and refer to them. These descriptive representations are not in their brains, but on their desks and in their libraries. The representations in the brain are different in kind—dynamically formed, changing in use, categorizations of categorizations *over time*, and multimodal (not just verbal), as means of *coordination*. Meaning can be written down (described), but words are not concepts; the map is not the territory.

This chapter illustrates how viewing human experience in a fresh way, applying a means–end approach, may be fruitful for suggesting new kinds of physical coordination mechanisms. A simple example is analyzed in great detail to bring out the properties of sequencing practiced behavior. These properties are described by a notation called an ICP diagram, representing the interactive coordination processes of neural maps. This diagram allows us to contrast neural processes with aspects of stored computer programs that we take for granted in our symbolic cognitive models: ordered steps, variable bindings, conditional statements, and subgoaling. The analysis begins to reveal how the brain accomplishes these structures and relations more flexibly, and hence, constitutes a new kind of computational device—one we do not fully understand and cannot yet replicate. Finally, the example reveals how talk about representations in the symbolic approach confused stored text and diagrams ("symbol structures") with active, always adapted processes, namely perceptual categorization, conceptual categorization of sequences of activation, and nonverbal forms of conceptualization (especially rhythm and imagery). The advice for AI research is to seek understanding of how the brain works, especially revealing how "multiple intelligences" (especially nonverbal) are interactively formed and coordinated in everyday behavior.

SENDING TWO MESSAGES: FORMS ORGANIZED BY ACTIVE PROCESSES

I examine in some detail how I typically used the Xerox-Lafite electronic mail system in the early 1980s (for simplicity, I use the present tense). The process is as follows: I decide to send a message to a particular person, and select *Send Mail* in the Lafite control window (Figure 1, top center). Then, perhaps before typing anything in the message window (W1), I remember that I want to send a message to someone else, so I select **Send Mail** in the control window a second time, in order to produce a second message window template (**W2**).

Why do I create a second window rather than using the first one? Why do I find it so easy to later return to the first window and send the message I first intended, when it may be unlabeled and I have no notes about what I intended to do with it? Why does it feel difficult to hold the first message in mind and reassign the first window to the second message?

The impression I have is that the first window, W1, is assigned; it embodies my intent; it already has meaning. I see W1 as "a message to Person 1." Using W1 to send a message to the second person means seeing it in a new way. My feeling is that this disrupts my thoughts. It is much easier and obvious to create a second window.

Using the terminology of Bamberger and Schön (1991), the physical structures visible on the screen, W1 and W2, are *reference entities*.

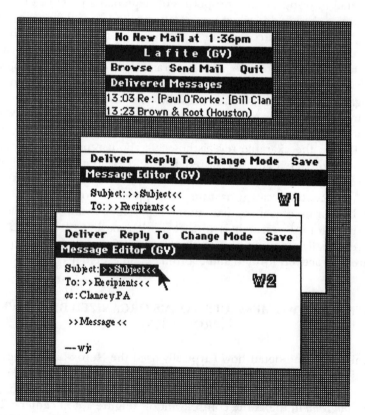

FIGURE 9.1.   Example of two active *Send Message* windows, labeled W1 and W2.

A reference entity serves to single out, externalize, hold for current attention some emergent object or relation. A reference entity serves the function of on-the-spot naming within, and as part of, the making process.

Related to these reference entities are activities, that I describe as "the process of sending a message to Person 1" and "the process of sending a message to Person 2." Crucially, I see W1 and W2 as being related to these activities—what I am currently doing and planning to do. Somehow, through neural processes inaccessible to me, W1 and W2 are bound or viewed as part of different activities.

To reassign W1 is to see it another way, to reperceive it. However, because W1 embodies the process of sending a message to Person 1, to see W1 in a different way is to *disrupt that process*. This is a crucial observation: Seeing materials in a different way may require disrupting an ongoing neural process, an active coordination between what we are seeing and what we are doing, that otherwise has no observable manifestation. Significantly, "doing" has the larger sense of what I am doing during this current E-mail session. In some sense, I am *still sending* that message to Person 1, even though I have shifted my focus to Person 2; the neural aspect of seeing and sending that message is still active. In cognitive jargon, we would say that I am still "intending" to send Message 1.

Instead of disrupting the first process, I *hold it aside* and start up a second process, embodied by W2. I send the second message and then return to W1. The windows on the screen serve as my external representation of messages I want to send. I do not even need to type in something in the TO: or SUBJECT: fields in W1. I can *remember how to see* W1. *I know what it means.*

The following aspects of this coordination are striking:

1. Visible spatial reminders on the screen allow me to coordinate multiple activities. I can interrupt what I am doing, both physically and mentally setting it aside, and pick up the activity later where I left off. I don't disrupt the interaction, I hold it active, keeping it current, but making it peripheral.
2. The capability to create multiple processes in the E-mail program facilitates my mental coordination. Activating the second *Send Mail* process in the mail program parallels and facilitates my allowing a second activity (sending a message to Person 2) to take form. Indeed, the idea of setting aside Message 1 and beginning Message 2 is afforded by the concreteness of W1 now in place, and the *Send Mail* button, allowing a repeated operation to occur. Selecting back and forth between W1 and W2, by buttoning the mouse in each window in turn, feels like shifting my attention back and forth between the activities of sending the two

messages. The effortless flow and context shift as windows shift forward and backward parallels my experience in thinking about the messages. The window I am seeing is the activity I am doing.

3. Completing the second message *first* is a bit odd. The impression is of a stack: I need to get rid of the second message before I can return to the first. The feeling is that the second message is more pressing. If I don't do it now, I will forget it. The idea of sending the second message arose effortlessly from the process of sending the first; but somehow, the second message, as an interruption that only came to mind as a second thought, needs to be handled immediately.

DISCUSSION: FIGURE–GROUND PRIORITIES

To develop these points further, consider that there are many alternative ways of using the Lafite system when you realize that you want to send two messages. Table 1 summarizes first how one might reassign the windows or reorder the sending of messages.

For example, one might keep the order (sending the first message first), but reassign the windows, so the first message is typed into W2, and one returns to W1 to send the second message. In the two cases where one uses W2 second, one might create W2 before or after entering a message into W1. For example, one might reassign W1 to the second message, then create a second process for the first message *after* sending off the second message. This gives six basic combinations. There are, however, other possibilities:

• Type in reminders about the contents of the first message before creating W2.
• Type in reminders about the contents of the first message after creating W2.
• Immediately type in reminders for the second message in W1, then create W2 and use it for sending the first message.

TABLE 9.1.
Alternative Ways of Sending Two Messages

	Keep interpretations	Reassign windows
Keep order	W1 <- msg1	W2 <- msg1
	W2 <- msg2	W1 <- msg2
Reorder messages	W2 <- msg2	W1 <- msg2
	W1 <- msg1	W2 <- msg1

The coordination I developed was to reorder messages, but keep interpretations without reminders. Assuming that this selection bears some relation to neural processes, what conjectures can we make about how neural processes are activated, held active, coordinated, and reactivated?

First, in my experience, *it is difficult to reassign* W1. The impression is that I would lose the process of sending the first message. There is no way to remember it, aside from reaching for a pad and making a note. It is difficult to switch contexts, to see W1 as being about (or for) the process of sending a message to Person 2. The meaning persists; perceived forms are coordinated with activities. To destroy or reassign perceived objects is to lose the coordination: To lose a way of seeing is to lose an activity.

Second, *it is difficult to do Message 1 before Message 2*. Message 2 is active now, after *Send Mail* was selected a second time. I'm doing *that* now. I don't want to disrupt Message 2 now. There would then be *two disruptions*. I need to keep going forward. (Later, we relate this observation to the inability to "move noun phrase references," a key pattern in Chomsky's Universal Grammar.)

It is difficult to *go back* to Message 1, given that Message 2 is in process already. Hence, I can hold in abeyance Message 1 and begin Message 2 easily, but I resist going back to Message 1! My sense is that I am finishing what's active now (and visually, it's the foreground window). Consistently, I sometimes (but rarely) start up a third message process and do it first. I have a sense of "the current process"—what I'm doing now.

Oddly, it seems easier to remember what I intend to do with W1 than to make the effort of typing in some TO: or SUBJECT: information as a reminder. Typing anything in W1, after already pulling down W2, feels like actually doing the first message—going back to it. Crucially, I immediately pull down a second window by buttoning *Send Mail* at the very moment that I realize that I want to send a message to a second person.

Thus, we have the curious and fortunate balance: It is difficult to reinterpret forms that are part of a sequence of activity (a chain of thought). However, it is relatively easy to recall how materials were previously perceived and engage in that process again. These possibilities work together here because interrupting the first process is perceived as a "holding aside," not a disruption, by the representation on the screen. The first message activity is held, not reorganized or ignored; it is peripherally visible on the screen. The activity is set aside like an object in the physical world, and can be picked up again at the click of the mouse.

The effect is like illusions that reorganize the visual field, such as the Necker Cube (seen in Figure 2), as well as the commonly known duck–rabbit and old–young woman. Selecting one of the windows makes that activity the *figure* and the other activity part of the *ground*. Fixing a figure–ground relationship on the screen by bringing W1 or W2 to the fore-

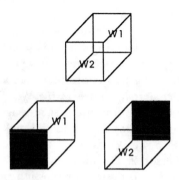

FIGURE 9.2.   Figure–ground relations between W1 and W2 shown as a Necker Cube.

ground   corresponds to making that activity, *"what I am doing now""* and making every other process in which I am engaged, *peripheral.* The figure–ground relation appears to be basic to the idea of focus of attention. Referring to the discrete manner in which we see forms as one thing and can shift back and forth, Arbib (1980) suggests that "The inhibition between duck schema and rabbit schema that would seem to underlie our perception of the duck-rabbit is not so much 'wired in' as it is based on the restriction of the low-level features to activate only one of several schemas" (p. 33).

WHY DID THE REMINDER OCCUR?

To better understand how the neural processes are created and held relative to each other, we introduce and use the ICP notation to show how the W2 process developed in the context of W1. Why did I experience the idea of sending a message to the second person, just when I was about to write to the first? When such an interruption occurs, I experience an image or name relating to the second person, a phenomenon that Bartlett identifies with the process of recollection. The activity of sending a message apparently enables an effortless beginning of the process of sending a different message. Building on this clue and Bartlett's analysis, I illustrate the relation of the two processes (Figure 3).

Figure 3 shows the coordination just after I have pulled down W2. Just after pulling down W1, a detail came to the foreground (e.g., the idea of another person or message). The diagram shows this second focus detail coming in from the side. Because of the materials available to me, I didn't experience a sense of disruption (an impasse). For example, without the multiple–process capability of Lafite, I might have been forced to turn

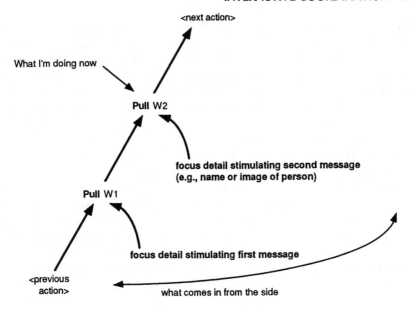

FIGURE 9.3. An ICP diagram: Process of sending second message viewed as a generalization of the active process of sending a message.

aside and write something down about Message 2 on a sheet of paper. Instead, I immediately repeated the current activity of writing a message, pulling down W2. By this coordination, I incorporated the detail; I made it "what I am doing now." The relation is asymmetric: I can button back and forth to *see the windows as different activities,* but I resist *actually doing* the first message activity after I have pulled down W2.

Notice that the constructive process is not a matter of seeing the first activity in a different way (W1 is not reinterpreted). Instead, the second activity is built around the spontaneously created idea of another message (and commentary about it, "Oh yes, I intended to send a note to Mike"). Because there is, in general, no content relation between the two messages, it is apparently the process of sending the first message itself—the active neural processes after W1 was pulled down—that brings the new focus detail to the foreground. The effect is that I recall the need to send a second message.

The two activities are parallel and coordinated, as if they indeed integrated in my understanding. Figure 3 is intended to represent this sequence; in some sense, *what I am doing now includes sending the first message.* Narrowly, my focus is on the second message, but broadly, my coordinated activity includes the first message. Furthermore, the activity of describing the second message or pulling down W2 is inseparable from the process of including the new focus detail coming in from the side in my activity. In terms of the ICP notation, the node labeled, "pull W2," represents a neural process that is activated just as the new focus detail comes to my attention. That is, there is a dialectic relation between the idea of sending a second message and the activity of doing so; in my experience, they come into being together. The new composition, represented by the node relating, "pull W1," and the focus of the second message, is created by the activity of sending the second message.

In contrast, a serial or parallel architecture would involve a different timing and different kinds of representation: The idea of sending a second message would be described internally by data structures that included some kind of reference to the general description of the procedure of sending a message, plus a reference to the topic of the second message. Reaching to select *Send Mail* would be interpreted as executing this procedure, and Figure 3 would be viewed as a representation of a stack, showing the order in which procedures and arguments were bound and invoked.

NEURAL MAP ACTIVATION OVER TIME

Figure 3 is not a representation of a stack, but of a sequence of links between neural maps. The ICP notation shows the relation of neural processes constructed over time by activating and composing maps. I conjecture that "Pull W2," literally, reuses the neural maps involved in "Pull W1," but coordinates them with different perceptual figures. Just as perceptual forms can be reused by different visual organizations (as seen in Figure 2), neural maps can be reused by different neural organizations. Just as I can slip back and forth between how I see the display or how I conceive my activity, a given set of neural maps can be simultaneously reorganized into a different, ongoing coordination.

Crucially, the production of one neural organization from the previous one is embodied in the timing of neural activations, so the next-next-next sequence is biased to be reconstructed. That is, the activation of a perceptual–motor map will activate the next map in sequence by virtue of having neuronal groups that are physically activated by groups in the previously active map. In the example of sending two messages, a given coordination is repeated, but composed with different perceptual and conceptual maps. This might be the most simple kind of sequencing: Doing something again, but acting on different objects in the world.

In this analysis, we are going beyond Edelman's focus on multimodal coupling of neural maps to consider how map activation occurs over time. Figure 4 illustrates how a given set of maps are reactivated at a later time. With similar inputs, there is similar output. The groups and the reentrant links that are activated are always prone to change because of changes in the external environment and changes in the correlations activated throughout the neural system. Broadly speaking, the theory of neuronal group selection (TNGS) claims that every activation is a *generalization* of past activation relations. Put another way, every activation is a *recategorization*, as opposed to a literal match or retrieval operation.

This recategorization is always occurring simultaneously within a larger sensorimotor coordination, involving conceptualization (at the level of maps of types of maps) and, often, in people, verbalization. By conjecture, *memory for sequence of activation* involves one map of maps activating another over time (Figure 5). This corresponds to Bartlett's (1932) notion of a schema as a *coordinating process.*

In Figure 5, we see *different* maps of maps linked to *different* higher–order maps. A perceptual detail may be a classification of a sound, a color, an object, a word, etc. The higher–order maps are physically linked by reentrant connections. However, the second higher–order map (labeled *time t'*) only becomes activated after the first map has become active (labeled *time t*). In this manner, it is conjectured that *maps of maps are sequenced over time via physical subsumption.* By conjecture, the number of possible connections in the brain is so large that there are sufficient links to establish a link between any sets of maps, as required by activity. Furthermore, all learning is categorization over time. This means that all learning is activation "in place" of preexisting links, which are composed over time into, and always within, sequences of activation. As Edelman states, there must be some way

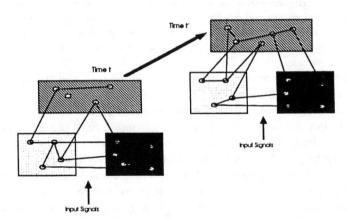

FIGURE 9.4.   Memory as recategorization: Inputs categorized similarly produce similar output relations. Circles are neuronal groups (perhaps thousands of neurons); lines indicate bidirectional activation; squares are maps; rectangles are maps of maps (adapted from Edelman, 1992; Figure 10-1, p. 103).

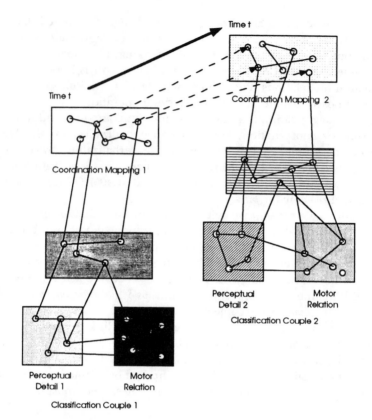

FIGURE 9.5.   Higher–order maps, including categorizations of global (cross-modal) maps, physically activate in sequence over time, serving as the memory of how perceptual details are coordinated within an activity. Note: Solid lines indicate coactivation in a circuit; dotted lines indicate activation over time.

of holding such activations so they can be compared and further coordinated, allowing for continuity in our experience.

This analysis is driven by two key observations about memory: First, Bartlett describes new conceptions as being *manufactured* out of previously active coordinations. How ways of seeing, moving, talking, etc. have worked together in the past will bias their future coordination, in the sense that they are physically connected again by the same relations. Second, I am building on Vygotsky's observation that every coordinated action (or descriptive claim, image, conception) is a *generalization* of what we are already doing (saying, seeing, categorizing). Putting these together, we tentatively view the ICP notation as showing a composition process over time (corresponding to inclusion of neural maps of the previous active coordination), such that each composing along the way is a generalization, qualified by details that specialize the neural construction, making it particular (focused on a thing) and unique.

INTENTION: INCORPORATING PROCESSES IN HIGHER–ORDER CATEGORIZATIONS

The coordination of sending two messages can be compared to a deliberate attempt to recall messages I need to send. Again, phrasing this in terms of Bartlett's model, I would first seek and construct a detail (e.g., an image of a journal paper might come to my attention) and then knit it together with a "main stream of interest" through a story relation (e.g., "I need to get back to Wendy"). I would probably create a list on paper of these activities.

In sending two messages, a generalization occurs immediately, without a sense of disruption (impasse) or need for a rationalizing story, because the new construction involves a *reactivation* of what I am currently doing. No seeking or manipulation of materials and reperceiving is necessary. Coordinating occurs when I say to myself, "Oh, yes, I intended to send a note to Mike." By this statement, I mark what I am doing now. The process of sending a second message is constructed directly from my currently active processes, my coordinated activity of looking at the screen and manipulating the mouse. I can compose the detail with my main stream of interest (the activity of sending messages) by simply doing again what I am already doing; I simply repeat the action of bringing down another message window.

By this analysis, the process of sending a second message is not a recursive procedure call, in the sense of storing a description of the procedure and its previous arguments (the topic of the first message). Instead, the neural links create physical structure "in place," such that a sequence of maps is constructed that includes the different ways of viewing the screen and my current activity. To do this with computer programs, we would have one copy of a procedure, *temporally* associated with different arguments (data). That is, the focus of a procedure is dynamically activated within an embracing physical structure, such that the containing structure *conceptually* relates the activity and the focus. In this way, I view the ICP diagram (Figure 3) as representing a sequence of conceptual compositions over time, with each new node in the sequence representing the concept of *what I am doing now*. This conceptualization (in these examples) simultaneously incorporates a particular focus, while broadening the previous conceptualization. Here, the broadening is such that "what I am doing now" (namely, sending messages) now includes two messages, but has a specific focus of the second message.

Significantly, in this simple example, the new focus detail *bears* the same relation to "Pulling down W1" as the first focus detail. I am able to see the second focus detail as *an instance* of *what I am already doing* (sending a message). The process of "sending the first message" (involving buttoning and following hand–eye, typing, information-entering processes) is reactivated, but with respect to a different figure (the name or image related to Mike that came to my attention). We can say that the two focus details, (essentially the topics of the two messages) are *correlated* by their composition with the conceptualization of sending a message. However, holding the two details together, the activity of deliberately relating the two topics (a crucial capability constituting higher–order consciousness), is very different from being in the activity of sending two messages. Grounded in the activity, the details are mutually exclusive. In *reasoning* about alternative actions, they are both active and related as details within an encompassing conceptualization of ordering, correspondence, cause, negation, identity, etc. (the fundamental reasoning processes emphasized by Piaget).

Shifting from one message activity to another, the previous focus becomes part of the background; the associated neural maps are still active, but I am not conceiving "sending W1" as what I am doing now. This is analogous to looking at the cube in Figure 2: "I am looking at the cube and seeing it as W1" or "I am looking into the cube seeing it as W2." An activity, a way of coordinating perception and action, is reenacted, but incorporating different perceptual categorizations.

In other circumstances, I might realize that the second focus detail might be another thing to mention in my first message, or something I can ask the first person to relay to someone else. In this case, the result would be a new composition of "What I am telling Person 1 now," with the second detail included. I conjecture that we build up next-next-next relations in this way—by a composition process—and have the capability to return to an earlier process state and read out the details (going forward) by reactivating containing generalizations. In this respect, our use of stories and how we construct stories—in the sequence of naming, framing, history-telling, and design (Schön, 1979)—has an underlying basis in this neural composition mechanism.

The tree form of the ICP notation (Figure 3) should not suggest that there is a data structure that is being traversed, inspected, or otherwise manipulated by some other process in the brain. Just as in perceptual reorganizations, in which lines get reorganized to form different angles and objects, neural maps get reorganized to form different figure–ground relations to foci and conceptualizations of what I am doing now. When I button back and forth between W1 and W2 I am recoordinating my activity. I conjecture that each buttoning back and forth results in a *new composition*, higher on the path shown in Figure 3. Indeed, the conceptualization of what I'm doing now becomes, "I'm buttoning back and forth on the screen" *(a categorization of the sequence).* That is, every activity must incorporate what is currently active as either figure or ground. The mechanism is not a process of moving pointers up and down a tree or restoring a previous organization by writing it into a buffer for execution. We are always moving forward, creating a new composition, albeit often a generalization of what we have done before.

DISTINGUISHING BETWEEN AWARENESS AND REPRESENTATIONS

The example of sending two messages illustrates that statements like "how the subject is representing the windows to himself" must be distinguished from "how the subject is *describing* the windows to himself." Indeed, like the fly coordinating his tongue with a passing fly or the blind man using the cane as an extension of his arm, a practiced message sender is perhaps not *representing* the windows any more than I am representing the location of the mouse on the desk, that I cannot see.

The experienced message sender is detecting previously categorized forms while coordinating the cursor and typing with an activity of composing a message. Our experience indicates that more of the screen becomes peripheral through practice. We are *apprehending relations,* and no longer *seeing forms.* The distinction between conscious and subconscious is then reframed as a distinction between figures and peripheral processes.

Contrast my experience in sending two messages with my asking an assistant to finish my work: He is given two identical, blank windows, already open on the screen. He is told to send two messages to different people. Window position has no representational significance, except he will probably use the front one first. Now, suppose I require that he assign the windows in the same manner as I saw them when they were created. I must represent these windows for him: "This is the window for Mark's message; here is the one for Wendy." Without a descriptive set of instructions, my friend can't replicate the activity I was engaged in: He needs to know what the two open windows represent.

The windows however, weren't representations to me, they were just part of my activity of sending messages. Commonly, we would say that in sending the two messages, I knew what the windows represent (or similarly, "what they mean"). Yet, this means that if asked, *I could tell you what I am doing,* not that I view the windows *as being representations.* For me, they are places in which I am composing messages—not representations of messages, but the real thing. I am not perceiving the forms as windows, but as spaces in which to type.

Given that the windows are identical except for spatial location, observers will say that they are examples of indexical representations (like the word "now"). Meaning is embedded in use; the process of seeing-as "registers" each of the windows as different activities. However, for me they aren't representations at all! They are reference *entities*, not references. They *are* the messages I am in the process of sending, not representations of them. Engaged in my activity, unlike the message program, I don't have a map or registration table that associates the windows with my message–sending processes. Their meaning is embodied in my activity, and held by active processes of categorizing.

The conceptual relation of my understanding *what I am doing now* isn't *between descriptions*. My understanding does not relate to neural processes and the world. Instead, seeing places on the screen is inseparable from interacting with them, what I am *doing* with them. As Ryle said, demonstrating know-how (doing) is not two things: knowing that (articulating facts) *plus* doing. What I am perceiving, my way of categorizing my experience, is literally part of the construction of what I am doing. I don't describe what I am doing when I return to W1; I simply reconstitute that process from the ground, making that place and the topic the figure of my conception.

RELATION OF THE ICP NOTATION TO STORED–TEXT PROCEDURAL MODELS

What does this analysis reveal about stored–program computer languages? We start with the null hypothesis that there is fairly direct mapping between the hierarchy of subgoals, the hierarchy, impasses, operators, and chunking in symbolic cognitive models and the activation relations of neural structures. It is very likely that the architecture we seek will not be constructed out of structures that cleanly map onto a modeler's domain terms and relations. We take care to distinguish categorized details (especially words) from categorizing processes that incorporate such details. In general, there is no simple mapping between words and conceptualizations. Nevertheless, we assume that conceptual coordinating involves recurrent relations between physical (neural) structures that are stable recategorizations of past neural activations, at some level corresponding to words, clichés, and the patterns of logical thought. By doing this, we shift from a stored–structure *manipulation* view to a process *construction* view.

The ICP notation is useful for comparing grammatical models to the flexibility that we claim is actually present in human conceptualization (Figure 6). Essentially, the primitive components of computational models—ordered steps (a sequence of operators in a problem space), variable bindings, conditional statements, and subgoaling—can be contrasted with

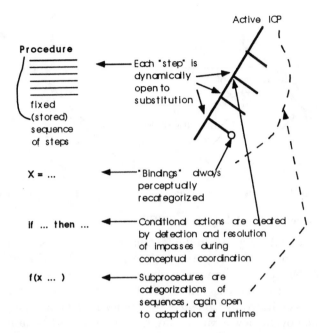

Active ICP

Procedure

fixed
(stored)
sequence
of steps

Each "step" is dynamically open to substitution

X = ...

"Bindings" always perceptually recategorized

if ... then ...

Conditional actions are created by detection and resolution of impasses during conceptual coordination

f(x ...)

Subprocedures are categorizations of sequences, again open to adaptation at runtime

FIGURE 9.6. Relation of stored procedures and rules to ICP construction.

classification, sequencing, and composition of neural maps. Furthermore, coordinated sequences constructed multidimensionally (from existing sequences, corresponding to grammatical orders) would be like remembering stacks (a sequence of procedural calls and variable bindings). In procedural terms, an ordering of steps and binding constraints could be reestablished without running the procedures themselves; this is what Soar's chunking provides. In terms of the ICP notation, a sequence of perceptual classifications (a next-next-next path) could be reestablished without recalling the specific actions that led to these perceptions in the past.

The ICP notation is a tool for visualizing where stored descriptive models are inflexible relative to the TNGS. It also reveals what Soar assigns to the "cognitive architecture," but doesn't explain it. Fundamentally, we need the ICP account to explain not only where the knowledge in the lower problem spaces come from, but also *why an operator hierarchy is constructed at all* and how operators—situation–action coordinations occurring at different points in time—can be *held active and related.*

Diagrams of classification couples (Figures 4 and 5) are a bit unwieldy. The ICP notation combines the maps of maps (rectangles) and secondary classification (e.g., coordinated motor relations) into a single node (Figure 7). Emphasis is thereby given to the sequence of perceptual details in the person's experience over time.

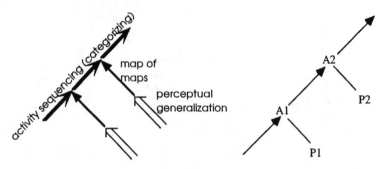

Note: A1 represents global maps or categorizations of global maps; P1 represents perceptual
details.

FIGURE 9.7.   Relation of ICP diagram to TNGS.

Each sequence node (e.g., A1) in the ICP diagram represents a conceptualization of global mapping. The perceptual detail (e.g., P1) included in the
associated global–mapping activation is shown. This detail is the focus of
attention (illustrated by the example of sending two messages). The next
node (e.g., A2) is activated in sequence, over time. This global mapping is
partially activated by the new environment, here, represented exclusively by
P2, another perceptual detail. Crucially, A2 and often P1, itself, are activated
by physical, reentrant links from the preceding global map, A1 (compare to
Figure 5). In people, this coordination is often associated with linguistic processes, so the person could say *what I'm doing now.* In using the ICP notation
to represent problem-solving protocols, we think of each transition (e.g.,
from A1 to A2) as being a shift in *what I'm doing now,* accompanied by a shift
in perceptual detail. More generally, the ICP notation shows simply *a sequence
of global mapping activations,* which in practiced form would not be accompanied by verbalizations (e.g., as in playing a musical instrument). Of special
interest is how perceptual details in a sequence are related.

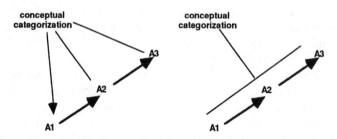

Note: The left diagram shows possible "feed-forward" activation to the head of the sequence,
      with couplings between the global map of the conceptual categorization and subsequent
      global map categorizations. We use the equivalent and simpler notation on the right.

FIGURE 9.8.   Conceptualization as categorization of sequences of activation.

Categorizing sequences of activation (e.g., A1-A2-) is a form of *conceptualization*, corresponding to creation of a subgoal hierarchy, such as Neomycin's task hierarchy (Figure 9). The categorization itself enables the capability to "activate or reconstruct portions of past activities of global mappings of different types—for example, those involving different sensory modalities. They must also be able to recombine or compare them." (Edelman, 1992, p. 109). For example, my conceptualization of "Pursue-Hypothesis" includes speaking a name for the idea (itself a complex perceptual–motor coordination), a visualization of the name in a tree diagram, and the first step of checking for exposure to a disease (that is, my understanding is now tied to my formal representation of the process).

Mapping a symbolic program's hierarchies onto neural processes is an attempt to explain how subgoal hierarchies are learned, or equivalently, in Soar's terms, how new problem spaces are learned. A key insight is that construction need not operate on textual representations, as both the dominant inductive and deductive models of machine learning suppose: Compositions may develop bottom-up from perceptual details—*in the very process of constraining what details are perceived.* In terms of the ICP notation, the sequence isn't necessarily included under something else that preexists, which is "running" or "executing" and monitoring every step. Instead,

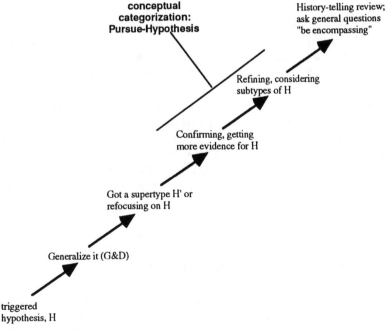

FIGURE 9.9. Habitual path in diagnosis, with a subsequence categorized as a new operator.

the brain is constantly creating a generalization of *what I am doing now,* and hence, constructing orderly, coherent sequences. An orderly, and eventually multileveled, pattern develops by the bias to redo a previous sequence, resee a kind of detail, and reestablish a cross-modal coordination.

To be specific, Figure 9 shows a plausible sequence of diagnostic activities corresponding to Neomycin's subtasks. Subsequences become segmented (chunked) and then categorized because steps always occur together and *they have a common kind of focus detail* (here, the category is *hypothesis*). These segments are now conceptual coordinations; activation is possible in a top-down manner by the inclusion of the higher-order category (e.g., "pursue-hypothesis") in another recurrent sequence. Goal-directed control then becomes possible if such a conceptualization can be held, biasing the activation of further sequences. A collection of diagrams, like Figure 9, has the same embedded structure as a conventional hierarchical notation. Instead of merely describing the hierarchical relations, the ICP notation argues that the inherent formative process is *categorization over time,* and these nodes are always adapted neural maps, not stored texts and *pointers* to locations in memory.

To summarize:

- *Chunks* are habitual sequences. The effect of practice is to establish reentrant links between perceptual details themselves, so attention to conceptualization drops out. In other words, a sequence of bindings is established from higher-order maps down to perceptual details and motor actions. (Note: Visual chunks, such as the arrangement of pieces on the chessboard, are nonverbal and nonsequential; they are *simultaneous categorizations.*)
- *Goals* are categorizations of sequences (or conceptualized coordinations) with a common kind of focus.
- A *subgoal hierarchy* is composed of categorizations of sequences (conceptualizations). The ordering dependency represented by the ICP notation is *temporal.* The hierarchical order of Figure 9 represents temporal dependency of activation, not a simple *spatial* property of physical inclusion of neural maps.

RELATING THE INNATE AND THE LEARNED: EVIDENCE FROM LINGUISTICS

The ICP perspective reifies two dimensions of organizers: On the one hand, relationships conceptually constructed in the past are organizing new utterances—previous sequences are being reactivated, generalized, and are operating on different levels of abstraction. On the other hand, the kinds of conceptual constructions that are possible, *de novo*, are deter-mined by the process of perceptual categorization, sequencing, reactivat-ing sequences, categorizing sequences (conceptualizing), and construc-tively composing sequences on different levels. This distinction has been primary in the linguistic theory of transformational grammar and is much misunderstood.

Berwick's (1983) summary of modern linguistic theory recapitulates the argument against mediating descriptions: (a) parse trees are not explicitly built, (b) the units of information are associated with individual words, and (c) surface structure is the product of many constraints acting in parallel. The idea of abstract rules describing classes of words and how they interact is replaced by a mechanism that determines how words interact to produce sequences by ordering and thematic constraints. Hence, syntax and seman-tics are effectively integrated. The phrase structure rules of early transfor-mational theory are reinterpreted as being an observer's abstractions over a set of sentences, not part of the mechanism itself.

Berwick's description still refers to dictionary entries and encoding of features. On the other hand, connectionism does not satisfactorily explain how orderings are learned and how this relates to other kinds of sequential learning.[1] The ICP notation provides a perspective that supports and improves upon Berwick's thesis. For example, Figure 10 shows Berwick's representation for a phrase structure rule in which a verb is indicated as having an inanimate object, as in the full sentence, "Sincerity frightens John." "Nanim" (corresponding to the word "sincerity") is a feature that "percolates to a higher node to carry out a compatibility check." (Berwick, p. 393).

The middle of Figure 10 shows the ICP notation for this sequence, in which Vt is a conceptualization of a kind of verb phrase. The relation of the ICP notation to Edelman's TNGS (see Figures 4 and 5) suggests that each of the nodes have a reentrant link to the categorization of the sequence (Vt).[2] Furthermore, as shown on the right side of Figure 1, the nodes at the head and the tail may have a special relation within the cate-

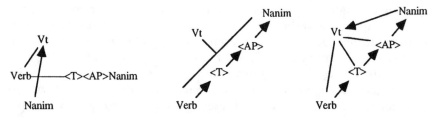

FIGURE 9.10.   **Representations of a phrase structure rule (left) shown by two forms of ICP notation, with a verb phrase (Vt) represented as a categorized sequence.**

gorization, allowing reconstructing the sequence from the end or activating the head via feed-forward activation. A conceptualization—a categorized sequence—unlike a felt path, may be reconstructed from the end because the subsuming categorization provides an activation link back to the head. Here, we have Berwick's representation, with no added feature tagged onto the Vt categorization—it is inherent in the sequence itself that the kind of verb is qualified by the object, Nanim, the last category in the sequence.[3]

The ICP representation in Figure 10 suggests that there may be a special relation between the categorization of the sequence and the head of the sequence. Indeed, Chomsky's X–bar theory of 1970 claims:

> A Verb Phrase *must* be expanded with a verbal "Head"—that is, what it means to be a Verb Phrase. Similarly, a Noun Phrase is always expanded as. . . N. . . . In short, every phrase of type "X" is grounded on a word of type X. Phrases, then, are merely projections of lexical items. . . . There is no specific phrase structure rule needed to describe the required constraints. (Berwick, p. 396)

However, the relation between the phrase categorization and the root is even more general—the ordering is the same for all kinds of phrases:

> Chomsky observed that not only does every phrase of type X have an X-based root, but also that the order of arguments of each phrase is fixed across all phrase types. For instance, in English, Verb Phrases are headed by Verbs, followed by optional Noun Phrases, Prepositional Phrases, and Sentential Phrases. Prepositional Phrases are headed by Prepositions, and are also followed by phrases of the same type. Similarly, for Adjectival Phrases. That is, once we have fixed the phrasal order XP->X NP PP, it is fixed for all phrasal types. (Berwick, p. 396)

This linguistic data suggests that a general sequencing coordinator is learned and applied systematically whenever speaking a given language. In ICP terms, a conceptualization that orders sequences within a phrase applies to all kinds of phrases. Only one kind of sequence categorization is applying throughout. The constraints referred to by Berwick are the activations in sequence and the formation of new phrase conceptualizations in accord with previous phrase conceptualizations. This suggests that learning a new kind of phrase conceptualization is generalizing an existing one; thus, constructing the categorization XP of the sequence X->NP->PP (where here "->" denotes the ICP sequence link). Perhaps it is better to allow for the fact that kinds of phrases are not necessarily learned separately, learning phrase ordering in a given language involves conceptualizing *what ordering means in that language*, which is one categorization—not many. As stated earlier, the constraints of transformational grammar are revealed in the ICP notation as being processes of sequential activation and recategorization of sequences, not stored dictionary entries as in a descriptive cognitive model. These observations fit Berwick's theoretical claims in relating modern transformational grammar to connectionism, and further support the ICP (*process construction*) perspective.

The "inability to move Noun Phrases" over multiple phrases reveals, from the other direction, a limitation in our ability to coordinate multiple conceptualizations. That is, the activation and sequencing process imposes a constraint that a subsumed phrase sequence can be moved "into the next higher sentence, but no farther." (Berwick, p. 405). So, we can understand "Who do I think that Mary likes," but not, "Who do I believe the claim that Mary likes?" Again, in phrase structure terms this "locality principle" is merely structural, based on *proximity*. The ICP notation suggests that a subsumed process may be *incorporated again* in the next sentence categorization, but not after that—a constraint of *activation* concerning physical construction of processes. However, this appears to merely restate (and support) the claim that each conceptualization is reusing or reactivating its previous construction. Again, there is no need for buffers or pointers: Constructing the next sentence is a process of *reactivating the previously active processes of the Sentence conceptualization*—hence, a, previously uttered "who phrase" is now available to be categorized within the new sequences "Mary likes . . ." "We do not actually 'move' NPs around." (Berwick, p. 406). In short, Chomsky's locality principle should be considered a constraint of process reconstruction, rather than a serial order of the surface structure which is its manifestation.

When linguistic observations are reformulated by the ICP notation, we find the kind of mechanism that Chomsky has argued for—a physiological process that structures conceptual content. The flexibility of "working from the head" or "working from the tail" suggests again, that physiologically, conceptualizations of phrase utterances are *circuits*, activating and available to be worked with as single processes. Although the head and tail are manifested in behavior at different points in time, they are incorporated in one categorization, couple (Figure 4). Further discussion of TNGS and consciousness (Clancey, In press) considers how the human brain allows us to hold active and coordinate multiple, competing sequences as "a soup of strings."

CONCLUSIONS

My interest, throughout, has been architectural; that is, describing the process mechanisms by which behavior is sequenced and composed has been my main focus. Following Bartlett's lead, I began by assuming that learning and memory should be viewed as the dynamic construction of coordinated sequences from *previous coordinations*. That is, *physical structures* are reactivated and reused in accord with how they categorically and temporally worked together in the past. With further examples from neuropsychology, I generalized the notion of coordination to multiple sensory systems and, especially in humans, multiple modes of conceiving. Fitting the original hypothesis that knowledge is not a body of text, this perspective recognizes, most of all, that verbalizations are not isomorphic to conceptualizations, and that scenes, rhythms, and melodies are other ways of organizing behavior. Hence, gestalt understanding, which appeared to our text-based mentality to be a prescientific concept like intuition, can now be understood as a *nondescriptive form of conceptualization*.

At the first order, we make no distinction between memory, learning and coordinating. The control regime of symbolic models, such as Neomycin's strategy rules, is replaced by temporal–sequential conceptualizing: reactivating, generalizing, and recoordinating behavior sequences (whether occurring as outward movement or private imagination). In this respect, knowledge is constructed as processes in-line and integrated with sensorimotor circuits. Cognition is *situated* because perception, conception, and action are physically coupled. Using this reformulation, cognition is not only physically and temporally situated ("knowledge is in the environment"), but *conceptually* situated as a tacit understanding of *what I am doing now.* In people, this conceptualization is pervasively social in content; hence, we see that the proponents of situated action are making psychological claims.

In accepting the broad patterns that the schema theories of cognitive psychology describe, we are able to go beyond other models as well, such as Lashley's serial organization and Edelman's perceptual categorization. Nevertheless, for the purpose of psychological theory (if not pedagogical design), we reject the idea of a body of knowledge, a store that is indexed, compared, instantiated, and applied. Putting such descriptions aside, we asked what *inherently developmental* process or architecture could Neomycin's strategy rules and MOPS scripts be describing?

This exploration presents a new research program and the methods of analysis point to new synthetic approaches. The Interactive Coordination Processes (ICP) notation is a means, not an end. The rules of a descriptive cognitive model are more convenient for classifying behavior, but the ICP notation is better for understanding development of sequences. By eliminating the mediating role of descriptions, we can intuitively show how "proceduralization" is not a secondary compilation step, but a constructive process that began in the evolution as sensorimotor coordination and became the process that we call *conceptualizing*, a means of holding active, ordering, and composing sequences. The ICP notation, although valuable for coarsely diagramming the phenomenology of cognition, imperfectly describes multimodal coordinations and must be assumed to still misconstrue the spatial and temporal properties of the neural mechanism.

The result is a sketch of an architecture for process memory, based on notions of coupling, activation sequencing, composing, figure–ground shifting—the neurological origins of the transformations and organizing principles studied by Lashley, Piaget, Chomsky, and Bateson. A more complete analysis (Clancey, In preparation), relates the verbal and visual to temporal-sequential, manipulo-spatial, and scene conceptualization. In analyses of dysfunctions and dreaming, we discover further evidence for specialized brain modules for conceptual organizing—hypothesizing that these are always mutually configured, neither parallel or serial-related in conventional terms, and have no existence as structures or capabilities apart from some integrated coordination in time with other processes.

NOTES

[1]I show in Clancey (In preparation) how the ICP notation could be implemented as a generalization of Simple Recursive Networks.

[2]Reentrant links would allow a conceptual categorization to "get back" to the head of a sequence (Figure 8, A1) and begin to activate subsequent categorizations (A2, A3). As the sequence is constructed, the overarching conceptual categorization is generalized and strengthened. Possibly, *the conceptual categorization is the first node in the sequence*, generalized to include the subsequent global maps, including them both temporally and by reentrant links. In this way, the sequence is subsumed within a global map but it is the global map itself, that operates by activating included maps as a process over time. The unit is a coordinated sequence over time. It is unclear how the end is marked. Closure might be conceived simply by the absence of further maps in sequence. Yet, some sequencing and timing mechanisms are required to prevent looping or stuttering. All of this is beyond Edelman's speculations and I cannot go further.

[3]This interpretation fits Small's theory, on which Berwick draws, that a thematic argument, such as a kind of NP, is a "concept structure," which is a "grouping of words." (Berwick p. 410) The difference is that we replacing "encodings in a dictionary" by categorizations of process sequences.

REFERENCES

Arbib, M. (1980). Visuomotor coordination: From neural nets to schema theory. *Cognition and Brain Theory, 4*(1), 23–39.

Bamberger, J. & Schön, D. A. (1991). Learning as reflective conversation with materials. In F. Steier (Ed.), *Research and reflectivity*. London: Sage.

Bartlett, F. C. (1932/1977). *Remembering—A study in experimental and social psychology.* Cambridge: Cambridge University Press. Reprint.

Berwick, R. C. (1983). Transformational grammar and artificial intelligence: A contemporary view. *Cognition and Brain Theory, 6*(4) 383–416.

Bickhard, M. H. & Terveen, L. (1995). *The impasse of artificial intelligence and cognitive science.* New York: Elsevier.

Clancey, W. J. (1993). Situated action: A neuropsychological interpretation (Response to Vera and Simon). *Cognitive Science, 17*(1), 87–107.

Clancey, W. J. (1997). *Situated cognition: On human knowledge and computer representations.* Cambridge: Cambridge University Press.

Clancey, W. J. (In preparation). Conceptual Coordination: How the Mind Orders Experience in Time.

Edelman, G. (1992). *Bright air, brilliant fire. On the matter of the mind.* New York: Basic Books.

Freeman, W. J. (1991, February). The physiology of perception. *Scientific American,* 78–85.

Gardner, H. (1985). *Frames of mind: The theory of multiple intelligences.* New York: Basic Books.

Merzenich, M., Kaas, J., Wall, J., Nelson, R., Sur, M., & Felleman, D. (1983). Topographic reorganization of somatosensory cortical area 3B and 1 in adult monkeys following restricted deafferentation. *Neuroscience, 8*(1), 33–55.

Newell, A. (1982). The knowledge level. *Artificial Intelligence, 18*(1), 87–127.

Polk, T. A. & Newell, A. (In press). Deduction as verbal reasoning. *Psychological Review.*

Rosenfield, I. (1992). *The strange, familiar, and forgotten.* New York: Vintage Books.

Sacks, O. (1987). *The man who mistook his wife for a hat.* New York: Harper & Row.

Schön, D. A. (1979). Generative metaphor: A perspective on problem-setting in social policy. In A. Ortony (Ed.), *Metaphor and thought.* Cambridge: Cambridge University Press.

Servan-Schreiber. (1991, September). Graded state machines: The representation of temporal contingencies in simple recurrent networks. *Machine Learning,* 7(2/3), 161–193.

Steels, L. & Brooks, R. (Eds.). (1995). *The "artificial life" route to "artificial intelligence": Building situated embodied agents.* Hillsdale, NJ: Erlbaum.

chapter 10

Cognitive Architecture: What Choice Do We Have?

Tim van Gelder
tgelder@ariel.unimelb.edu.au
Department of Philosophy
University of Melbourne

C entrally located in some of the most fiercely contested terrain in the
philosophy of cognitive science are questions of the general form of
human cognitive architecture. Mainstream orthodoxy, of course,
holds that the human mind is some kind of computer (Haugeland, 1978);
the task of cognitive science is simply to work out, in more detail, what kind
of computer it is, and in particular what its functional architecture is like
(Pylyshyn, 1984). Although a wide variety of considerations favor the so-
called classical approach, ranging from abstract philosophical arguments
to the empirical virtues of particular cognitive models, there is also a wide
variety of difficulties. However, the existence of these difficulties has failed
to persuade many to abandon the computational model, and one important reason is the perceived lack of decent alternatives. In what follows,
rather than try to describe any specific conception of cognitive architecture that might compete with the classical one, I will briefly sketch some of
the terrain so as to reveal some of the great amount of room that there
actually is for alternative conceptions.

In a recent well-known description and defense of the heart of so-called
"classical" cognitive architectures, it was maintained that mental representations must be symbolic in the sense that they have a combinatorial syntax
and compositional semantics, and that mental processes must be structure-
sensitive in the sense that they are defined over that combinatorial structure (Fodor & Pylyshyn, 1988). These requirements do not in themselves
amount to an actual specification of cognitive architecture, Pylyshyn has

described cognitive architecture as the functional architecture of a "cognitive computer," and to specify this is quite a demanding business:

> The set of mechanisms needed . . . includes the basic operations provided by the biological substrate, say, for storing and retrieving symbols, comparing them, treating them differently as a function of how they are stored, (hence as a function of whether they represent beliefs or goals), and so on, as well as such basic resources and constraints of the system as a limited memory. It also includes what computer scientists refer to as the "control structure," which selects which rules to apply at various times. (Pylyshyn, 1984, 30–31)

To specify that representations be symbolic and processes be structure-sensitive is just to select a very broad class of cognitive architectures. Nevertheless, this specification can be used as the basis of inquiry into the range of alternative conceptions of cognitive architecture, for if there were any alternative to the computational approach, it would presumably be one that was constructed around some *different* kind of representation, or some *different* kind of process, or (most likely) both.

On the side of representation, inquiry into the possibility of alternative cognitive architectures leads directly to what is in fact a traditional philosophical project, the general taxonomy of kinds of representation. We are looking for some genuinely different (i.e., nonsymbolic) kind of representation that might constitute the medium of at least some significant portion of genuinely cognitive functioning. Taxonomies of forms of representation standardly admit only two generic kinds: the symbolic (propositional, sentential, logical, etc.) and the imagistic (pictorial, analog, iconic, etc.). Yet it is usually also agreed that imagistic representation is, at best, highly limited in its utility for cognitive functioning. This has led many people to assume that there really is no interesting alternative to classical cognitive architectures. If there are different approaches to the study of cognition, it would seem that they must be approaches to the *implementation* of classical architectures rather than direct competitors.

During the 1980s, talk of *distributed* representation became increasingly common, particularly in connectionist circles but also elsewhere. Might distributed representation be a third genus that could form the basis of an alternative conception of cognitive architecture? The possibility is surely worth looking into.

Determining whether distributed representation forms a third genus of representation requires clarifying the meaning of the term "distributed." In one common usage, a representation is distributed if it is somehow "spread out" over some relatively large portion of the available representational resources. In this sense a database might be distributed over many machines, or a mental representation might be distributed over many thousands of neurons. It is fairly clear that when the term is used in this way, distributed representation is not another genus of representation alongside the other major kinds. Rather, distributedness is just a property that representations of any particular kind might or might not have; i.e., just a feature of their implementation.

However another sense of the term "distributed" is more common in the cognitive science literature and also more theoretically interesting. The core of this sense is *semantic superposition*. Roughly, this is where many items are simultaneously represented by just one representation. It can be thought of as the situation where the representations of many individual items are simultaneously distributed (in the previous sense of being spread out) over the very same chunk of the representational resources. You cannot point to one chunk of the resources and say "there is the representation of item A" and to another *different* chunk and say "there is the representation of item B."

Fortunately this intuitive idea can be given a reasonably rigorous characterization. The key move is to take over the quite general mathematical notion of a distributing transformation. This is an operation that takes some function $f(s)$ and transforms it into another function $g(t)$ in such a way that the value of $g(t)$ at any point t depends on the value of $f(s)$ at every point s. The Fourier transformation is a classic example. Now, it turns out that all standard cases of distributed representation that can be mathematically characterized fit into this distributing transformation framework. That is, in all standard cases of distributed representation, if we regard the function f as a mathematical description of the *items* to be represented, and we regard g as a mathematical description of the *representation* of those items, then g is a particular distributing transformation of f (see Figure 10.1).

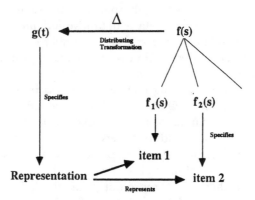

Note: If S is domain of f, each represented item *i* is specified by the restriction f_i, of f to some subdomain S_i of S. For more detailed explanation see (van Gelder, 1992a).

FIGURE 10.1   The generic structure of distributed representation.

This realization paves the way for a general definition of the notion of distributed representation. The basic idea is that particular distributing transformations give you particular schemes of distributed representations: plug in a function describing some contents at one end and the transformation will give you a function describing a distributed representation of those contents at the other. A representation is distributed if it belongs to such a scheme.[1] So, for example, hidden unit patterns in the archetypal connectionist three-layer feedforward backpropagation network standardly count as distributed representations according to this scheme, where $f(s)$ specifies the input items (the activations on the input nodes), $g(t)$ specifies the representation (the hidden layer activity pattern) and Δ is the transformation that transforms one into the other—fixed, of course, by the particular pattern of synaptic connections between the input and hidden layers.

Is distributed representation defined this way really a distinct genus? That is, are the categories of symbolic, imagistic, and distributed representation disjoint? The way to address this question is to ask whether the conditions that a representation must satisfy to belong to one kind (e.g., symbolic) directly conflict with the conditions it must satisfy to belong to another (e.g., distributed). The answer is that if all three kinds are defined in ways that are both reasonably precise and the most useful for *other* theoretical purposes, then it turns out that there are in fact such conflicts (van Gelder, 1990b). Basically, both symbolic and imagistic representation impose characteristic locality requirements—representational content must correspond to parts of the representation in distinctive ways—but these locality requirements are incompatible with semantic superposition, the core of this refined concept of distributed representation.

Our main interest in distributed representation has been as a possible representational basis of a whole alternative conception of cognitive architecture. It is still too early to deliver definitive judgments on the form of human cognitive architecture. However, a number of considerations indicate that distributed representation is an interesting candidate in at least some arenas. For example, connectionist models based on distributed representation have been showing increasing success in accounting for psychological phenomena (Quinlan, 1991). Second, nobody has yet established any clear limitations on the expressive power of distributed representation (i.e., what kinds of things you can or cannot represent this way). It is particularly important to realize that complex symbolic structures such as sentences of natural language can be represented in distributed form, and then such representations used as the medium of nonclassical cognitive processing (Pollack, 1990). (In such cases, it is the *content* of the representations—that which they represent—that is symbolic; the representations themselves are not symbolic.) And third, in especially stark contrast with the case of symbolic representation, distributed representation appears to be fundamentally compatible with what we currently know about the detailed structure of the brain, both at the level of gross organization and at the level of the wiring details. On the other hand, certain practical difficulties seem inherent to distribution, such as the problem of catastrophic interference (French, 1992). And, the flip side of the fact that nobody has established clear limits on the expressive power of distributed representation is that it is still unclear how extensive that expressive power actually is.

Representation is only one very broad aspect of cognitive architecture. Its essential counterpart is processing. If we are considering the possibility that distributed representation lies at the heart of a whole alterative conception of cognitive architecture, what alternative general form of cognitive processing might go with it? We are looking for a characterization pitched at roughly the same high level as the claim that, in so-called classical architectures, "the principles by which mental states are transformed . . . are defined over structural properties of mental representations" (Fodor & Pylyshyn, 1988).

The most extensive use of distributed representations has occurred in connectionism, and so one way to address this question is: what is the general form of cognitive processing found in connectionist networks? It is, however, rather difficult to give any neat answer to this question. One reason is that connectionism is highly diverse, and connectionist networks are used to implement a wide variety of operations. Of course, all connectionist networks can trivially be regarded as transforming patterns of unit activity, but this characterization is too vague and general to be of any use. (For one thing, classical structure-sensitive processing can take the form of transformations of patterns of unit activity, and so the desired contrast has been lost.) We need some more interesting general conception of processing that is typical of connectionist networks using distributed representations.

One example of such a conception is the idea that connectionism is really nothing more than latter-day associationism; connectionist processes are not classically structure-sensitive but rather serve merely to associate unstructured activity patterns in accordance with shallow statistical properties of the environment (Fodor & Pylyshyn, 1988). This cannot be right, however. When appropriate, connectionist networks using distributed representations do exhibit sensitivity to combinatorial structure, though this sensitivity takes a nonclassical form. This feature of connectionism has been demonstrated in practice ([Pollack, 1990], [Chrisman, 1991]) and articulated in theory (van Gelder, 1990a). Whatever else connectionism may or may not be, it is not a term of simple-minded associationism; and whatever else the interesting alternative to classical processes might be, it is not mere statistical replication.

Another kind of answer that some found tempting was that the basic form of processing in distributed connectionist networks is *pattern recognition*. One of the more prominent exemplars of this approach has been Paul Churchland, who has maintained that processing in such networks is fundamentally a matter of *prototype activation* (Churchland, 1988). (Activation of the prototype for a given input can be thought of as recognizing that input as an instance of the relevant pattern.) This approach also has problems. A conception of connectionist processing as prototype activation may fit early networks whose basic mode of operation is either simple settling to an attraction (e.g., Hopfield nets) or transformations of patterns of activity from one layer to another (e.g., classic backpropagation networks). However, the prototype-activation model has been losing its applicability and appeal as connectionism has matured and diversified. This is especially true in the case of advanced deployments of recurrent networks in which input is best seen as exerting a subtle overall influence on the evolving behavior of the network (Port, 1990).

Equally important, pattern recognition, although certainly central to various aspects of cognition, cannot itself be the general form of cognitive functioning. There are basic aspects of cognition, such as language use and motor control, that have quite the wrong general character to be thought of as some kind of pattern recognition (van Gelder, 1993). Thus, even if pattern recognition were the general form of processing in connectionist networks, it could not serve to play the role of primary interest here, that of a conception of the general form of cognitive processing that can stand as an interesting alternative to the classical one.

A third kind of answer was that sketched by Paul Smolensky in his well-known 1988 discussion of connectionism (Smolensky, 1988). His suggestion was that we think of connectionist networks as dynamical systems whose state is the activation values of all the units at a given time and whose evolution equation is the differential (or difference) equation that governs how these activation values evolve over time. Processing in connectionist networks is then just *state-space evolution in connectionist dynamical systems* (p. 6).

This characterization of connectionist processing is sufficiently general to encompass most if not all connectionist work. However, in contrast to the suggestion that cognitive processing in connectionist networks is simply transformations of activity patterns, it does not achieve this by being virtually contentless itself. Just as the classical conception of cognition as computation is the result of applying a particular general conceptual framework (computation theory) to the study of cognitive systems, so the conception of cognition as evolution in connectionist dynamical systems is the result of bringing to bear another and quite different general conceptual framework, that of dynamical modeling and dynamical systems theory. The characterization of connectionist cognitive processing stands to inherit the sophistication and resources of that more general framework. Moreover, partly by virtue of its breadth, this characterization is not subject to various immediate and obvious objections, as were the previous characterizations.

Recall that our interest in the nature of processing in distributed connectionist networks was subordinate to a more general inquiry into the possibility of alterative kinds of cognitive processes that might form the basis of a whole alterative conception of cognitive architecture. Smolensky's characterization of connectionist processes can easily be generalized in a way that is appropriate to this wider interest. Before doing this, however, it is useful to lay out a still more general way of thinking about the nature of cognitive processes—one that is so general as to embrace the classical conception itself. This is the *Dynamical Cognition Hypothesis*, as laid out by Manco Giunti (Giunti, 1991).

For current purposes, a dynamical system can be thought of as any self-contained system whose state changes over time in a way that can be captured in relevant detail by some set of rules or equations. In thinking about a system as a dynamical system we need to specify at least three things: the space of states that the system can occupy, the set that will be used to represent "time" (usually the integers or the real numbers), and the rules or equations that govern how the states of the system change over time. The Dynamical Cognition Hypothesis is the claim that all cognitive processes are a matter of state-space evolution in dynamical systems, or *dynamical processes*, for short.[2]

If Smolensky is right in his characterization of connectionist processes, then connectionists should be happy to subscribe to the Dynamical Cognition Hypothesis, since connectionist networks are just special cases of dynamical systems, and connectionist processes just special cases of dynamical processes. A little less obvious is the fact that all classical theorists should be equally happy to subscribe to the Dynamical Cognition Hypothesis, since their computational systems are also special cases of dynamical systems. To see this, consider that paradigm of a computational system, the Turing Machine. If the Turing Machine is a dynamical system, it must be possible to specify the state space, the set that represents time, and the evolution rules or equations. Turing Machines are usually not described in such terms, but this kind of description can be obtained by fairly trivial manipulation of standard presentations. Thus, consider Minsky's famous four-symbol, seven-state universal Turing Machine (Minsky, 1967), usually described by means of a machine table of the following kind as shown in Table 10.1. (The first square tells us that if head is currently in state 1 and the symbol in the cell over which the head is positioned is a Y, then change that symbol to _, move left, and change head state to state 1; and so on.) The state space for this machine is the set of possible states the machine as

TABLE 10.1.
Machine table

	1	2	3	4	5	6	7
Y	_L1	_L1	YL3	YL4	YR5	YR6	_R7
_	_L1	YR2	HALT	YR5	YL3	AL3	YR6
1	1L2	AR2	AL3	1L7	AR5	AR6	1R7
A	1L1	YR6	1L4	1L4	1R5	1R6	_R2

a whole can be in. Normally we think of the state of a Turing Machine as just its current *head* state, but for a dynamical treatment the state has to encompass all aspects of the system that change over time; thus the total state of the Turing Machine must also include the current location of the head and the current contents of every cell on the tape. Since the tape is unbounded in both directions, there is an unbounded number of cells and hence an unbounded number of state variables. That is, the Turing Machine has, in theory, an infinite-dimensional state space, though in practice it is always sufficient to consider it as having a certain finite (possibly large) number of dimensions. Although we use the word "space," the state space is not simply a high-dimensional extension of the everyday notion of space with its three real-valued dimensions. The head state variable can take, as values, the integers between 1 and n, where n is the number of head states of the Turing Machine; the head position variable takes integers, and the variables specifying individual cell contents can take, as values, any *symbol* in the alphabet of the machine. The state space is thus not simply numerical (the values taken by some variables are not numbers) and highly discrete. The high dimensionality of the state space creates a problem in representing the state of the machine at a given time; one relatively convenient method is to use the schema

$$\cdots a_{i+3}\ a_{i+2}\ a_{i+1}\ q\ a_i\ a_{i-1}\ a_{i-2}\ a_{i-3} \cdots$$

where a_α is a variable specifying the contents of cell α, q specifies the current head state, and q is located immediately to the right of the cell over which the head is located; that is, no separate head location variable is in this schema.

To represent time for this Turing Machine, it is convenient to take the integers. (Note that for this purpose we could use any set at all that had a strict ordering.) What about the evolution equation? An evolution equation tells us how the total state of a system changes as a function of its current state; for a system that is discrete in time, it tells us what the total state of the system, S_{t+1}, will be as some function F of its previous total state S_t.

Now, any given square in the machine table only specifies the change in three variables depending on their own current value. It leaves implicit that all other variables stay the same, or that, more precisely from a dynamical point of view, their change happens to be null at this time step. To obtain a genuine evolution equation we have to convert the table to an equation of the form $S_{t+1} = F(S_t)$; this means converting all the individual rules in the table into one large rule specifying transitions in total state. The first square in the table, if translated into a specification of a total state transition, tells us that if at time t the system is in state

$$S(t) = \ldots . a\, a\, a\, a\, 1\, Y\, a\, a\, a \ldots .$$

then at time $t + 1$ it should be in state

$$S(t+1) \ldots . a\, a\, a\, 1\, a\_a\, a\, a \ldots$$

The evolution equation for Minsky's machine thus turns out to be the rather tedious conditional:

$$S(t+1) = F(S(t)) = \ldots . aaa1a\_aaa \ldots . \text{ if } S(t) = \ldots . aaaa1Yaaa \ldots .$$
$$\ldots . aaa1a\_aaa \ldots . \text{ if } S(t) = \ldots . aaaa1\_aaa \ldots .$$
$$\text{etc.}$$

Standardly, a computation in a Turing Machine is thought of as a sequence of discrete symbol manipulating steps. From a dynamical point of view, a computation is a sequence of total state transitions, and thus traces out a particular trajectory in the machine's discrete symbolic state space. In fact, from a dynamical perspective, computation can be regarded as a matter of *touring* the machine's state space.

In all of this there is of course nothing special about Turing machines. The same general points hold true for any computational system, including the kind of symbolic machines used in the mainstream computational approach to cognition (von Neumann machines, LISP machines, production machines, etc.) and so also of particular cognitive models on such machines, such as those developed within the SOAR production system framework (Newell, 1991), though actually specifying the state-space and the evolution equations for such systems would be highly tedious in practice.

The fact that both connectionist and classical conceptions of cognition can be subsumed under the Dynamical Cognition Hypothesis does not mean that this hypothesis is either trivially true or useless. It is not trivially true because not every phenomenon is dynamical in the relevant sense. Many kinds of phenomena are such that we currently have no good reason to believe that they can be described in relevant detail by some specifiable set of rules or equations that tell us how the state of the system is changing in terms of its current state. These include legal systems, football matches, interpersonal relations, and a host of others; for these phenomena we use other, less strict, methods for understanding the way they change. The Dynamical Cognition Hypothesis is the relatively strong empirical hypothesis—and methodological assumption—that cognitive phenomena are rather more like the motions of the planets or the behavior of a Turing Machine than they are like these other kinds of nondynamical phenomena.

The Dynamical Cognition Hypothesis is philosophically useful because it makes it possible to locate current competing schools of thought in cognitive science within a common field. Previously, it was as if one school says cognition is chalk, while another says it is cheese. Now, we can see that it is as if one school says cognition is apples, while the other says it is oranges— that is, both agree that cognition is a kind of *fruit*, and it is simply a matter of determining what *kind* of fruit it really is. Knowing that we trying to sort out kinds of fruit enables us to formulate questions and hypotheses, and utilize methods, not available before. In particular, the perspective afforded by the Dynamical Cognition Hypothesis makes it possible to envisage the possibility of forms of cognitive processing that are neither classical nor connectionist, and to formulate an alternative to the classical conception of cognitive processes which, although inspired by Smolensky's characterization of connectionist processes, is more suitably general.

There is a long list of basic properties that dynamical systems can have. They can be linear or nonlinear, continuous or discrete, high or low dimensional, have state variables taking numerical or non-numerical values, and so on. These basic properties can be thought of as delineating a vast space of possible kinds of dynamical system. Thus, Turing Machines considered as dynamical systems are discrete in time, high dimensional, digital, etc.. These properties make them very different from classic examples of dynamical systems such as pendula or planetary systems, and in fact makes it possible to think of their operation (and that of computational systems more generally) in nondynamical terms.[3] That is, computational systems are dynamical systems whose behavior is best understood and manipulated using the conceptual tools of computation theory rather than traditional dynamical modeling and contemporary dynamical systems theory.

Occupying a rather different region of the space of possible dynamical systems are typical connectionist networks. These are standardly continuous, nonlinear, numerical systems with evolution equations specifying the change in value of any given state variable (unit activation) as a sigmoidal function of the values of the other state variables; this sigmoidal function has, as parameters, the current settings of the connection weights. When connectionism was enjoying its initial resurgence of popularity in the early to mid-1980s, it was common to try thinking of their operation in terms that were borrowed from computationalists—that is, in terms of the sequential and orderly manipulation of static representations. As connectionism has matured, however, the trend is to understand their operation in increasingly pure dynamical terms.

So one way to understand the disagreement between classical computationalism and connectionism is to see them as differing primarily over where, in the space of possible dynamical systems, cognitive systems are most likely to be found. But to see this is to realize immediately that computationalism and connectionism may not be the only interesting options. Cognitive systems may be dynamical systems from neither the computational nor the connectionist corner. And, in fact, recent years have seen the rapid emergence of a wide variety of dynamical models that are both noncomputational and nonconnectionist. Like connectionist networks, these models are standardly numerical, nonlinear, and continuous, but they differ in being usually low dimensional and governed by quite different differential equations. They are analyzed solely using the tools of dynamical modeling and dynamical systems theory. Theorists who work with such models consider themselves neither computationalists nor connectionists but rather *dynamicists*. In a number of domains these purely dynamical models currently provide the best available accounts of all the relevant data; see, for example, the work of Busemeyer and Townsend in that core cognitive area, decision-making under uncertainty (Busemeyer & Townsend, 1993).[4]

The most cautious way to provide a general characterization of cognitive processes that can stand as an alternative to the classical conception, then, is to suggest simply that cognitive processes are noncomputational dynamical processes—that is, they are a matter of state-space evolution in dynamical systems quite far removed from standard computational systems. This general characterization can then be tightened in various ways as modeling attempts reveal some varieties of noncomputational dynamical system to be more fruitful than others. For example—and this is currently one of the most interesting directions in which it can be tightened—we might conjecture that cognitive processes are really a matter of state-space evolution in nonlinear systems with continuous numerical state variables that change simultaneously and interdependently in a way that is governed by differential equations. This characterization would embrace much but not all connectionist work and much nonconnectionist dynamical work as well.

So far I have been suggesting that currently, anyone searching for a nonclassical conception of cognitive architecture might on one hand look in the direction of distributed representation, and on the other look in the direction of noncomputational dynamical processes. What is the relation between these two? Obviously they can come together, as they do in much connectionist work. This kind of marriage is in fact quite a natural one, for a number of reasons. Distributed representations find their most straightforward implementations as numerical vectors, and hence can be the state of a nonncomputational dynamical system. Moreover, simultaneous interdependency among state variables is an ideal environment for semantic superimposition, the very heart of distribution. And if the parameter settings that fix the particular equations that govern the system are themselves taken to constitute a representation (as in the case of the weights in a connectionist network) this representation is inherently distributed, since the same set of parameter settings underlies all the different behavioral trajectories that the system exhibits.

Nevertheless, distributed representation and noncomputational dynamical processes are conceptually independent and quite separable in practice. By pointing in these directions, we are not picking out a single unified class of cognitive architectures, but rather two large and overlapping classes. However, doing this satisfies the original goal—surveying some of the range of alternatives to the classical approach—as well as specifying a single class. The fact is that far from computational cognitive architectures being the only game in town, there is a wide field of semi-explored and unexplored alternatives. It would be rash indeed to discount swiftly the possibility that the human cognitive architecture might be found quite far from the computational lamppost, under whose fading light most investigations have thus far been conducted.

NOTES

[1] More precisely: suppose we have a distributing transformation Δ. Let G be the range of this transformation, i.e., the set of functions g such that $g = \Delta f$ for some function f. G can be regarded as a set of descriptions of entities that may be functioning as representations. The scheme of distributed representations defined by Δ is the set of representations R such that (a) R represents contents $c_1, \ldots, c_n$ ($n \geq 2$); (b) there is a function g in G such that g effectively specifies R; and (c) there is a function f that effectively specifies $c_1, \ldots, c_n$ and such that $g = \Delta f$. A representation is distributed if it belongs to the scheme of distributed representations defined by some distributing transformation.

[2] Superficially, Giunti's approach to these issues differ markedly from that I have been recommending in other places (van Gelder, 1995; van Gelder & Port, 1995). In fact, our approaches are fundamentally compatible; the entire difference boils down to the definition of "dynamical system" one uses. Broad definitions, like the one used by Giunti, subsume computational systems. Narrower definitions preserve a contrast between digital computers and dynamical systems. It is just a matter of convenience, given one's philosophical purposes, which perspective one adopts.

[3] For a discussion of the deep differences between thinking of a system computationally and thinking of it dynamically, see (van Gelder, 1995).

[4] For further examples, see the selection in (Port & van Gelder, 1995).

REFERENCES

Busemeyer, J. R. & Townsend, J. T. (1993). Decision field theory: A dynamic-cognitive approach to decision making in an uncertain environment. *Psychological Review, 100*, 432–459.

Chrisman, L. (1991). Learning recursive distributed representations for holistic computation. *Connection Science, 3*(4), 345–366.

Churchland, P. M. (1988). *A neurocomputational perspective.* Cambridge MA: MIT Press.

Fodor, J. A. & Pylyshyn, Z. (1988). Connectionism and cognitive architecture: A critical analysis. *Cognition, 28*, 3–71.

French, R. (1992). Semi-distributed representations and catastrophic forgetting in connectionist networks. *Connection Science, 4*, 365–377.

Giunti, M. (1991). Computers, Dynamical Systems, Phenomena and the Mind. Doctoral Dissertation, Indiana University.

Haugeland, J. (1978). The name and plausibility of cognitivism. *Behavioral and Brain Sciences 1*, 215–226.

Minsky, M. (1967). *Computation: Finite and infinite machines.* Englewood Cliffs, NJ: Prentice-Hall.

Newell, A. (1991). *Unified theories of cognition.* Cambridge MA: Harvard University Press.

Pollack, J. B. (1990). Recursive distributed representations. *Artificial Intelligence, 46,* 77–105.

Port, R. & van Gelder, T. J. (1995) *Mind as motion: Explorations in the dynamics of cognition.* Cambridge MA: MIT Press.

Port, R F. (1990). Representation and recognition of temporal patterns. *Connection Science, 2,* 151–176.

Pylyshyn, Z. W. (1984). *Computation and cognition: Toward a foundation for cognitive science.* Cambridge MA: Bradford/MIT Press.

Quinlan, P. (1991). *Connectionism and psychology.* Chicago: University of Chicago Press.

Smolensky, P. (1988). On the proper treatment of connectionism. *Behavioral and Brain Sciences, 11*, 1–74.

van Gelder, T. (1990a). Compositionality: A connectionist variation on a classical theme. *Cognitive Science, 14*, 355–384.

van Gelder, T. (1990b). Why distributed representation is inherently non-symbolic. In G. Dorffner (ed.) *Konnektionismus in artificial intelligence and Kognitionsforschung.* Berlin: Springer-Verlag.

van Gelder, T. J. (1992a). Defining "distributed representation." *Connection Science, 4*, 175–191.

van Gelder, T. J. (1993). Is cognition categorization? In G. V. Nakamura, R. M. Taraban, & D. L. Medin (Eds.), *Categorization by humans and machines.* San Diego: Academic Press.

van Gelder, T. J. (1995). What might cognition be, if not computation? *Journal of Philosophy, 91,* 345–381.

van Gelder, T. J. & Port, R. (1995). It's about time: An overview of the dynamical approach to cognition. In R. Port & T. van Gelder (Eds.), *Mind as motion: explorations in the dynamics of cognition.* Cambridge MA: MIT Press.

chapter II

The Cognitive Architecture of Vision and Action[*]

M.A. Goodale
goodale@uwo.ca
Department of Psychology
University of Western Ontario

Michael A. Arbib
arbib@pollux.usc.edu
USC Brain Project
University of Southern California

ARCHITECTURE AS METAPHOR

Our approach to the cognitive architecture of vision begins with a simple question: How does the brain transform sensory input into useful motor output? To answer this question, we examine the role of vision in guiding the actions of frogs, monkeys, and humans, and we use this account to develop an evolutionary perspective on the origins of the underlying architecture. We go on to suggest that this relatively ancient function of vision in guiding a basic repertoire of actions preceded its role in constructing the more complex perceptual representations that permit knowledge of the world and the objects and events within it.

Cognitive Architecture is often defined by comparison with Computer Architecture, suggesting that there is a fixed design for the hardware that

[*]The research described in this chapter was supported in part by Grant MA7269 from the Medical Research Council of Canada to M.A. Goodale, Grant NOOO14-92-J-4026 from ONR, and a grant from the Human Frontier Science Program to M. A. Arbib. This chapter is based on the separate oral presentations given by Goodale and Arbib at the Inaugural Conference on Cognitive Architecture, Rutgers Center for Cognitive Science, October 31–November 2, 1991.

can be separated cleanly from the software. Such separation makes little sense when we seek an architecture for cognitive neuroscience, and so we offer a different perspective by looking at the different senses of the architecture of buildings:

1. The art/science of designing buildings
2. The design of a particular house
3. A collection of special features

An example of the first might include the principle that "water goes to the kitchen," and an example of the third might include "there are tiles on the kitchen floor." In this chapter, we use the term architecture in the first two senses: 1) We offer "schema theory" (for a recent review, see Arbib, 1992) as a general methodology for cognitive science inspired by the findings of human neuropsychology; and 2) we analyze specific regions of the brain in specific animals. The database for the analysis comes from the study of the behavior of neurological patients and the behavior of normal and brain-damaged animals.

Schema theory is distinct from "computationalist" approaches that embody the "language of thought" in that schema theory is based on the interaction of dynamic systems rather than on systems of explicit symbol-processing. Although the specification of schemes is compatible with their implementation as neural networks, schema theory is also different from "connectionism"—if that effort is limited to the use of learning protocols for adapting a randomly structured network to some specific task. Rather, we offer an approach, rooted in the study of the brain as the organ of mind and behavior, that recognizes that different parts of the brain have evolved as neural networks with radically different structures. Thus, we must emphasize design (and evolutionary history) perhaps even more than learning in seeking to understand how complex tasks (mental or behavioral) are played out over networks of schemas, themselves implementable in neural networks, which interact through a multilevel process of "cooperative computation."

Pylyshyn (1991) has remarked that the architecture for vision is not the general architecture for thought, and that perhaps language uses a different architecture from reasoning. Such remarks might suggest a "new dualism" in which only thought and reasoning have true cognitive architecture, whereas vision and other such functions are peripheral. Yet just as an architect may speak of the distinctive architecture of homes, factories, and airport terminals, so can we talk about the distinctive nature of different cognitive systems, while attempting to provide the beginnings of a unified perspective on perception and action, language and thought. In short, we seek an integrated architecture cognitive neuroscience (sense 1)—a science of minds and the brains that implement them—while using this general framework to chart the particularities of specific systems (sense 2).

By suggesting how even the highest cognitive systems might have evolved from basic systems for sensorimotor integration, we hope to gain insights that would not be achievable if, for example, a cognitive skill, such as language, were viewed as a totally new symbolic system with no evolutionary antecedents. This chapter, however, carries the story from instinctive aspects of visuomotor behavior only as far as the more abstract forms of human visual perception, leaving the implications for language for later studies (but for early essays in this direction, see Arbib and Caplan, 1979; Arbib, Caplan, and Marshall, 1982; and Arbib, Conklin, and Hill, 1987).

The key question in the context of cognitive architecture is this: How do different systems evolve? In other words, when are they truly distinct? Although both the heart and the kidneys manage body fluids, it may well be that their genetic basis (and thus, their structure) diverged so far back in evolution that little is to be gained from studying them within a common architecture, though even here we may gain understanding by looking at shared cellular mechanisms (a subarchitectural issue?) as well as the systems analysis of how water moves through different body compartments (which is an architectural issue). In the study of the human brain, the linkage seems far more direct. The human brain occurs rather late in mammalian, let alone, vertebrate evolution. We are thus justified in viewing those parts of the brain involved in cognitive functions as being recently evolved extensions of systems that were present in the ancestors we share with many other vertebrates (for an elaboration of this argument, see Goodale, 1983, 1988). In the last sentence, we try to avoid the trap of viewing evolution as linear (cf. the critique by Gould [1989]). It is not that frogs, rats, monkeys, and humans represent successive stages in evolution. Instead, they share ancestors who evolved to yield the different brains we see in the modern species. These brains exhibit enough commonalities to encourage their comparative study under the banner of neuroethology—the study of neural mechanisms of animal behavior—with a real expectation of gaining insights into the architecture of cognitive neuroscience. In this spirit, we start with a study of approach and avoidance behavior in the frog, arguing that it reveals a set of functions that are similar to those expressed by homologous areas in the mammalian brain, including the human brain, and that understanding this commonality can allow us to see more clearly what is also distinctive about the human visual system.

SCHEMAS FOR DETOUR BEHAVIOR IN FROG AND TOAD

To a very rough first approximation, the ability of a frog to find food can be reduced to the ability to tell small moving objects from large moving objects. A frog surrounded by dead flies will starve to death, but the frog will snap with equal enthusiasm at a moving fly or a pencil tip wiggled in a fly-like way. A larger moving object can trigger an escape reaction. Thus, at a very simple level, we might imagine that the brain of a frog has a basic pattern-recognition routine (what we shall call *perceptual schemas*) for recognizing small moving objects (food-like stimuli) that, when activated, will in turn trigger the motor schema for approach (*motor schema* is our term for a control-system producing action). More generally, multiple schemas may be coactivated to control subtle behaviors (Cobas and Arbib, 1992). Moreover, perceptual schemes provide a parametric description that can be used to tune and calibrate the motor output. When the frog recognizes prey, it does not simply respond by launching itself in a standard or random direction, but rather it turns and snaps at the position in three-dimensional space where the prey is located. Similarly, when confronted with a possible predator, such as a looming visual stimulus, the frog tends to jump in the opposite direction or in such a way that it moves out of the path of the predator.

There are many models that incorporate more than the simple perceptual schemas for prey recognition. One such model, admittedly not very biological, was motivated by data like that in Fig. 11.1 in which we see single frames from a movie of a frog observing a worm through a semitransparent grating or barrier (Ingle, 1976). Instead of launching itself directly at its prey as would occur if no barrier were present, the frog reacts appropriately, detouring around the barrier (as we see in progress in the fourth frame) to get its prey. For this to happen, the perceptual schema for recognizing prey must be augmented by the perceptual schema for recognizing a barrier, and there can no longer be a simple direct path from prey recognition to the triggering of approach behavior. Rather, there must be some way for this path to be modulated by the recognition of the barrier to yield an indirect detour, rather than the direct response.

FIGURE 11.1.   When a toad sees a worm behind a barrier, it will detour rather than snapping directly (Ingle, 1976).

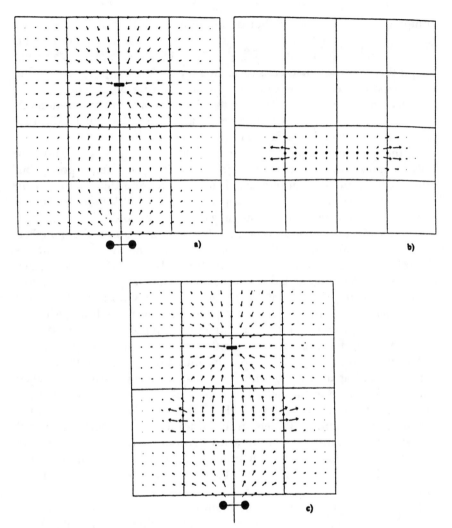

FIGURE 11.2.

In Figure 11.2, the potential fields depicted represent an exploratory attempt at defining a set of primitive fields that will interact in interpreting a complex scene. Each field provides, for each position in the ground plane, a vector showing the direction and strength of a movement the animal might make were it situated at that position. (a) A single prey object sets up a radially symmetric attractant field whose strength decays gradually with distance from the prey. (b) A single barrier object sets up a repellent field whose effect is more localized to its point of origin than is that of the prey field. The barrier field is not radially symmetric but has a lateral component that is stronger but decays more rapidly with distance than does its opposing component. (c) The effect of the interaction of the fields from several barrier objects arranged to form a fence is to provide a strong lateral thrust at the fence ends. The lateral components produced by the interior posts is effectively cancelled by neighboring posts. The net field produced by the interaction of all of the elements of the configuration can then be thought of as tracing out a set of paths, most of which are diverted around the fence ends (Arbib & House, 1987).

In the particular situation under consideration, the animal must not only recognize prey and barrier (a line of small, vertical fence posts), but must locate both of them in space. If it can recognize that the prey is in front of the barrier or at most a tongue's length behind, then the animal indeed will snap directly. But if the prey is further behind the barrier, then the animal must use its recognition of where the prey is and where the barrier is to come up with a path that will carry it around the barrier towards the prey. In a model developed by Arbib and House (1987), perceptual schemes for prey and barrier drive motor schemas that compete and cooperate to yield the overall behavior (Fig. 11.2). They postulated that the ground plane in front of the animal is represented in the brain, with the worm being represented as a global attractor: each point in the arena has a vector pointing towards the worm, with the vectors decreasing in length with distance from the prey, but not vanishing (Fig. 11.2a). Each fence post is represented as a local repellor, such that the animal will be repelled either to the left or to the right if it comes close to the fence post, but will not be affected if it is further away (Fig. 11.2b). When the actions of individual fence posts are combined, strong vector fields to the left and right of the fence are produced. If all this activity is combined, the field shown in Fig. 11.2c is generated, which when integrated yields trajectories that pass either to the left or the right of the fence and then continue en route to the prey.

It is not our claim here that the brainstem of the frog implements the potential field algorithm in its neural circuitry. Rather, the crucial point is that it is possible to construct an evolutionary account of how such a system might arise (Fig. 11.3). First, the elements of the prey-recognition system—perceptual schema, motor schema, and motor-pattern generator (MPG)—coevolve so that activity in the prey-schema (a perceptual schema) can represent a goal in such a way that the approach-schema (a motor schema) provides the right control signals for the MPG to determine a path to the prey. Then, the detour system evolves by combining a perceptual schema for stationary objects with a new motor schema that *modulates* the effect that the original approach-schema has on the motor pattern generator.

In this section, then, we have seen how useful it is to move between models and neurobehavioral data in detailing the cognitive architecture of

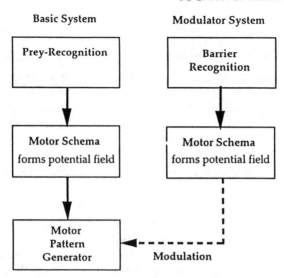

FIGURE 11.3. The evolutionary refinement adding detour behavior to prey-approach by modulating the basic system for approaching prey.

the frog's visuomotor system. In addition, we have seen how an evolutionary perspective can assist in constructing possible interactions between different schemas within a visuomotor network. The arguments that we have presented are summarized *and extended* below as three principles of cognitive architecture.

Principle 1.   Cooperative computation of schemas. The functions of perceptual-motor behavior can be expressed as a network of interacting schema instances.[1] The method of interaction of schema instances is "cooperative computation" (competition and cooperation) so that "computations" that are often seen as the province of traditional symbol-based processing are carried out by distributed "neuron-like" methods that do not involve explicit symbolic control.

Principle 2.   Interaction of partial representations. A multiplicity of different representations must be linked into an integrated whole. Such linkage, however, may be mediated by distributed processes of competition and cooperation. There is no one place in the brain where an integrated representation of space plays the sole executive role in linking perception of the current environment to action.

Principle 3.   Evolution and modulation. New schemas often arise as "modulators" of existing schemas, rather than as new systems with independent functional roles. It is the thesis of this chapter that such schema interactions provides the general mechanism for Cognitive Architecture, serving as a basis not only for coordinated motor actions, but for planning and intelligent behavior (including the use of language, which is beyond the scope of this paper). But we also shall see that the transition from frog-like to human brains involved many evolutionary innovations in the nature of schema interactions. In the previous examples from frog and toad, the partial representations are formed on a retinotopic basis. More generally, they may involve abstract representations of knowledge about types of objects in the world, or more abstract planning spaces.

SCHEMAS FOR REACHING AND GRASPING

Vision can be used to guide a wide variety of actions, from eye movements to locomotion to prehension. In what follows, we will focus on prehension—or, more specifically, the visual control of the arm and hand movements that constitute reaching and grasping. During prehension, not only does the hand move toward an object that it is to grasp, but it preshapes itself in a way that is clearly adapted to the shape of the target (Jeannerod & Biguer, 1982), although the preshape is somewhat larger than the object itself. An early model of this (Arbib, 1981) shows a perceptual schema that can locate the object and then activate perceptual subschemas that recognize the object's size and orientation (Fig. 11.4). The parameters describing where the object is, how big it is, and its orientation can then be passed

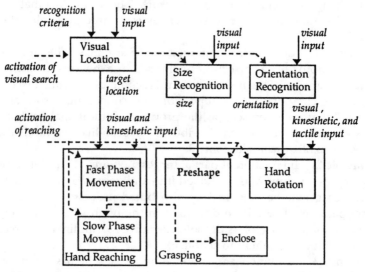

Note: Dashed lines: activation signals; solid lines: transfer of data (Adapted from Arbib, 1981).

FIGURE 11.4. Hypothetical coordinated control program for reaching and grasping.

to the motor schemas. One motor schema moves the arm to carry the hand in a ballistic movement which, when completed, triggers a slow adjustment movement to the final position of the hand. At the same time, two motor subschemas of the grasp schema are activated to achieve the preshape. Once the preshape is achieved, however, the grasp schema engages in no further processing until the handreaching schema activates the enclose subschema when the hand is in the right place for tactile guidance of the hand as it grasps the object.

But how is the preshape determined? For the purpose of the control of action the task of the perceptual schemas is not so much to recognize the object as a ball or pencil in any generic sense as it is to anatomize the object in terms of parameters such as size and orientation that are crucial to the task of grasping. They can then pass these parameters to the various motor schemes for moving and preshaping the hand. We now introduce two concepts—virtual fingers and opposition spaces—which have been used to describe human grasping. Arbib, Iberall, and Lyons (1985) analyzed the task of picking up a mug, not directly in terms of what the five fingers do, but rather in terms of three virtual fingers. The first (always the thumb) places itself on top of the handle. Virtual finger 2 goes through the handle, and can contain one, two, three, or even four fingers. Whatever fingers remain constitute virtual finger 3. The concept of the virtual finger tells us how to replace analysis of hand movements directly based on the mechanical degrees of freedom of individual fingers by analysis of the functional roles of the forces being applied in carrying out some task. But, having agreed to analyze the hand in terms of these virtual fingers, how do we specify the movement of these units? Iberall, Bingham, and Arbib (1986) argue that a variety of **opposition spaces** provides the appropriate coordinate systems. In *pad opposition* the pad of the thumb opposes the pad of the virtual finger; the opposition space is the axis along which the finger pads move to provide that opposition. *Palm opposition* is a power grip, opposing a group of fingers (the first virtual finger) with the palm acting as a second virtual finger; the axis determines the movement of the first virtual finger towards the palm. *Side opposition* opposes the thumb to the side of another finger, or may be used to grasp an object between two adjacent fingers.

Of course, when an object is grasped, the virtual fingers moving along the opposition axis may come to rest their opposing surfaces on the object between them, rather than making direct contact with each other. This makes possible a theory of preshaping. One task of vision is to determine, from the retinal input, an opposition space embedded in the object that is to be the target for the position of the appropriate opposition space of the hand. There is a safety margin extending the opposition space beyond the boundaries of the object. Preshaping forms the hand so that the opposing surfaces of the virtual fingers will be correspondingly separated. An approach vector, between the origin of opposition space and the center of the opposition vector, distinguishes the orientation and distance of the hand relative to the object. A virtual finger configuration must be moved from its current state to a desired state, under the control of a motor schema. As the hand preshapes to meet this specification (the Preshape Schema), the arm transports it (Move Arm Schema) and the wrist rotates it (the Orient Schema) to approximately the right position. Note that the target position of the wrist depends on the proposed preshape of the hand— the arm controller must know the offset of the wrist from the center of the opposition space as embedded in the object if it is to transport the hand successfully to its goal. Thereafter, the position of the hand is adjusted to align the two opposition spaces (that in the hand with that in the object) and the virtual fingers then close along the aligned axes to grasp the object firmly under tactile control (the Enclose Schema).

Recent experimental work (e.g., Paulignan et al., 1991a,b) has called into question two specific assumptions on which the model of Fig. 11.4 rests: (a) The transport phase involves a ballistic motor schema (in other words it generates a movement that cannot be changed once initiated but must proceed to completion), followed by a slow adjustment schema under the control of feedback to bring about the final positioning of the hand by the arm, (b) The preshape of the hand is maintained until the same signal that initiates the adjustment subschema also triggers the enclosed schema. It now appears, however, that instead of running off independently, the transport and grasp components of prehension are highly interactive. Control-theoretic models that remedy these shortcomings have been developed by Hoff and Arbib (1992, 1993), but further work is required to address new data. Jakobson and Goodale (1991) have recently shown, for example, that although the opening of the hand during a grasping movement was closely correlated with the size of the object, it was also affected by the amplitude of the required reach. Thus, maximum grip aperture increased as a function of an increase in either object size or distance. Moreover, they found that the transport component too was affected by both object size and distance with peak velocity increasing as a function of an increase in either variable (although the effect of distance is more dramatic). These results suggest that the perceptual schemas analyzing object location and object size do not have independent effects on the motor schema specifying the grasp and the reach respectively. A number of other studies have also revealed complex interactions between the transport and grasp. Wing, Turton, and Fraser (1986), for example, demonstrated that requiring subjects to reach more quickly produced a corresponding increase in the maximum aperture of the hand. More recently, Gentilucci, Castiello, Corradini, Scarpi, Umilta, and Rizzolatti

(1991) found, like Jakobson and Goodale (1991), that changes in object distance affect the size of the grasp as well as the velocity profile of the reach itself. In addition, they observed that the kind of grasp required (a precision grip with the index finger and thumb or a whole-hand grip) significantly affected the kinematics of the transport component. When subjects used a precision grip to pick up a small object, they accelerated more slowly, achieved a lower peak velocity, and spent more time in deceleration than when they used a whole-hand grip to pick up a larger object. These results underscore the highly interactive nature of the motor schemas underlying the production of the transport and grasp components of prehension: different distal components (precision versus wholehand grip, for example) appear to be associated with different patterns in the transport component, and increases in the required transport speeds (or time) are associated with increases in the amplitude of the grasp. Nevertheless, although all these observations offer new directions for modelling the schema control of prehension, they fit well the general approach to cognitive architecture of vision that we have adopted and indicate the close coupling between vision and action.

On the basis of the observations and arguments that we have reviewed in this section, the following two principles can be added to our list of Principles of Cognitive Architecture.

Principle 4. The task of perceptual schemas is not so much to recognize objects in any generic sense as it is to anatomize the object in terms of parameters that are crucial to the ongoing behavior of the organism.

This principle is far more far-ranging than it appears because the simple activation of one or a few motor schemas from the current stock may not always be well-suited to the organism's well-being in future environments. This opens the way for further evolution of the ability to evaluate alternative courses of action and to learn from experience. The necessary corollary, however, is that the animal cannot predict which environmental features are most relevant to immediate needs let alone to the long-term acquisition of adaptive knowledge and behavior.

Principle 5. Cognitive architectures can be open systems that change with experience. The emergence of new schemas rests on perceptual schemas that provide data not only to guide immediate action but also to support (covert or overt) exploration of alternatives; the evolution of new behaviors involves not only the modulation and extension of existing behaviors but also the inhibition of old behaviors that are less adaptive than the new acquisitions.

This is one of the reasons why competition is as much a part of the cooperative computation of schemas/schema instances as is cooperation: the various partial representations (Principle 2) are in no way guaranteed to be consistent, and dynamic interactions in general will be required to yield a coherent course of action.

THE WHAT, WHERE, AND HOW OF VISION

The previous discussion of reaching and grasping in humans provides a functional analysis of interacting schemes that further exemplifies the principle, based on our study of approach and avoidance in frog and toad, that a multiplicity of different representations must be linked into an integrated whole in action-oriented perception. In this section, we look at the way in which these presentations are played out over the human brain. But first we look at two results that relate studies of frog (and toad) to the attempt to understand the human visual system and its role in the control of action. These studies show the division of function between the superior colliculus (the mammalian brain region homologous to the frog's tectum) and cortical regions in mammals. We will then turn to evidence that the cortical regions of monkey and human brain that are implicated in vision have a diversity of function that is best understood within the framework of "action-oriented perception" that we have previously established.

A famous example of the attempt to place human cognition in an evolutionary context rooted in mechanisms for instinctive behavior is provided by the study (Humphrey, 1970) of "What the frog's eye tells the monkey's brain." It had long been known that the role of tectum in directing whole body movements in frog is analogous to the role of superior colliculus in directing orienting movements in cat and monkey. It had also been believed by neurologists that a monkey (or human) without a visual cortex was blind. Humphrey argued, however, that a monkey without a visual cortex should have at least as much visual ability as a frog, but that such monkeys had not been taught to pay attention to available visual cues. To demonstrate this, he gave two years of attention training to a monkey in which primary visual cortex had been removed. Remarkably, after extensive training, she was able to use visual cues to grab at moving objects, and to use changes in luminance— such as an open door—for navigation, even though delicate processes of pattern recognition were never regained. Moreover, it was discovered shortly after this that humans without primary visual cortex could also see in this sense—but they were not conscious that they could see. Such patients could point accurately toward small lights placed in their blind half field, even though they failed to report seeing the stimuli to which they pointed. This phenomenon is often referred to as **blindsight** (Weiskrantz, 1974) and it is assumed that many of the residual visual abilities in individuals with blindsight depend on circuitry involving the superior colliculus (a.k.a. the optic tectum). The superior colliculus functions as a "where" system.

From What and Where to What and How

Ungerleider and Mishkin (1982; see also Mishkin, Ungerleider, & Macko, 1983) noted that monkeys with lesions of inferotemporal cortex were profoundly impaired in visual pattern discrimination and recognition, but less impaired in solving landmark tasks, where the location of a visual cue determines which of two alternative locations is rewarded. Quite the opposite pattern of results was observed in monkeys with lesions to posterior parietal cortex. On the basis of these behavioral observations and a wealth of anatomical and electrophysiological data, they distinguished two visual systems in extrastriate visual processing, both originating in primary visual cortex, V1: a ventral stream projecting from V1 to inferotemporal cortex which they characterized as the "object vision" pathway and a dorsal stream projecting from V1 to posterior parietal cortex which they described as the "spatial vision" pathway. The ventral stream, according to Mishkin and Ungerleider, enabled the organism to identify what an object was, whereas the dorsal stream enabled it to tell where the object was. This is at first sight confusing, since we have already seen that the superior colliculus functions as a where system. Note, by the way, the crucial choice of "a" rather than "the." Our examination of visually guided behavior in frogs has taught us that a function that might appear unitary to introspection may involve diverse schemas distributed across multiple brain regions. The where of prey catching involves neural networks in the optic tectum, and the where of barrier avoidance during locomotion involves the pretectum. But for Ungerleider and Mishkin, what and where appeared to be general-purpose computations that the monkey or human could apply to any one of a number of visually guided responses. But as we have been at pains to emphasize throughout this paper, the computations that are performed by different networks in the visual system are shaped (in both the evolutionary and the experiential sense) by the requirements of the particular outputs that they serve (cf. Principles 4 and 5).

Goodale and Milner (1992), while still accepting that the ventral system plays the major role in the perceptual identification of objects, suggest that the dorsal system mediates the required sensorimotor transformations for visually guided actions directed at such objects. Although Goodale and Milner have characterized this distinction as what versus how, they recognize that each of these processing pathways requires information about both the spatial location and structural features of objects (albeit within different coordinate frameworks). They also recognize that the how system consists of a number of different sensorimotor networks that are assembled in different combinations for different actions.

In Figure 11.5 the aperture between index finger and thumb plotted as a function of object width for the patient (DF) with visual form agnosia

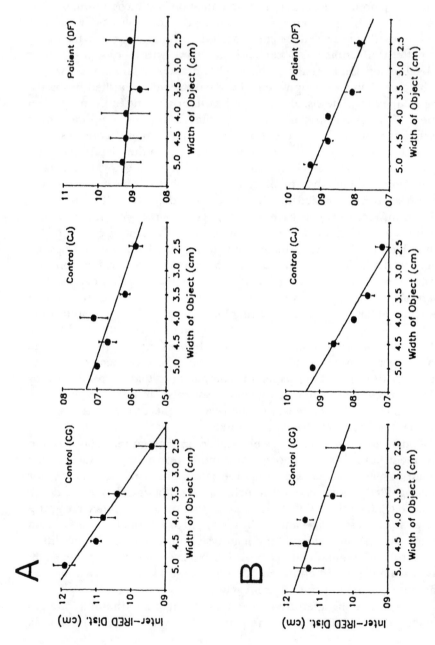

FIGURE 11.5.

and two age-matched control subjects (CG and CJ) in two tasks. For the task plotted in panel A, the subjects were asked to indicate manually the front-to-back dimension of each of five different blocks of equal area (25 cm^2) but different dimensions (ranging from 5 × 5 cm to 2.5 × 10 cm) placed directly in front of them at a viewing distance of approximately 45 cm. The distance between the index finger and thumb was measured opto-electronically. For the task plotted in panel B, the subjects were asked to reach out and pick up each target object. The maximum aperture between the index finger and thumb, which was achieved well before contact with the object, was again measured optoelectronically.

Goodale, Milner, Jakobson, and Carey (1991) studied the visually guided behavior in a patient (DF) who developed a profound visual form agnosia following carbon monoxide poisoning in which most of the damage to cortical visual areas was apparent in areas 18 and 19, but not area 17. Despite her profound inability to recognize the size, shape, and orientation of visual objects, DF showed accurate hand and finger movements directed at the very same objects. When asked to indicate the width of a single block by means of her index finger and thumb, for example, her matches bore no relationship to the dimensions of the object and showed considerable trial to trial variability (see Fig. 11.5). Yet when she was asked simply to reach out and pick up the block, the aperture between her index finger and thumb changed systematically with the width of the object, as in normal controls (Fig. 11.5). A similar dissociation was seen in her responses to the orientation of stimuli and most recently, to the shape of objects (Goodale, Meenan, Bülthoff, Nicolle, Murphy, and Racicot, 1994). Thus, even though DF's ability to perceive the size, shape, and orientation of objects in the visual world is severely compromised (presumably because the output from primary visual cortex to inferotemporal cortex is damaged), she is still able to use information about these same object features to calibrate skilled movements directed at those objects (presumably on the basis of intact projections to posterior parietal cortex).

Thus, even though we relate both the reaching and grasping systems to the dorsal how system, we see even here the further decomposition of specialized subsystems. This structure of semi-independent systems that are linked for the visual guidance of increasingly sophisticated tasks exemplifies the general notions summarized in Principle 2. But Principle 2 speaks not only of multiple representations but also of the processes of competition and cooperation that integrate them. As we further explore the relation between the what and how systems, it is not enough to dissect more carefully a variety of specialized subsystems. We must also solve the binding problem. In general, the various aspects of our visual recognition of, and motor interaction with, an object are seamlessly joined.

Visual and Attentional Requirements for Perception and Action

Schemas serve to represent, at least, perceptual structures and distributed motor control. A crucial point that we have not stressed until now (cf. Note 1) is that schemas may be instantiated. For example, given a schema that represents generic knowledge about some domain of interaction, we need several schema instances, each suitably tuned, to subserve our perception of several instances of that domain. The invocation of generic knowledge by the process of schema instantiation is, as we shall see, particularly important in providing our perceptual experience of the world (as distinct from the on-line control of particular actions). Unlike serial computers, the brain can support concurrent activity of many schema instances for the recognition of different objects and the planning of action, and at the same time, support the activity of schemas controlling the constituent movements of various motor acts.

In the primate visual system, basic processes like edge detection, depth mapping, and motion detection are also replicated over arrays of neurons that allow these processes to be replicated for parallel implementation over the entire visual field. However, we have evolved to learn to recognize, discriminate, and respond to visual patterns of a dazzling variety, from lions to cars to differential equations. But to replicate the machinery for recognizing all these objects so that it could be applied simultaneously in each small region of the visual field would require an inordinate increase in neural circuitry—quite apart from the massive connections that would be needed to solve the problem of how learning gleaned from experience gained with an object in one locale would be distributed to all the copies of the circuitry for recognizing the object at other locales. Our visual versatility depends on an evolutionary innovation—the ability to focus attention on one part of the visual field and then bring perceptual schemas to bear on just this foveal sample. In this way, it is no longer necessary to replicate perceptual machinery to such a great extent. At the cost of some serial scanning of the image, great computing power is gained without an inordinate increase (large, yes, but not inordinate) in the volume of circuitry that must be deployed.

For example, we can grab an object whose movement is sensed in the peripheral visual field if only a generalized grasp is required, but if we are to preshape the hand to grasp the object appropriately, then we must first foveate the object. We see here the continuity in discontinuity in the evolution of cognitive architecture. We have seen that the role of tectum in directing the whole body movements of frog and toad is akin to the role of superior colliculus in directing eye movements and thus in setting the frame for arm and hand movements in monkey and human. This is the continuity. The discontinuity is that the superior colliculus (and other cortical pathways that have emerged) need not commit the monkey or human to an overt course of behavior, as in approach or avoidance, but can instead gather information that can be used in planning before the organism is committed to action. To this it must be added that shifts of attention are not only overt; that is, involving eye movements. Neural circuitry can enable us, for example, to attend to different letters of a word even while we maintain the same fixation point. Many cells (e.g., in area 7a in the dorsal stream) are modulated by such covert switches of attention to different parts of the visual field (Bushnell, Goldberg & Robinson, 1981). Attentional modulation, however, can be found in neurons in many parts of the cortex, including area V4 and the inferotemporal region within the ventral stream (Moran & Desimone, 1985). Indeed, in the example of attention to particular letters of a word, it is likely that the critical process is attentional modulation in the ventral rather than the dorsal stream. We conclude that spatial attention is physiologically non-unitary (Rizzolatti, et al., 1985), and may be as much associated with the ventral system as with the dorsal.

VISUAL PERCEPTION AND THE EMERGENCE OF PLANNING

Figure 11.6 provides a functional view of the what vs. how distinction. A variety of low-level visual processes can provide the input both to reactive control systems (control of locomotion by optic flow, visual guidance of prehension, etc.) and for processes of high-level vision that may yield conscious knowledge of the current scene. Our thesis is that although these pathways are in some circumstances separable, action-oriented visual perception will normally rest on the integration of their functioning.

Analysis of the location, size, shape, and orientation of an object can set the parameters that motor schemas need to guide an action successfully, and we have reviewed a number of cases in which dedicated neural circuitry has or may have evolved to implement the specific perceptual and motor schemas involved. This is indicated by the "Reactive Control" path of Figure 11.6. The perception of complex scenes, however, involves rather different mechanisms that transcend particular views and particular locations in egocentric space. In everyday life, our behavior depends on the recognition of many different objects, and an appreciation of their changing positions. Consider the act of walking across the street; the recognition of cars, pedestrians, and the shop you are walking toward all enter into determining your pattern of movement. At least two kinds of interactive visual processes are at work here—contrast the process of locating the shop

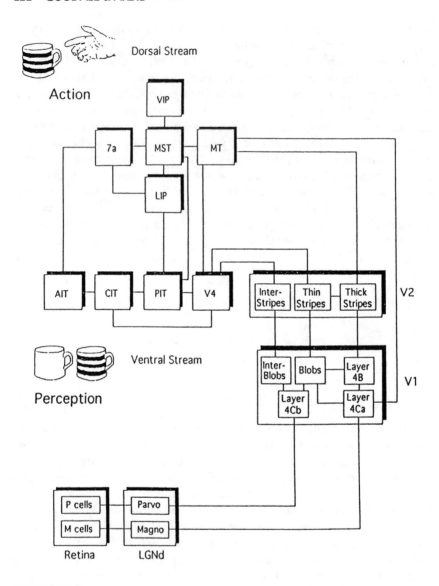

FIGURE 11.6.

and setting your overall path with the process of actually crossing the street (which may depend more on dedicated perceptual and motor schemas for the avoidance of moving objects, using cues from optic flow, than on the recognition of the identity of a specific car or bus). We have relatively few neural data on the processes of **high-level vision** supporting our perceptual experience (based on our knowledge of objects in the world; the right-hand path in Fig. 11.6) as distinct from **low-level vision** (processes of edge-finding, figure-ground separation, motion perception, and so on, that do not depend on the nature of the objects as distinct from their general physical properties). Some of these low-level processes provide input to the dedicated action systems of the dorsal stream, some to the more perceptual, knowledge-related systems of the ventral stream, and some, perhaps the majority, to both. Thus, our strategy here will depart from our usual emphasis on schema models based on behavioral and lesion analysis of animals and humans. Instead, we will describe a specific system for high-level computer vision, and then use it to develop a number of hypotheses about the way in which scene understanding may be implemented in the human brain (extending the argument in (Arbib, 1989), Sections 5.2 and 7.4). This allows us to discuss explicitly the problem of schema instantiation which, we claim, must be faced in bridging between cognitive science and neuroscience.

As in most computer vision systems, the VISIONS computer vision system developed by Riseman and Hanson (1987; see also, Draper, Collins, Brolio, Hanson and Riseman, 1989) employs low-level processes to take an image (e.g., a color photograph) and, working independently of object-specific knowledge, extract multiple representations, including regions, lines, surfaces, and vertices, tagged with features such as color, texture, shape, size, and location. Given a pair or sequence of images, other processes can yield further information such as depth and motion. The result is an intermediate representation (a set of partial representations) of the image that may be updated as interpretation proceeds. The interacting schemas that encode recognition routines for houses and walls and trees provide the processes to grab different features of the intermediate representation and come up with the overall interpretation of the image.

In Figure 11.7, interpretation strategies are stored in schemas that are linked in a schema network in Long Term Memory (LTM). Under the guidance of these schemas, the intermediate representation is modified and interpreted by a network of schema instances that label regions of the image and link them to a three-dimensional geometry in Short Term Memory (STM). [From (Weymouth, 1986)]

The knowledge required for interpretation is stored in LTM (long-term memory) as a network of schemas, and the state of interpretation of the particular scene unfolds in STM (short-term or working memory) in the form of a network of schema instances (Fig. 11.7). The user starts the interpretation process by invoking an arbitrary number of initial schemas. These may reflect general visual goals, such as "interpret this image as a road scene," or more specific needs, such as "find the sidewalk in this image." Each schema instance has an associated activity level (or confi-

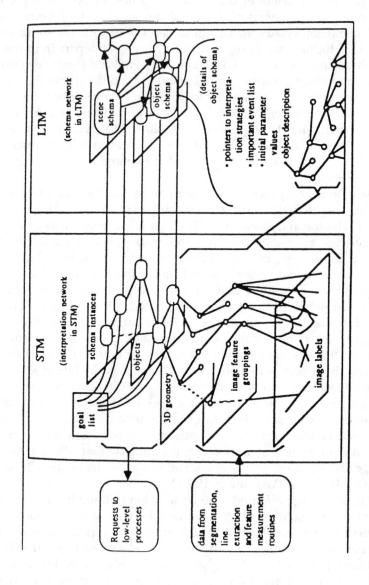

FIGURE 11.7.

dence level) that changes on the basis of interactions with other units in the (dynamically reconfigurable) STM network. The STM network makes context explicit: each object represents a context for further processing, using to advantage the relations among objects. When a schema instance is activated, it is with an associated area of the image and an associated set of local variables. Multiple instances of a given schema are normally associated with separate portions of the image. The structure of STM is further constrained in part by relationships encoded within LTM, both those between schemas for interobject relations and those within a schema for geometric relations of parts.

In addition to schema instances, the STM contains hypotheses and goals. A **hypothesis** asserts that a particular object provides the interpretation of a portion of the image. The hypothesis is posted (in the sense of posting something up on a bulletin board) when the relevant schema instance achieves a threshold in its confidence level, and will then include parameters descriptive of the object so recognized.

Contrast schema activation—when an instance starts to process—with schema firing or propagation—when an instance posts a hypothesis that can affect the activity of other schemas. A schema instance may set as a **goal** the confirmation that a certain context applies; and posting the goal may in turn lead to the forming of a schema instance to check whether a posited object occurs in a certain portion of the image (in the following example, recognizing a roof sets the goal of finding a wall-region beneath it in the image).

Active schema instances set out to accomplish their goals as independently acting agents. As part of recognizing their particular scene or object, schemas may invoke other schemas to recognize subparts of their objects, or to recognize spatially, functionally, or contextually related objects. The set of schemas that another schema invokes is flexible. A schema for recognizing houses, for example, may only invoke a schema for recognizing a wall if one of its hypotheses needs additional support. Otherwise, it may never invoke the wall schema. Thus the network of schema instances changes dynamically in response to the viewer's needs (e.g., goal-driven activation of schema instances) and the image (which dictates which schemas another schema will activate). It should also be noted that, once activated, the wall schema (or any schema) becomes an independent process, which can outlast the schema that invoked it, or even contradict that schema's hypotheses.

However, to see this as providing a step towards a general Cognitive Architecture, we must contrast the style of VISIONS with the action-oriented perception of animals and humans. In VISIONS, an image is supplied, goals are set, and the process of scene interpretation proceeds to conclusion. The result is a network of parameterized schema instances linked to portions of the image. In a human or animal, in contrast, the sensory input is constantly changing, in part because of the organism's control of its sensors. The process of interpretation in action-oriented perception involves a network that links instances of perceptual schemas to motor schemas, providing parameters and changing confidence levels. As their activity levels reach threshold, certain sets of these motor schemas create patterns of overt behavior. And so the action-perception cycle continues (Neisser, 1976; Arbib, 1981).

To see the way in which perceptual demands change as action proceeds, consider a driver instructed to turn right at the red barn. At first the person drives along looking for some crude perceptual event (something large and red), after which the perceptual schema for barns is brought to bear. Once a barn is identified, the emphasis shifts from identification of the barn *per se* to recognition of spatial relations appropriate to executing a right turn "at" the barn, but determined rather by the placement of the roadway, the position of cars, and so on.

In classical AI, explicit planning precedes execution, taking the form of a centralized sequential deliberation based on goals and a world model to yield a sequence of actions. Such an approach may impose unrealistic requirements for modelling and perception since all relevant information must be available before planning begins. This makes it hard to adapt the plan to events not predicted by the model. In reaction to this, some critics have advocated reactive planning in which selection and execution of actions are inextricably intertwined. Such reactive systems are parallel and distributed, with a priority scheme that is fixed at compile-time. There is no deliberation, and no model. Inhibition/suppression rules determines which modules will control action, on the basis of current input.

Such reactive systems, however, are hard-wired, difficult to design, and completely data-oriented. The analysis of the VISIONS system makes it clear that schema theory embraces a more general form of planning involving generativity to form novel patterns of schema activation that may require the creation of novel networks. We must now see how to extend the VISIONS computational strategy to provide a computational analysis of action-oriented perception in which planning is intertwined with execution, in which the plan may be updated as action proceeds, and in which planning is a process emerging from the cooperative computation of multiple agents rather than being imposed by a separate executive planning system. As we shall see towards the end of the paper, this shift towards cooperative computation can offer some insights into how the high-level perceptual machinery of the ventral stream of visual processing in the primate brain may interact with the visuomotor action systems in the dorsal stream to create dynamic and responsive visual behavior.

TOWARDS A NEURALIZATION OF SCHEMA-BASED
VISION AND ACTION

In this section, we spell out some of the ways in which the VISIONS system falls short of being a model of the brain mechanisms of visual perception. In doing so, we make explicit the outlines of a fresh appreciation of how different brain regions interact in the planning and execution of visually guided behavior. VISIONS is a computer system that takes a single photograph and produces a generic interpretation by breaking the image into a number of segments, each of which can be labeled by hypotheses posted by perceptual schemas when those schemas achieve a high confidence level for that segment. Note that this is very much a hybrid of dynamic and computer science terminology. The schema is an active process, but when its confidence level passes a threshold, it posts a symbolic description of the object the perceptual schema is designed to recognize, and links it (in a computer implementation, this is done with a pointer) to the region processed by the schema to achieve this high confidence. The aim is to provide a symbolic description of a static scene. In action-oriented perception, however, current sensory stimulation is always interpreted within the ongoing state of the organism. The organism does not generate a single representation of the visual input of, say, the last minute or two. Rather, the representation is dynamic and task-oriented. In trying to open a bottle, much of the visual environment will be ignored, but the spatial relationship between bottle opener and bottle cap (as well as related tactile feedback) will be continuously updated, and will undergo a discontinuous updating once the bottle cap is removed. The representation of the current input is thus elaborated within the context of, and contributes to the updating of, an already formed schema assemblage (the structure of working memory), and the structure of that representation is strongly conditioned by the current goals, tasks, and motivational as well as emotional state of the organism.

The clear interaction of data-driven and hypothesis-driven activity in the action-oriented perception of the organism can be modeled within an extended VISIONS framework when we note that schema instantiation in VISIONS can be hypothesis-driven as well as data-driven. Thus, the general architecture of schema instances, hypotheses, and goals exemplified by VISIONS is well-suited for use in the action-perception cycle once the system is broadened to allow goals to be set by needs of the organism beyond mere visual interpretation.

Let us take stock, then, of our current stage of defining our broader framework. We suggest that what must be changed from VISIONS is one, the inclusion of motor schemas and of goal schemas for other than perceptual goals; and two, the continual dynamic interaction of working memory with changing sensory input rather than convergence to a static interpretation.[2] Even with these changes, however, this general architecture is not computationally efficient as it stands. Creating an instance of every schema for every region of an image to determine for which pairs (s,r) of schemas and regions there is a high value of activity is prohibitively expensive, whether in time on a serial computer or in space in a fully parallel implementation. The mechanism in the brain is likely therefore to be something like this: Low-level mechanisms can isolate regions with sufficient salience to become the focus of attention; these regions provide input to a variety of networks (some specialized, such as those supporting face recognition; others tuned more by experience than by evolution) which proceed through a hierarchy of interacting descriptors to provide vigorous firing of those neural patterns that code for certain generic schemas. These then provide the inputs to working memory (coding both the schema and the locus where it has gained a high confidence level) which allow the process of scene recognition to proceed, both by data-driven and hypothesis-driven mechanisms.

The VISIONS architecture in the form described previously has no focus of attention mechanism. It allows unlimited spawning of schema instances which then all compete and cooperate before a final consensus is achieved. In a serial computer implementation of the system, a rigid schedule must be enforced, with one process active at a time. In the brain, the matter is more subtle. A multiplicity of different brain regions are dedicated, not only to a variety of processes of the kind referred to as low-level vision, but also to many specialized schemas for tasks from face recognition and object identification to the grasping of objects and local navigation around them. Indeed, as we have suggested, the schemas supporting the high-level visual perception of objects and events in the world form part of a network cluster that can be differentiated both anatomically and physiologically from the schemas underlying the production of skilled visuomotor acts directed at those objects and events. Moreover, the brain also has vital and interactive control structures within each of these twin streams of processing for shifting attention from one region of the visual array to another. What remains to be understood is how these shifts of attention are integrated with the unfolding structure of STM as perceptual analysis proceeds within the context of the action-perception cycle.

These considerations lead us to a new hypothesis: The what system of inferotemporal cortex provides a stock of perceptual schemas deriving their input from the low-level vision systems of primary visual cortex; the how systems of parietal cortex, which also derive low-level visual information from primary visual cortex (as well as from the superior colliculus, via the pulvinar) provide an array of visuomotor transformations (or motor schemas) that are reciprocally connected with motor circuitry in the premotor cortex and project to pontine motor nuclei in the brainstem. These how systems maintain a coordinated representation of currently executing motor schemas within an overall action frame, but the what system provides the schema-processing power only for the current field of attention, providing information to the how system about the function-dependent features of the required action. Thus a working memory is required, presumably in frontal cortex, to integrate the output of the what system, to yield a neural encoding of a network of schema instances, each tagged with a confidence level and various parameter values, and linked to the world frame of the organism. This STM (working memory) maintains a graphical representation of the world in which schema instances are not active processes, but are patterns that link a schema to a region of the world (not necessarily visible or within reach), and encode the current schema parameters, both confidence levels and perceptual or motor descriptors. This working memory can then mediate processes of competition and cooperation between schema instances, but the data-driven updating of a particular instance must await the shift of attention that can provide appropriate input to the active circuitry of its schema, which will then update the working memory for that schema instance accordingly. STM holds a representation of data relevant to a particular course of behavior, a memory that must be updated as the behavior proceeds or as unexpected contingencies arise. This ability underlies the capability of the system to combine explicit planning based on look-ahead evaluation of multiple alternatives with reactive planning that enables an autonomous system to act promptly should an unexpected emergency arise.

We may note here a controversy about the nature of AI fomented, for example by Brooks (1986), which sets an ethologically inspired heirarchy of levels of control, each biasing rather than replacing the one below it, in opposition to the classical view in AI of abstract operators applied to uniform representations. More subtly, the "neuralization of VISIONS" that we have just developed explains a complex cognitive function through the interaction of hard-wired schemas, implemented in specifically evolved circuitry, and abstract schemas that are developed through learning and experience in general-purpose circuitry. An intelligent system needs to combine the ability to react rapidly (jumping out of the way of an unexpected vehicle when crossing the street) with the ability to weigh alternatives abstractly (deciding on the best route to get to the next appointment).

In our proposed cognitive architecture, the STM is a working memory that holds a representation of data relevant to a particular course of behavior, a memory that must be updated as the behavior proceeds or as unexpected contingencies arise. This ability underlies the capability of the system to combine explicit planning based on lookahead evaluation of multiple alternatives with reactive planning, which enables an autonomous system to act promptly should an unexpected emergency arise. Our earlier analysis of neurological studies, however, makes it clear that the STM is not a unitary structure embodied in one brain region, but is distributed across many brain regions maintaining diverse partial representations of the organism, its world, and the state of their interactions. As Goodale and Milner (1992) have emphasized, this distribution reflects, among other things, a difference in the nature of the representations required for the identification of meaningful objects and the nature of those required for the visuomotor transformations underlying actions directed at those objects.

We, like Goodale and Milner, have called the dorsal (parietal) system the how system. But if we are in a complex situation, we must recognize which object it is appropriate to interact with, and for what purpose, before the how system can generate the appropriate motor parameters. If, then, object recognition is mediated by the ventral system, the question of how to act must be mediated through dynamic interaction of the ventral system with a variety of other areas. To take a simple example, suppose one sees two plums on a plate. The dorsal system is able to provide the visuomotor transformation to guide the arm and hand in picking up one of the plums, but it may be the task of the ventral system to recognize which plum is the riper and thus help determine the "focus of attention" of the dorsal system. In a more complicated situation, action is determined by goals and prior input as much as, if not more than, by current sensory input. This requires processes that appear to involve the prefrontal cortex, which indeed is known to play a crucial role in a variety of tasks involving working memory. Moreover, Fuster (1989), has reviewed the role of prefrontal cortex in processes that elaborate, store, and—during the course of behavior—update a plan of action. We hypothesize that, at each stage of action, prefrontal cortex, through its extensive system of reciprocal interconnections with parietal cortex (Goldman-Rakic 1987), focuses the attention of the dorsal system so that it may elaborate visually-based parameters for action. Again, through these reciprocal connections, parietal cortex can apprise the prefrontal system of the progress of motor execution as controlled by premotor cortex, as well as reporting any obstacles to execution of the current plan. This allows the prefrontal system to update the plan, through a mixture of off-line and reactive planning, as the task unfolds.

We thus argue that the planning, coordination, and execution of complex visually guided actions in primates requires a subtle interaction between the ventral and dorsal streams of visual processing in cortex (as well as interactions with critical subcortical visual areas such as the pretectum, the superior colliculus, and the accessory optic nuclei). Both the ventral and the dorsal streams have reciprocal connections, not only with each other, but also with important motor and memory-related regions of premotor and prefrontal cortex that have been implicated in the planning of action (for review, see Milner & Goodale, 1993; 1995). The nature of the complex interactions between these different regions we are only just beginning to understand. Nevertheless, it is clear that the anatomy and physiology of particular interactions are sufficiently detailed that a number of interactive models can be proposed that involve combination of off-line and reactive planning routines, extending the Dominey & Arbib (1992) model of prefrontal-parietal interactions subserving working memory for the control of sequential saccades.

In this paper, we argue that a satisfactory Cognitive Architecture should be a hybrid, in which specialized mechanisms for instinctive behavior provides a basis for, and function in tight interaction with, general-purpose mechanisms (e.g., in inferotemporal or prefrontal cortex) for a variety of acquired behaviors, including (but by no means limited to) those we classify as rational. The contrast between the inflexibility of frog visuomotor coordination and the flexibility of human visual perception and action makes explicit the contrast between those schema assemblages that are evolutionarily hard-wired into patterns of competition and cooperation between specific brain regions, and those which can, through multiple instantiations (both data and hypothesis driven) yield totally new forms to develop novel skills and to represent novel situations.

NOTES

[1]In later studies we will discriminate between a schema as a generic specification of a process and a schema instance as a particular application of that process. For example, in recognizing three chairs in a room, we may invoke three instances of the perceptual schema for chair recognition. In the examples discussed in this section, however, we have not found it necessary to invoke the distinction.

[2]The antepenultimate paragraph of Wittgenstein's *Tractatus Logico-Philosophicus* reads as follows: "My propositions serve as elucidations in the following way: anyone who understands me eventually recognizes them as nonsensical, when he has used them—as steps—to climb up beyond them. (He must, so to speak, throw away the ladder after he has climbed up it.)" Some readers of earlier drafts of this paper have read us as asserting the "nonsense" that the VISIONS architecture is a good computational framework for modeling neural mechanisms of action-oriented perception. But it would be better to say that it provides a computationally explicit rung on the ladder. The present section seeks to suggest the other steps that must be taken in building the desired cognitive architecture. When it is built, the ladder, including the review of the VISIONS system, can be, if not thrown away, at least safely stored in the historical toolshed. To make the point in another way, we may recall Warren McCulloch's dictum: "Don't bite my finger; look where I'm pointing."

REFERENCES

Arbib, M. A. (1981). Perceptual structures and distributed motor control. In V. B. Brooks (Ed.), *Handbook of physiology: The nervous system II. Motor control.* Bethesda, MD: American Physiological Society, pp. 1449–1480.

Arbib, M. A. (1989). *The metaphorical brain 2: Neural networks and beyond.* New York: Wiley-Interscience.

Arbib, M. A. (1992). Schema Theory. In S. Shapiro (Ed.). *The encyclopedia of artificial intelligence.* New York: Wiley-Interscience, pp. 1427–1443.

Arbib, M. A. & Caplan, D. (1979). Neurolinguistics must be computational. *Behavioral and Brain Sciences, 2,* 449–483.

Arbib, M. A., Caplan, D., & Marshall, J. C. (Ed.) (1982). *Neural models of language processes.* New York: Academic Press.

Arbib, M. A., Conklin, E. J., & Hill, J. C. (1987). *From schema theory to language.* New York: Oxford University Press.

Arbib, M. A. & House, D. H. (1987). Depth and detours: An essay on visually-guided behavior. In M. A. Arbib & A. R. Hanson (Eds.), *Vision, brain, and cooperative computation.* Cambridge, MA: A Bradford Book/MIT Press, pp. 129–163.

Arbib, M. A., Iberall, T., & Lyons, D. (1985). Coordinated control programs for control of the hands. In A. W. Goodwin & I. Darian-Smith (Eds.), *Hand function and the neocortex.* Berlin: Springer-Verlag, pp. 111–129.

Brooks, R. A. (1986). A robust layered control system for a mobile robot. *IEEE Journal of Robotics and Automation, RA-2,* 14–23.

Bushnell, M. C., Goldberg, M. E., & Robinson, D. L. (1981). Behavioral enhancement of visual responses in monkey cerebral cortex. I. Modulation in posterior parietal cortex related to selective attention. *Journal of Neurophysiology, 46,* 755–772.

Cobas, A. & Arbib, M. A. (1992). Prey-catching and predator-avoidance in frog and toad: Defining the schemas. *J. Theoretical Biol., 157,* 271–304.

Dominey, P. F. & Arbib, M. A. (1992). A cortico-subcortical model for generation of spatially accurate sequential saccades. *Cerebral Cortex, 2,* 153–175.

Draper, B. A., Collins, R. T., Brolio, J., Hanson, A. R., & Riseman, E. M. (1989). The schema system. *International Journal of Computer Vision, 2,* 209–250.

Fuster, J. M. (1989). *The prefrontal cortex: Anatomy, physiology, and neuropsychology of the frontal lobe* (second edition). New York: Raven Press.

Gentilucci, M., Castiello, U., Corradini, M. L., Scarpa, M., Umilta, C., & Rizzolatti, G. (1991). Influence of different types of grasping on the transport component of prehension movements. *Neuropsychologia, 29,* 361–378.

Goldman-Rakic, P. S. (1987). Circuitry of primate prefrontal cortex and regulation of behavior by representational memory. In V. B. Mountcastle, F. Plum, & S. R. Geiger (Eds.), *Handbook of physiology section 1: The nervous system, Volume V: Higher functions of the brain, Part 2* (pp. 373–417). Bethesda, MD: American Physiological Association.

Goodale, M. A. (1983). Vision as a sensorimotor system. In T. E. Robinson (Ed.). *Behavioral approaches to brain research* (pp. 41–61). Oxford University Press: New York.

Goodale, M. A. (1988). Modularity in visuomotor control: From input to output. In Z. Pylyshyn (Ed.), *Computational processes in human vision: An interdisciplinary perspective.* Norwood, NJ: Ablex.

Goodale, M. A., Meenan, J. P., Bülthoff, H. H., Nicolle, D. A., Murphy, K. J., & Racicot, C. (1994). Separate neural pathways for the visual analysis of object shape in perception and prehension. *Current Biology, 4,* 604–610.

Goodale, M. A. & Milner, A. D. (1992). Separate visual pathways for perception and action. *Trends in Neuroscience, 15,* 20–25.

Goodale, M. A., Milner, A. D., Jakobson, L. S., & Carey, D. P. (1991). A neurological dissociation between perceiving objects and grasping them. *Nature, 349,* 154–156.

Gould, S. J. (1989). *Wonderful life: The burgess shale and the nature of history.* New York: W. W. Norton & Company.

Hoff, B. & Arbib, M. A. (1992). A model of the effects of speed, accuracy and perturbation on visually guided reaching. In R. Caminiti (Ed.), *Control of arm movement in space: Neurophysiological and computational approaches.* Heidelberg, New York: Springer-Verlag.

Hoff, B. & Arbib, M. A. (1993). Models of trajectory formation and temporal interaction of reach and grasp. *Journal of Motor Behavior* (in press).

Humphrey, N. K. (1970). What the frog's eye tells the monkey's brain. *Brain Behavior and Evolution, 3,* 324–337.

Iberall, T., Bingham, G., & Arbib, M. A. (1986). Opposition space as a structuring concept for the analysis of skilled hand movements. In H. Heuer & C. Fromm (Eds.), *Generation and modulation of action patterns* (pp. 158–173). Berlin: Springer-Verlag.

Ingle, D. (1976). Spatial vision in anurans. In K. V. Fite (Ed.), *The amphibian visual system* (pp. 119–140). New York: Academic Press.

Jakobson, L. S. & Goodale, M. A. (1991). Factors influencing higher-order movement planning: A kinematic analysis of human prehension. *Experimental Brain Research, 86,* 199–208.

Jeannerod, M. & Biguer, B. (1982). Visuomotor mechanisms in reaching within extra-personal space. In D. J. Ingle, R. J. W. Mansfield, & M. A. Goodale (Eds.), *Advances in the analysis of visual behavior* (pp. 387–409). Cambridge, MA: The MIT Press.

Milner, A. D. & Goodale, M. A. (1993). Visual pathways to perception and action. In T. P. Hicks, S. Molotchnikoff, & T. Ono (Eds.), *Progress in brain research. The visually responsive neuron: From basic neurophysiology to behavior.* Amsterdam: Elsevier.

Millner, A. D., & Goodale, M. A. (1995). *The visual brain in action.* Oxford University Press: Oxford, p. 248.

Mishkin, M., Ungerleider, L. G., & Macko, K. A. (1983). Object vision and spatial vision: Two cortical pathways. *Trends in Neuroscience, 6,* 414–417.

Moran, J. & Desimone, R. (1985). Selective attention gates visual processing in the extrastriate cortex. *Science, 229,* 782–784.

Neisser, U. (1976). *Cognition and reality: Principles and implications of cognitive psychology.* San Francisco: W.H. Freeman.

Paulignan, Y., Jeannerod, M., MacKenzie, C., & Marteniuk, R. (1991a). Selective perturbation of visual input during prehension movements. 2. The effects of changing object size. *Experimental Brain Research, 87*, 407–420.

Paulignan, Y., MacKenzie, C., Marteniuk, R., & Jeannerod, M. (1991b). Selective perturbation of visual input during prehension movements. 1. The effects of changing object position. *Experimental Brain Research, 83*, 502–512.

Pylyshyn, Z. (1991). Opening remarks, Inaugural conference on cognitive architecture, Rutgers Center for Cognitive Science, October 31–November 2.

Riseman, E. M. & Hanson, A. R. (1987). A methodology for the development of general knowledge-based vision systems. In M. A. Arbib & A. R. Hanson (Eds.), *Vision, brain and cooperative computation* (pp. 285–328). Cambridge, MA: A Bradford Book/The MIT Press.

Rizzolatti, G., Gentilucci, M., & Matelli, M. (1985). Selective spatial attention: one center, one circuit, or many circuits? In M. I. Posner & O. S. M. Marin (Eds.), *Attention and Performance XI* (pp. 251–265). Hillsdale, NJ: Erlbaum.

Ungerleider, L. G. & Mishkin, M. (1982). Two cortical visual systems. In D. J. Ingle, M. A. Goodale, & R. J. W. Mansfield (Eds.), *Analysis of visual behavior.* Cambridge, MA: The MIT Press.

van Gisbergen, J. A. M., Robinson, D. A., & Gielen, S. (1981). A quantitative analysis of generation of saccadic eye movements by burst neurons. *J. Neurophysiol., 45*, 417–442.

Wang, D. L., Arbib, M. A., & Ewert, J. P. (1991). Dishabituation hierarchies for visual pattern discrimination in toads: A dialog between modeling and experimentation. In M. A. Arbib & J.-P. Ewert (Eds.), *Visual structures and integrated functions. Research notes in neural computing 3* (pp. 427–441). Springer-Verlag.

Weiskrantz, L. (1974). The interaction between occipital and temporal cortex in vision: an overview. In F. O. Schmitt & F. G. Worden (Eds.), *The neurosciences third study program* (pp. 189–204). Cambridge, MA: The MIT Press.

Weymouth, T. E. (1986). Using object descriptions in a schema network for machine vision. Ph.D. Thesis and COINS Technical Report 86–24, Department of Computer and Information Science, University of Massachusetts at Amherst.

Wing, A. M., Turton, A., & Fraser, C. (1986). Grasp size and accuracy of approach in reaching. *Journal of Motor Behavior, 18*, 245–260.

chapter 12

Speculations on Structure and Communication in Planning

Stacy C. Marsella
marsella@isi.edu
Information Sciences Institute
University of Southern California

INTRODUCTION

What relation do we expect between a computational model of cognition and some data it purports to explain? A minimal answer is that computational models are sought whose mapping from input to output explain or are coincident with some data.[1] If a model's relevance is simply in terms of its input and output than the task of constructing it is reasonably well-defined once we choose the computational framework, or stuff, in which to model, whether it be neural nets, production system, lisp, etc. Any framework that admits models that can behave like a finite automata will suffice in the confines of a finite set of data to be modelled. A researcher need only exercise a choice as to which framework to use, for all these frameworks provide sufficient flexibility in which to realize some fixed finite map between input and output pairs in some data.

However, the choice turns out to be critical if we are concerned with how a model achieves the map [Pylyshyn, 1984]. The task of modelling within a computational framework forces the researcher to fix additional aspects that govern how the framework realizes the map. Depending on the framework, these aspects could include the algorithm, input/output coding, settling parameters, etc. In other words, these aspects, such as the algorithm employed, are convolved with the computational framework.

In this paper, I come from a certain perspective to the question of how a computational model achieves a mapping from input to output. I am not too interested here in how researchers might exercise[2] free will in choosing a computational framework and model. Rather, it's the free will of the

235

subjects under study that interests me; their concern for how the model achieves the map.

This interest follows from what I consider to be a most striking phenomenon about human problem-solving capabilities, contrary to some prevailing wisdom,[3] its plasticity. Even in a situation as arcane as a problem-solving task contrived in some laboratory, subjects manage to muddle through. To a remarkable degree, humans have an ability to perform arbitrarily set-up computations, to form arbitrary maps.

Call this ability to attempt an arbitrary map "first order arbitrariness." In general, some arbitrary computation is realized by associating, or bringing together, processes or processes and data. We can roughly characterize approaches to computation by the degree to which they impose restrictions on how this bringing together occurs. So, for instance, some frameworks for modelling cognitive processes are quite liberal in this regard. They allow arbitrary data or processes to be associated in arbitrary ways. They allow a "second order arbitrariness," an arbitrariness in how the system is programmed. For example, the connectionism/backpropagation of the PDP model [Rumelhart, et al. 1986] and Soar's "elaboration phase" and "working memory" [Newell, 1990] exhibit this second order arbitrariness.

Of course, this second order arbitrariness is tied up with carefully thought-out conclusions about appropriate features of a cognitive architecture (e.g., content addressable memory) or the way in which the architecture is programmed (e.g., via "learning"). But it also runs counter to what would be called good programming practice in software design methodology. To wit, ease of programming, program repair, program modularity all depend on how arbitrary data/processes are associated. In writing programs, one does not bring arbitrary components together in arbitrary ways if there is to be any hope of keeping track of what the program is doing. Loosely, arbitrary approaches lead to arbitrary stories about how the program works. And a programmer cannot tell herself an arbitrary story when writing or modifying programs. As a consequence, this second order arbitrariness leads to an opacity as to how a program works, how processes and data are associated.

Likewise with regard to modelling human problem solving, I think models that admit such second order arbitrariness go too far.[4] The reason I think that concerns the nature of the plasticity that subjects exhibit, specifically the regularity and preferences they exhibit as well as the algorithms they appear to employ while problem solving, all points that will be touched upon in this paper.

The moral of the story I propose to tell is that perhaps we are studying a well-evolved system, one in which its apparent limitations are rather useful features. Like the paradox to be learned from software design methodology, far from being in conflict, a system's limitations may actually be key to its flexibility and the elegance of the algorithms it realizes.

One of the keys to seeing the beauty of a well-designed system where others might see limitations is to have the right "architectural bias," for, as we just mentioned, the computational framework is convolved with, and therefore taints, the algorithm. And indeed I will bring to the discussion what I consider to be fundamental architectural constraints on any complex intelligent system, constraints that *a priori* might legitimately be taken into consideration when developing cognitive models. Particularly, an intelligent system operating in the world is going to be a logically and physically distributed system, a system comprised of communicating processes. Therefore, in the context of that architectural reality, are their constraints on how arbitrary processes and data are associated appropriate constraints on the second order arbitrariness?

By analyzing the tasks of deriving and executing plans this paper hopefully will shed some light on these questions. A lot of what is discussed is not simply emergent from the modelling of the data. What I discuss is a speculative prelude to the collection of better data. However, data is discussed, albeit in a creative fashion. What I hope to do is to further understanding, mine if no one else's, as to what it might mean for the design of the architecture and the algorithms realized within it if we presume, as I think we must, that humans are very plastic, distributed, or communicating systems living in a distributed world.

PLANNING

As I started to write this paper, ostensively on planning, I realized there may be a problem of perspective. You and I may not agree on what planning is. I have read many times, and at times compliantly written, that agents, human or artificial, plan in order to derive some (partially) ordered set of actions which when applied to a starting state achieve some goals in some future state of the world. Of course, that is at best overly optimistic and to some extent misses the point. Only the most foolishly optimistic agent would expect to derive a complete successful plan. In defining a goal, deriving a plan, and executing it, an agent has only limited knowledge of future states of the world or what its goals and capabilities will be in those states. Further, an agent has limited computational resources (including time) with which to derive the plan. Nevertheless, the success of a plan when it is executed hinges on the accuracy of this knowledge and the agent's unrestricted ability to reason about it.

One response is simply to ignore the uncertainties that arise in executing and monitoring a plan that a planner may derive. This is essentially the classical Artificial Intelligence approach to planning. In the classical approach, planning is some partial function from problems to solutions, the latter being described as partially ordered sets (*posets*) of actions. The use of the term function is meant to be noncommittal concerning how it is implemented. Rather, the point is that a problem is fixed as an initial and goal-state pair, and, given such a pair, the planning returns or derives a poset of actions, any total order of which, when executed, transforms the initial state into a final state that satisfies the goal. This view of planning presumes the planner has a correct model of what the world, and the effect of its actions, will be when the plan is executed. This, in turn, enables the trivialization of the execution task. In truth however, there will be gaps in knowledge of current and future states of the world and the effects of other agencies in that world—gaps due to sensory, memory, and computational limitations. To compound the matter, the greater detail a plan has, the greater likelihood that specific aspects of the plan will fail due to an inability to predict unforeseen events and actors.

Another response is to ignore the uncertainties that arise from the variegated goals/plans themselves by adopting a purely reactive view of planning. In this view, agents are not functions from problems to complete plans. They don't plan at all but rather are some sort of stereotyped goal satisfaction machine that reacts to perceptual events.

But if agents do plan in order to solve novel problems and plan with some expectation vis-a-vis execution, albeit not with the expectation of simply achieving goals, why do they plan? What I assume in this paper is that agents plan in order to have a plan. Now, in my flippant way, I don't intend that to be a tautology. Agents need plans in order to reduce uncertainty. They plan in order to establish constraints as to what they might do, when to do it and how they must be prepared to perceive it, all to exercise some control over what may happen in the future, hopefully in accordance with their goals.[5] Thus, the uncertainty the planner deals with is both internal, for example, knowing how and when to act or perceive, as well as external, for example, exercising control over an uncertain future.

Specifically, I presume that an agent's plan and behavior are realized within a distributed system, the components of which are distinct, potentially temporally discontinuous, and therefore need to be coordinated. The need for coordination stems from the fact that an agent's planning behavior comprises logically distinct subtasks, such as plan derivation, execution, and monitoring. Plan derivation derives plans for solving some problem, plan execution performs the actions in the plan, and monitoring monitors the world, in part to determine whether the actions had the desired effect. Together, these subtasks constitute a task decomposition of the overall "planning behavior."

Since very distinct modalities are associated with derivation, execution, and monitoring, the task decomposition must be realized via a computational and architectural decomposition, at least to the extent that distinct processes (and devices) are involved in realizing these tasks. Furthermore, these processes must be coordinated, a requirement whose satisfaction is complicated by the fact that derivation, execution, and monitoring may temporally overlap to varying degrees. Plan derivation to some degree precedes execution and monitoring but it need not precede them in toto and in fact can be driven by them. Thus the coordination must be across time and have the ability to coordinate on partial realizations of the subtasks, if the system is to have some semblance of coherence over time.

The subtasks in this decomposition are not independent, for how one subtask is achieved impacts how another is achieved. In fact, the tasks are not only dependent in terms of what they compute but also in terms of how they compute. The nature in which the individual subtasks are realized impacts the particulars of their coordination, and, vice versa, the nature of the coordination impacts how the individual subtasks are realized.

The initial role of the plan in this mix of subtasks is to express a starting framework for bringing the distinct components of this distributed system into coordination, in a fashion consistent over time with the goals. However, the dynamics involved in achieving this coordination is important. One of the fundamental concerns in such a distributed system is the communication required to achieve coordination. Realizing effective communication is particularly difficult in a planning system, a system which over time is solving novel or arbitrary problems in dynamic worlds. So, for instance, the question is not only how to coordinate the subtasks but also how to simplify that coordination over time. There must be some kind of pressure to simplify, or minimize, the communication required for coordination. Taking these dynamics into account, the intent of planning is to exercise control over the various components of the system so as to achieve coordination more effortlessly and thereby reduce an agent's uncertainty about the behavior of the components, including the sensing of the world, which comprise it.

You see, as I told you, we probably don't have the same view about what planning is, probably to your benefit. Nevertheless several questions immediately come to mind. What is the evidence in support of, or in contradiction to, this view? Are there formal consequences to this view? In the rest of this paper, I will attempt to shed some light on these questions, or at least refine them. In the next two sections, I will address briefly some earlier research concerning the plan derivation subtask and its relation to human problem solving. I will then discuss the overall task decomposition both abstractly and in relation to some human data. I conclude with an attempt to bring the threads of this discussion into synchronization.

PLAN DERIVATION—DECOMPOSITION AND REGULARITY IN EFFECTIVE SEARCH

In contrast to some autonomic, reactive, or stimulus-response behavior, the distinguishing presumption of plan-based behavior is that the behavior is in some way motivated or mediated by a plan derived by the agent. Therefore, understanding planning requires us to address how plans are derived.

Within AI, planning research has explored many approaches to deriving plans. Most employ some form of decomposition; in particular, a recursive procedure that decomposes goals into easier to solve subgoals. By itself, decomposition addresses only part of the planning derivation task; any such procedure is incomplete since the information used to derive a solution to a subgoal, as well as the nature of the solution, depends very much on when in the overall planning the solution to the subgoal is derived and where in the overall plan it is executed. For instance, assume you want to take a trip in your car and one of the subgoals is to check the engine fluids. If "check fluids" is the first subgoal for which you derive a solution, you may simply choose to do the checking at home prior to driving off. However, perhaps you derive the solution to a "check fluids" subgoal after you plan the route to your destination and thereby notice that early on your route will take you right by the garage of a trusted mechanic. Thus you might decide alternatively to solve "check fluids" by having your mechanic do it, which in turn may impact how fast you drive during that initial leg of the journey, out of fear of damaging the car. In such a case, there is said to be a dependency between how subgoals are solved. And therefore the order in which you plan out subgoals as well as the order in which you execute their solutions can impact the plan that is derived.

To make these points more concrete, consider the simple problem in Figure 12.1. As we can see from this figure, the domain consists of a square grid of locations where some of these locations are occupied by tiles denoted by a letter A, B, or C. The primitive actions allowed in this domain consist of moving a single tile up, down, left, or right to an immediately adjacent location if that location is not already occupied by some other tile. The goal for this problem is the conjunction of two conditions on a goal state: both tiles A and B must be at the top of the grid as indicated.

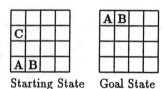

Starting State   Goal State

FIGURE 12.1.   An example sparse sliding tile problem.

There are several ways to solve this problem. That is important. If we are interested in subject's "free will," how they choose to solve problems, than we best give them a choice. Still, all the ways of solving the problem must deal in some way with the dependency caused by the placement of tile C. Whether tile C is moved or tiles A and B just go around it, interactions ensue between the primitive actions. Note that the dependency impacts the planning in two distinct ways—both in how the solutions to moving tiles A, B, and potentially C are planned as well as in the order the actions that realize the solutions are executed.

Solutions to this problem can be classified into three categories, the Go-Around, the Toggle, and the Clear-Out. We can loosely characterize these solutions as follows. The Go-Around involves movement of the goal tiles around obstructing tiles. The Clear-Out clears obstructing tiles from the paths of the goal tiles. The Toggle shuffles the obstructing tiles between the paths of the goal tiles. To exemplify, Figure 12.2 depicts a Go-Around, a Toggle, and a Clear-Out solution to the example problem. Each solution is denoted by arrows that depict the paths taken by the various tiles. Note these are quite different solutions with differing sets of actions and differing pattern of interactions between actions, interactions in the sense that an action may enable or potentially inhibit another action. Therefore, not all alternative possible orders of the set of actions in a solution also realize a solution. In the Go-Around, the pattern of interactions are such that various actions that move tile A must precede various actions that move tile B. Roughly, the reverse is true for the Toggle, all three moves of tile B must precede the last two moves of tile A. Finally, in the Clear-Out, tile C is cleared out first and the actions that move tiles A and B need not be ordered with respect to each other.

Given that the differing solutions differentially impact the plan derivation task, the question arises as to whether plan derivation should take a prescriptive or postdictive approach during derivation to handle these differences. Briefly, this is an issue within AI because unexpected interactions may impact the search for a plan and require costly backtracking over the plan search. The fact that differing solutions have differing patterns of interaction suggests that a prescriptive approach is required to avoid unexpected interactions and the cost of backtracking. Nevertheless, the tradi-

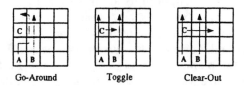

Go-Around   Toggle   Clear-Out

FIGURE 12.2.   Different solutions to example problem.

tional AI approaches have been mainly postdictive. In contrast, the REAPPR planning system and its derivative (Bresina, Marsella, & Schmidt, 1987, Marsella, 1993) explored a prescriptive approach. An analysis of this prescriptive approach can be found (Marsella, 1993). Some formal results from that work will be used here.

However, distinct from the efficiency issue, additional data is to be addressed if the concern is to elucidate human planning behavior. When humans solve such sparse tile problems, they typically exhibit considerable regularity. In particular, once subjects hit upon a clearing-out approach,[6] they tend to stick with it, transferring the approach to similar problems; for example, tile problems with different numbers of blocking tiles at different locations (Schmidt, et al. 1986). And, consistently, when subjects use a clear out, they will first clear nongoal tiles from the paths that the goal tiles will take. And, just as important, subjects don't always use the same approach on the same problem.

Certainly, there are many ways to characterize such behavior. But we need to do more than simply characterize its regularity. We need to characterize the planner's ("subject's") ability to (structurally) exhibit this regularity in problem solving and the ability to acquire this regularity (Marsella, 1993). Both issues are critical, given that testing of behavior is over some finite set of problems. For, given some set of problems amenable to this Clear-Out strategy, it is trivial to weakly characterize the planner's ability by defining a function that is observational adequate—a function that maps problem descriptions to solutions that are consistent with a Clear-Out strategy for those problems. Yet such a weak characterization fails to provide a principled account as to how the observationally adequate function arises or even how to define the sets of problems and solutions that constitute the domain and range of the function. Those sets are not *a priori* fixed for the planner, or the planner's hardware. Further, if we accept a weak characterization, then the changes to the function's domain over time have to be modelled, for the regularity a subject exhibits is not static—limited to behavior on some problem that is consistent with a specific solution or specific strategy.

What is needed is a characterization for the class of Clear-Out solutions that satisfies a kind of descriptive adequacy (Chomsky, 1965). In particular, a characterization that is not some ad hoc description of the hardware that is either opaque to the planner or fixed for the planner. The description is available to (penetrable by) the subject in its planning. This is evidenced by the fact that subjects can exhibit solutions that are not consistent with varying strategies and, quite simply, a subject can be successfully informed. The description the planner possesses must be of a form that the planner can plan in accordance with or at least can employ to guide its acquisition. Of course, this claim plops me down into an argument of longstanding in cognitive studies (which I won't replay here) and also breaks company with traditional approaches to planning in AI research (which I also won't replay here). But in fact this is not so controversial if we accept that people plan. By its very nature planning presumes some degree of transparency.

As previously stated, subjects exhibit considerable regularity when solving tile problems. Specifically, they tend eventually to use the clearing out approach and do so across different problems. They also tend first to clear nongoal tiles from the paths that the goal tiles will take. This suggests that subjects distinguish, in kind, blocking tiles from goal tiles. And since blocking tiles are moved first, the movement of goal tiles must be differentiated from movement of blocking tiles, grouped in some fashion, and temporally ordered with respect to each other. Finally, blocking tiles are not *a priori* specified, since knowing which tiles are blocking and where they can be cleared to requires knowledge of the paths that goal tiles will take.

A strategy that satisfies such requirements can be described in terms of the three components depicted in Table 12.1. First, there is a decomposition of the problem into two subproblems. One subproblem consists of planning the paths for A and B tiles and the second subproblem involves the planning to clear those paths. Secondly, note that it is necessary to plan the paths for tiles A and B prior to planning for the blocking tiles (e.g., tile C in Figure 12.1) because what constitutes a blocking tile and the location to which it must be moved depends on how the A and B subproblems are solved. Thus an ordering on the planning of subproblems must be imposed. Finally, the clearing of the paths must be executed before the step that moves tiles A and B along these paths. That fact comprises the third component of the strategy, the execution order.

There are several significant features to this strategy. It has generality, in the sense that it is not a description of a particular solution to a particular problem but rather is a high-level description of solutions to a class of problems. This high-level description is realized by forming groups and ordering their planning and execution. Specifically, the strategy involves decomposition of the problem, along with specification of the order in which the derived subgoals are planned and executed. These are distinct specifications; the order in which the subproblems are planned must be

TABLE 12.1.

The Clear-Out Strategy

- Decomposition:
  - —Subproblem 1: Plan straight upwards paths for tiles A and B.
  - —Subproblem 2: Plan the clearing of those paths.
- Plan Derivation Order: Plan Subproblem 1 before Subproblem 2.
- Execution Order: Execute solution to Subproblem 2 before Subproblem 1.

---

the reverse of the order in which the solutions to those subproblems are executed. The knowledge of these orderings must be explicitly stated as part of the strategy in order to directly and correctly realize a Clear-Out solution. Also, the planning of the clearing subproblem depends on a description of how the solution to the "A and B" subproblem is planned out. A description of the paths taken is required, not just where tiles A and B end up.

Imposing Orders on Hierarchical Groupings: the HPO Model

The above representation of a Clear-Out strategy has considerable structure, including decomposition into subproblems and orderings on those subproblems. In this section, I try to be more precise about the implications that structure has for plan derivation and execution.

Decomposition into subproblems logically denotes a conjunction. In this Clear-Out example, the goal can be achieved if the paths of the Goal tiles are derived "and" those paths are cleared. If, more generally, we presume that subproblems can be further decomposed, as is the case in AI, then the history of such recursive decompositions into conjunctions of subproblems (subsubproblems, etc.) can be represented hierarchically, as what is termed an AND tree. Each node in an AND tree is a (sub)problem with the children of a node representing the decomposition of the (sub)problem.

Therefore, representing the realization of a Clear-Out strategy as described in Table 12.1 directly result in one node (presumably the root) in an AND tree, representing the overall problem. The direct children of that node would be the two subproblems denoted in Table 12.1 with their children representing how those subproblems were solved. However, by itself the AND tree is not sufficient to describe the Clear-Out strategy in general terms. We need to settle on some formalism for the knowledge represented in the strategy for the order in which the planner is to derive the solutions to the subproblems and the order in which to execute those solutions.

Partial Orders

Ordering knowledge is typically described via a partial order relation. The partial order relation models the possible ways to order a set, for instance, the possible ways of ordering a set of actions so they achieve some goal. More carefully, a partial order is a binary relation P (set of ordered pairs) on a set A which is reflexive, antisymmetric, and transitive. We write $a \prec b$, if $(a, b) \in P$. A partial order in which every pair of elements is comparable is called a total order, sequence, or chain (depending on mood). A partial order in which no pair of elements is comparable, so that P is the empty relation, is called an antichain.

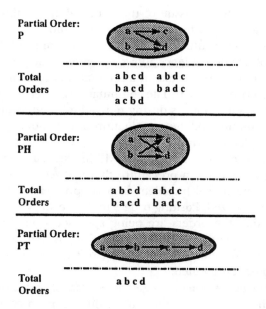

Partial Order:
P

Total Orders

a b c d	a b d c
b a c d	b a d c
a c b d	

Partial Order:
PH

Total Orders

a b c d	a b d c
b a c d	b a d c

Partial Order:
PT

Total Orders   a b c d

FIGURE 12.3.   Some partial orders.

For example, in Figure 12.3, various partial orders are depicted that model alternative ways to order four specific actions denoted by the letters a, b, c, and d. The directed edges describe the partial order relation. The partial order for the graph at the top of Figure 12.3 is $[(a, c)(a, d)(h, d)]$. The partial order relation describes the precedence for the execution of actions. So in the top graph, action c must be executed after the execution of action a. Note that a partial order relation is closed under transitivity but the transitive edges will not be drawn here.[7] An equivalent way of describing a partial order is to list all possible sequences, or total orders, of the elements of the set consistent with the partial order. Figure 12.3 also depicts the set of total orders consistent with each partial order.

In particular, note that the top and middle graphs in Figure 12.3 are similar except that the top graph is consistent with an additional total order, since the additional relation in the middle graph, (b, c), rules out the total order a c b d. The bottom graph in Figure 12.3 is totally ordered or, in other words, only one total order is consistent with it. Note also a partial order provides a compact way to represent alternative orderings when there are numerous alternative orders.

Hierarchical Partial Orders

To reiterate, the Clear-Out strategy specifies both an order on plan derivation and an order on execution. The orders are central to the generality of the strategy. Besides the issue of the expressibility of this strategy, the intent behind the orders is to control planning without the reevaluation or retraction of previous planning decisions. The expression of such knowledge on subproblem dependency allows a planner to be prescriptive about making choices that correctly take into account subproblem dependencies as the planner derives the plan. The computational intent is to avoid either the reordering of subproblems during derivation, the reordering of components of the solution, or the reevaluation of dependency between subproblems as the plan is derived.

However, that knowledge is employed within a search procedure that we are presuming is recursive, a procedure that realizes a solution by recursively decomposing a (sub)problem into subproblems until "primitive" problems are recognized. Positing orders in this recursive context leads to the constraint that the orders are being specified over the equivalence classes realized by the recursive decomposition, as denoted by the AND tree's hierarchical structure. This ends up restricting the class of partial orders that can be represented.

To simplify the exposition of this restricted class of partial orders, it's useful to discuss them in terms of the artifact the recursion creates, the AND tree. For example, consider an AND tree, consisting of a set of nodes N, each node annotated with partial orders on planning and execution. For simplicity, let us first consider just one of the annotations, say the execution order—the same structural characteristics hold for the planning order, although it need not be the same order. Given any internal node, N0, let P0 be the partial order on execution *realized* by the annotated subtree rooted at N0 and let E0 be the partial order on execution *annotated* in N0. Thus E0 is a partial order on N0's children and, by construction, P0 can be expressed by the *composition* graph $P0 = E0[P1, \ldots, Pk]$, where $P1 \ldots Pk$ are the partial orders realized by the subtrees rooted at $N1 \ldots Nk$ respectively, the children of N0. In such a graph, E0 is termed an external factor and the $P1 \ldots Pk$ are internal factors (Golumbic, 1980). The composition graph is formed as follows, for every edge (Ni, Nj) in E0, make each vertex of Pi adjacent to each vertex of Pj. Because of the hierarchical nature of the AND tree, a similar partial order composition can be done for the $P1 \ldots Pk$ and moreover it can be done for any internal node in the tree. In this way, the AND tree expresses a hierarchically annotated partial order.

The restriction on the possible orders that can be represented this way is related to the depth of the tree, the deeper the tree, the greater the restriction. For, instance, the partial order that was depicted earlier, at the top of Figure 12.3 can be represented only in a tree of depth 1. To remove this relation to depth of the tree (or recursion depth), let's presume that any node's partial order annotation (the external factors) are specified using a representation language that is also hierarchical or embedded. That is, it has the form *ordering-scheme* = (*order* $term_1 \ldots term_k$), where order is either *seq* (a linear order, or chain, of $term_1 \ldots term_k$) or *par* (the $term_1 \ldots term_k$ are unordered, i.e., an antichain) and where each $term_i$ is either a child node in the tree or any embedded ordering-scheme.[8]

Positing this constraint enables a certain uniformity between the hierarchical nesting of the tree and the hierarchical nesting of the representation external factors (the Ei). So, for instance, any partial order that can be represented in this scheme can be represented in a depth one AND tree or in a tree where all the external factors are depth one—either a chain or antichain.

Not every partial order can be represented in this hierarchical fashion, which is to say equivalently that not every partial order has such a recursive graph decomposition. I call a partial order that can be represented as such a *hierarchical partial order.*

Now, an annotated AND tree is an AND tree in which each node in the tree has a unique node label and each interior node (nonterminal node) has a planning partial order annotation and an execution partial order annotation. Annotations are of the form (order-rel $term_1 \ldots term_n$), where order-rel is either a total order (seq) or an antichain (par). The BNF of these annotations is presented in Table 12.2. The child node labels in an annotation are drawn from the set of node labels that name the immediate children of the node at which the annotation occurs, under the constraint that each child node label occurs exactly once in the annotation. That is to say, there is a fixed one-to-one and onto mapping between child node labels in the annotation and the actual children of the node that is being annotated.

Considering just one of the annotations at each node in the tree, either the planning or execution annotation, then the resulting collection of annotations realize what I call a HPO, as follows. Replace each child node label in the root node's annotation with the annotation at that child in the plan. Repeat this replacement with any new labels until only terminal nodes remain. This realizes a restricted form of partial order decomposition structure of the form P0 = E0(P1 . . . Pn) where the P1 . . . Pn are also hierarchical partial orders and E0 is an ordering relation that is either a chain or antichain over the set P1 . . . Pn. Note this decomposition should

TABLE 12.2.
BNF for Planning and Execution Order Annotations

{*order annotation*}: = ({*order-rel*} $term_1 \ldots term_n$)

{*order-rel*}: = *seq* | *par*

$term_i$: = {*order annotation*} | {*child node label*}

not be confused with the plan trees decomposition since the Pi of this decomposition can represent either a node label or an embedded annotation. We fix the convention that the HPO on the singleton set x is written (seq x). Also the convention for graph decompositions is to write them as E0(P1 . . . Pn). We follow that convention when we talk of graph decompositions but you should note that the syntax of the plan node annotations place the parentheses around the entire annotation.

Note we can always represent a HPO, P0 = E0(P1 . . . Pn) as P0 = E0'(Pa Pb) where Pa = Ea(P1. . . Pi) and Pb = Eb(Pi + 1 . . . Pn), $1 < i < n$, where Ea, Eb, and E0' are all chains (i.e., seq) if E0 is a chain, or are all antichains (i.e., par) if E0 is an antichain. Nothing restricts the level of the HPO at which this restructuring occurs, and thus HPO can always be restructured so that every decomposition is binary.

In subsequent sections, additional characteristics of HPOs will be discussed when needed. A more careful analysis can be found in (Marsella, 1993).

Characterizing Plan Derivation

The fact that an HPO on a set A recursively partitions elements of that set follows from the fact that their specification reifies a desire to specify strategies within a plan derivation framework that uses recursive decomposition. With the encoding of a strategy, especially within a decomposition framework, there can be considerable benefit to the efficiency of the problem solving search, as discussed in (Marsella, 1993).

However, search efficiency was not the central focus here, regularity in deriving solutions to problems is the focus. The main point to be gleaned from this discussion concerns how to express the regularity exhibited by subjects so that the derivation of the plan is suitably controlled. The form in which the strategy was expressed presumed a problem solver that could make reference to, and control, its own planning and execution subproblems. This is a novel, rather perspicacious view of planning. To borrow terminology from the introduction, the strategy gives the planner access to a story about its own planning and execution when solving the Clear-Out. At the same time, that access is tightly controlled because the description is at a level of abstraction controlled by the decomposition. Thus the story is not excessively convoluted by details of how the subproblems are solved, rather it is a general story that is applicable across problems.

The regularity imposed in how a plan is derived also impacts the structure of the plan. Consistent with the decomposition, hierarchy is critical to realizing a naming regimen over parts of a plan. This abstraction hierarchy allowed the simple algebraic-like BNF for HPOs. At the same time, an HPO's par annotation allow discontinuous constituents in the solution string. These two features end up being useful when we link it up to a subsequent point, that the structure of a plan impacts how it is communicated.

PLANS, STATES OF THE WORLD, AND MONITORING

It has been reported (Schmidt, et al. 1986) that in solving sparse sliding tile problems, human subjects exhibit a preference for solutions consistent with a Clear-Out strategy. Specifically, once subjects exhibit Clear-Out solutions, they persist in exhibiting them on problems presented subsequently that are amenable to a Clear-Out approach. In the previous section, the need for, and benefit of, expressing this regularity was the basis for arguing that intelligent agents (human and machine) must have something akin to a hierarchical and modular representation that drives their plan derivation. However, the sliding tile domain typically admits many solutions to any particular problem and many different orderings of the actions in a solution. To appreciate why a specific solution preference might exhibit itself, it is useful to characterize the structure of alternative solutions.

Partial Order Structure and the State Space

Figure 12.4 reiterates the simple problem presented earlier in Figure 12.1. Figure 12.5 reiterates the three different kinds of solutions to the example problem, the Go-Around, the Toggle, and the Clear-Out, as first depicted in Figure 12.2.

Figure 12.6 depicts various partial order relations on the execution of the three solutions. The nodes or vertices in these graphs represent actions

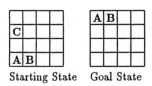

Starting State   Goal State

FIGURE 12.4.   An example sparse sliding tile problem.

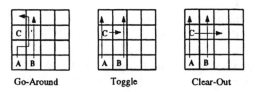

Go-Around   Toggle   Clear-Out

FIGURE 12.5.   Three solutions to example problem.

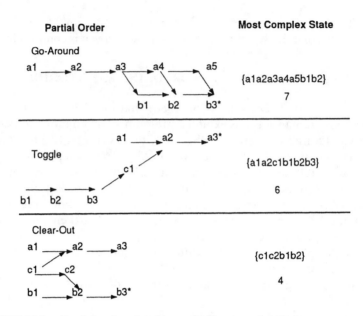

FIGURE 12.6.   Partial orders for three solutions.

and the labels on the nodes denote the actions; for example, a1 signifies the first movement of tile A. As before, the directed edges between nodes represent direct precedence; transitive edges have not been drawn. Thus, for instance, in the "Go Around" solution, action a1 directly enables a2 and a3 directly enables b1. A path from a1 and b1 in the Go-Around means that a1 must precede b1. Next to each partial order in Figure 12.6 is a field titled "Most Complex State." For the time being, ignore that field, we will return to it presently.

So for the Go-Around, the first poses (partially ordered set) depicted in Figure 12.6 represents all possible total orders (sequences) of the specific five motions of tile A and three motions of tile B that achieve the goal. There are five such total orders, specifically:

a1 a2 a3 a4 a5 b1 b2 b3
a1 a2 a3 a4 b1 a5 b2 b3
a1 a2 a3 a4 b1 b2 a5 b3
a1 a2 a3 b1 a4 a5 b2 b3
a1 a2 a3 b1 a4 b2 a5 b3

The second graph depicts the Toggle partial order. This is the optimal solution in terms of the number of actions. This partial order also represents five total orders, specifically:

b1 b2 b3 c1 a1 a2 a3
b1 b2 b3 a1 c1 a2 a3
b1 b2 a1 b3 c1 a2 a3
b1 a1 b2 b3 c1 a2 a3
a1 b1 b2 b3 c1 a2 a3

Finally, the partial order of the eight actions comprising the Clear-Out is represented, where the second motion of tile C is constrained to occur before the second motion of tile B—this is what distinguishes the Clear-Out from the Toggle. By a significant margin, the Clear-Out realizes the weakest partial order, in the sense that more total orders are consistent with it, a total of 140.

Solutions with weak partial orders are significant because they allow freedom in how actions can be grouped and ordered with respect to each other. In the Clear-Out poset of Figure 12.6, tiles A and B can moved in any order once tile C is cleared. For instance, tile A can be moved to its goal first (i.e., the sequence of actions **c1c2a1a2a3b1b2b3**), tile B can be moved to the goal first (**c1c2b1b2b3a1a2a3**), or the movements of tiles A and B can be grouped (**c1c2a1b1a2b2a3b3**).

In addition, we can also consider what the structure of the resulting poset implies about the states of the world in which the poset's actions can be executed. For every action in the poset, there is a subset of possible states in which that action can be executed in a fashion consistent with the poses. Again consider the Clear-Out poset of Figure 12.6. Action **a2** can be executed in any state resulting from a sequence of actions executed in the initial state that includes the execution of actions a1 and c1 but excludes a2 and a3. Let's denote states using the prefix of actions that create them. In particular, { } is the initial state of the world, a state in which either actions **a1, b1,** or **c1** is executable and {a1} is the state that results from performing action **a1**. Whereas {a1} is some (partial) model of the state of the world, no commitment is being made to how that model is realized. Specifically, the model should not be confused with its naming convention, "{a1}," that actually informs us which action occurred that transformed { } into {a1}.

Now for each set of states that some action can be executed in, let's pick a representative, or candidate, state from the set. An action's *candidate state* is the state labeled with those actions that **must** be executed. Note this is not necessarily unique, since the states {a1c1} and {c1a1} both satisfy the "must" criteria for action a2 in the Clear-Out poset. Yet, due to the partial order, there is a single set of actions that *must* precede an action, even though in terms of the state set there may be different orderings of that set of actions. In such a case we can safely pick one ordering, under some criteria as lexicographical order, and that criteria can be uniformly applied to any other action.[9] The set comprised of all the candidate states is called the *candidate set*. The candidate set provides a way to root the partial order in world states.

Consider how the structural differences in the partial orders of Figure 12.6 impact their candidate states. Clearly, the partial orders differ according to the nature of the states in their respective candidate sets. In particular, define the number of actions in a state s bracket description to be its *projection complexity*, a rough measure of how far into the "future," in terms of action sequence length, a planner must reason in generating the plan. Similarly, the projection complexity of an action is the projection complexity of its candidate state and the projection complexity of a poset is the maximal projection complexity of its member actions.

In Figure 12.6, the most complex candidate state is noted to the right of each partial order and the corresponding action is marked with an asterisk. Under this metric, the Clear-Out is notably better, as we would expect given its weaker partial order.

Discussion: The Connection Between Actions and States

Planning does not happen in a stateless vacuum. In this section, that is essentially the only assumption being made about how solutions are generated, that they are generated in some form and that form permits the relationship between action and state to be considered.

The need for states should not be contentious. Assuming an agent has the ability to plan, to sense, to act and to react, or even just to sense and to learn to react, it must reason over possible plans of actions. To generate these plans of actions and to monitor their execution, a planner must reason explicitly or implicitly about (partial) states of the world and thus have a concern for how the structure of its plan of actions maps to the states of the world it posits and senses. This is so even if an agent is just sensing and reacting, for its current reaction must be predicated on what its future reactions will be and at some level the space of action sequences will have to be considered.[10]

The various classical and reactive algorithms in AI planners employ very different approaches for generating and/or reasoning about these states. Actual states may be explicitly generated (e.g., [Fikes, Hart, Nilsson, 1971]), or implicitly generated (e.g., [Sacerdoti, 1977, Chapman, 1987, Tate, 1977, Schmidt, 1986]), or may even be compiled into some form of behavioral or reactive plan (e.g., [Agre & Chapman, Schoppers, 1987]). However, irrespective of how plans are derived, the issue is thus raised as to the structure of actions and world states that a planning agent posits. Whatever modelling framework is employed to describe such an agent, they must reason about actions and the (partial) states of the world in which the actions will be executed.

Therefore, we have taken the view here that we can structurally characterize the solution via the poset that is implicit in a solution and consider the relation between the poset and the states of the world. This allowed us to question the nature of the map between these action posets and states of the world, and to raise this question while ignoring specifics of how the planner generates the solution.

Stripping out the states of the world makes more apparent how various solution structures differ with respect to the modelling of intermediate states of the world. Two related differences were identified in the various solution types subjects exhibit in solving the problem of Figure 12.4, the weakness of partial order and projection complexity. However, this is simply the start. It is with the analysis of planning as a behavior realized in a distributed system that these differences take on added significance and bring us back to the question of how plans are derived.

COMMUNICATION: A DISTRIBUTED AGENT IN A DISTRIBUTED WORLD

Agents that operate in the world, operate in a world distributed across an agent's own internal faculties or processes, distributed across other agents or forces, as well as distributed across internal processes and perception of external processes. This distributed quality impacts the behavior of the agent. In particular, as a consequence an agent cannot plan or compose behavior based on some global analysis of this distributed system. There is no homunculus that has such knowledge. Nevertheless, agents must plan. The impossibility of planning is the best argument for why it is necessary. It behooves an agent to find mappings between these distributed components, mappings that exhibit sufficient regularity to allow agents to act effectively in the world. The role of the plan is to provide a framework under which the processes that give rise to behavior are coordinated or at least have individual behaviors whereby the overall system adapts or learns how to become coordinated in an uncertain world.

The Clear-Out strategy discussed in the previous section gives preliminary witness to the utility of coordination. The strategy worked because it provided a framework by which the plan derivation task's generation of the subproblem solutions could be ordered distinct from the execution task's ordering on the execution of the solutions. That coordination enabled communication of information such as the path that needed to be clear. However, the coordination of each task was based on a hierarchical structure fixed across derivation and execution tasks that nevertheless posed little direct relation on the coordination between the tasks, other than the presumption that derivation precedes execution. Clearly however, the coordination must be more sophisticated, particular if we factor in the task of monitoring the world. This section considers the issue of coordination, or more precisely communication, between tasks such as derivation and execution, assuming from the start that derivation, execution, and monitoring are distinct processes that must coordinate their behavior.

An Aside on Communicating Processes

Given distinct processes, there is a technical question as to how the processes share information and coordinate their behavior. Two traditional approaches are via shared memory or via some communication across a channel. However, I presume that shared memory is not a viable approach. One reason for such a presumption is that there exist purely logical arguments to be made against a shared memory approach, arguments that are not specific to the planner's "hardware."[11]

A classic example in point involves two (or more) processes trying to increment the value of a variable in shared memory by one (Hoare, 1985). Call these processes **A** and **B**. Both processes read the variable's value and then write the incremented value back to shared memory. Thus, in total four subprocesses comprise **A** and **B** and certain interleaves of those four subprocesses interfere with each other. For instance, if they proceed in the following order:

1. **A** reads the value of the shared variable
2. **B** reads the value of the shared variable
3. **A** writes the incremented value to the shared variable
4. **B** writes the incremented value to the shared variable

The final effect of these four steps is that the variable is incremented by one, not by two. The lesson is that accesses to a shared memory have to be tightly controlled to avoid such interferences. This leads to a concomitant negative impact on the concurrency of associated processes, and, for instance, the real time behavior or interrupt response time. In fact, when it is utilized, the trend in shared memory is to realize it as a communication.

Where does this leave us? I will assume planning behavior is realized via communication between distinct processes. This position has formal consequences, which I believe can be shown to correlate with what can observed in the behavior of human agents.

Logical Constraints on Plan Communications

Let us consider the nature of the communication between derivation, execution, and monitoring under the pattern of linkage depicted in Figure

12.7. Roughly, the derivation task communicates what actions can be executed, monitoring determines whether those actions are in fact executable in the current state of the world, and execution performs the actions. The significance of this linkage will become clear as we proceed, but the concern here is not only the pattern of linkage. The logical characterization of the communications over the links, or communication channels, is also important.

In characterizing the communication, the terms *presumptions* and *constraints* will be used. Presumptions are *a priori*, fixed characterizations of how this thought experiment is being set up. Constraints, on the other hand, are essentially desirable criteria for the communication to work well. In either case, what follows is not intended to be an argument that this is the only way to relate planning tasks. In fact, it is a deliberate simplification since it ignores very difficult questions about the complex ways that planning, execution, and world monitoring are contingent upon one another. The purpose is to lay out one alternative simply enough so that we can begin to understand the implications of assuming a distributed system behavior.

Derivation and Execution

Let us start by presuming that the derivation task communicates to the execution task what action to execute. That is:

- Execution Presumption: The execution task needs to be told which actions to execute and when to execute them.

Note that this is a logical or qualitative constraint on communication as opposed to quantitative or bandwidth constraint.

We will also presume that:

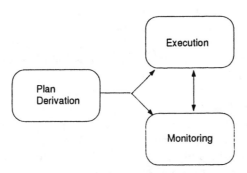

FIGURE 12.7.   The communication linkage between processes.

- Knowledge Presumption: Partial orders characterize the planner's knowledge of which actions to execute and are therefore the basis for what it communicates to the execution task.

This characterization of the knowledge is not meant as a commitment to how the planner derives orderings on actions. Rather, it's simply a statement that overall behavior of the plan derivation task, as a black box communicating with other tasks in a distributed system, is consistent with this knowledge presumption. This is an important distinction. For instance, we may not want to commit to a presumption that plan derivation creates a complete plan and without a complete plan, there cannot be the fixed set (of actions) required by the definition of a partial order. Nevertheless, even if partial orders are assumed just to characterize the communication, they still represent a restriction on what is communicated. In particular, a partial order's antisymmetry and the fact that the partial order is over a fixed set both impose a restriction on the communication, albeit I expect, a useful one in a distributed system.

There are also several constraints that we may want to impose on the relation between planning and execution. One is that the execution task can potentially exhibit every behavior entailed by the plan. Note that this is essentially a constraint that insures that no behavioral uncertainty arises from the communication.

- Behavioral Constraint: The communication between planning and execution must potentially support all possible behaviors entailed by the plan.

In fact, we may also impose a more stringent constraint, that the communication realizes a relation between planning and execution such that the execution task can recover from the communication exactly the knowledge entailed in the plan.

- Knowledge Constraint: The communication between planning and execution must support the recovery of the plan by the execution task.

Note that such a constraint opens the possibility of the execution task decoupling from the derivation task.

Monitoring Action Execution

In addition to the communication between plan derivation and execution. there is assumed to be communication between derivation and monitoring. Based on the information provided by the derivation task, the monitor must determine whether the actions prescribed are truly executable in the world. We make the assumption here that the derivation task communicates the same information to monitoring that it communicates to the execution task:

- Monitoring Presumption: The monitoring task needs to be told which actions to monitor for.

However there are different constraints on execution and monitoring. Whereas the execution task must know what to do next, the monitoring task must know what to "look for" next. What must be monitored depends very much on the partial order. Particularly, if the set of actions communicated to monitoring have differences in terms of the states in which they can be executed, monitoring must derive how to distinguish states accordingly; for instance, by acquiring more complete knowledge of the partial order from plan derivation. In addition, the distinctive characteristics of those distinguished states must be monitored so that they, in fact, can be distinguished. Finally, monitoring must communicate to execution not just that the current actions are executable but which action. In other words, the pattern of communications gets far more complex than initially suggested. To simplify this task, we can propose a rather strong simplification on monitoring for the currently executable actions such that the states in which they can be executed are identical:

- Monitoring Knowledge Constraint: Ideally, the communication between plan derivation and monitoring is such that for a set of actions, α, which are communicated by the plan as currently executable (but therefore, have not yet been executed), the set of states in which an action can be executed is identical across actions in α.

Under this constraint, monitoring need not uniquely determine for each action in the set communicated by the plan whether it is executable. They can be monitored for jointly and it can be left to execution as to the order of their execution.

General Constraints

Ideally, tasks in a distributed system should be decoupled as much as possible. If the distributed system is cooperating via communication, that in effect means it is desirable to minimize the communication under some qualitative or quantitative measure.

- Minimization constraint: All things being equal, the communication between tasks should be as minimal as possible.

Similarly, it is desirable to reduce the overhead associated with maintaining the communication.

- Simplicity constraint: All things being equal, the communication between tasks should be as simple as possible in terms of the overhead of both generating and interpreting the communication.

These constraints are obviously not an exhaustive consideration. For instance, we might also want to posit conditions on the behavior of the overall planning system if part of the system fails. However, this discussion suffices for the discussion that follows.

Discerning Implications

Now, assume we have a planning system comprised of just two tasks, one that derives a plan of execution and another that actually controls its execution, realized as two communicating processes. In other words, the former is essentially a reasoning component and the latter is some form of intelligent controller for an activator or motor unit. In addition, there is a communication channel by which those two tasks communicate. This leaves out the monitoring issue, but we will get back to that. The two diagrams in Figure 12.8 depict two different instances of such a task arrangement. On the left in each diagram is the plan derivation subtask/subprocess along with the partial order that it must communicate to the execution task. The execution task is depicted on the right. In between, the arrows depict the communication between the tasks, each arrow being labeled with the content of the communication. Consistent with the Execution Presumption, the plan process communicates to the executor which actions can currently be executed and the executor communicates which action it just executed. With respect to the temporal ordering of these communications, time flows downward. Finally on the far right is depicted the plausible inferences that the executor could make about the original partial order given the history of the communications. If the communication history does not support a unique inference, the ambiguity is marked by a question mark, with the alternative inferences enclosed in a box.

Consider first the top diagram. The communication starts with the plan process communicating that either action **a** or **b** can be executed. The executor reports back that it made the choice of action **b**, while inferring that **a** and **b** are unordered (no edges between them). The plan response is that action **a** can be executed and the subsequent communication from the executor is that **a** was in fact executed. The plan process responds finally with the choice of either **c** or **d**.

This pattern of communication in fact supports all the possible behaviors, all possible total orders, consistent with the partial order. Which behavior is exhibited depends on the choices made by the execute process. Thus, this satisfies the Behavioral Constraint.

However, this comes at a certain expense. There is considerable repetition in the communication of actions to the execution task. In the example, Action **a** is communicated twice to the execution task. Although not depicted in the examples of Figure 12.8, it is possible even in this simple plan of four actions for an action to be communicated three times before it is executed. That would occur if the execution task had chosen to execute **a** first, then **c**. In that case, the action **b** would be communicated three times to the execution task.

Furthermore, the plan derivation task must keep track of the communications coming from the execution task to know which actions to commu-

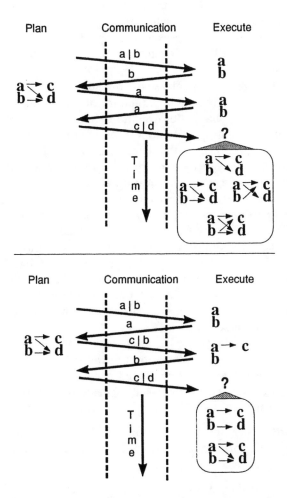

FIGURE 12.8.   Two different communication histories for the same plan.

nicate next. The communications are required to search the partial order for what can be done next.

There is yet another concern. At the bottom of Figure 12.8, a different communication history for the same partial order is depicted. In either history, the execution process ends up with considerable ambiguity in its inferences about what the underlying partial order is. That is, there is no guarantee that the two processes will have the same "view." Accordingly, the Knowledge Constraint is not satisfied.

Finally, there is the question of monitoring. Recall we made the presumption that monitoring received the same sequence of communications from planning that was received by execution. However, the communication "C—D" violates the Monitoring Knowledge Constraint since the set of states in which actions C or D, inclusively, can be executed differ from the set of states in which C can be executed. Specifically, C can be executed after only action A, but D can be executed only after both actions A and B have occurred.

These failings are inescapable, given the structure of the partial order that is being communicated and the nature of the communication. Note the partial order's "Z" shape. Because of its shape, this is called the Z partial order. There is no graph decomposition for this Z partial order, a fact which generally complicates the communication of its structure. For instance, consider the specific pattern of communication being exemplified here whereby we are communicating what actions can "currently" be executed. At the onset, that means actions **a** and **b** will be grouped, but there is no way to uniformly relate that group to the subsequent actions nor is there any way to partition it and then associate the parts with the subsequent actions, for **c** and **d** must be executed after **a** but only **d** must be executed after **b**. This difficulty arises whenever a "Z" subgraph exists in a partial order. We use the term "Z-full" for any partial order that has a subgraph isomorphic to this Z partial order. As we will see, there is an interesting relation between the Z partial order and the Hierarchical Partial Orders (HPOs) discussed earlier.

However, there is always a most conservative inference that the execution task can derive that entails a subset of the sequences denoted by the original partial order, so that the inferred partial order is said to be *consistent* with the original partial order. That suggests that it is possible to satisfy a weakened constraint:

- Consistent Constraint: The communication between planning and execution must support the recovery of a plan by the execution task that is consistent with the original plan.

Alternatively, we can satisfy the knowledge constraint if the class of partial order that is being communicated is restricted suitably.

Restricting the Class of Partial Orders

Recall that in Figure 12.8, the two alternative communication histories were consistent with the inference by the execution task of three different partial orders. Of the total of six partial orders, only one was consistent with both histories. If a restriction is placed on the class of partial orders being communicated, then the communication can capitalize on that restriction. For instance, consider Figure 12.9.

Notice the pattern of the communications. The plan process communicates a set of actions and each subsequent communication is simply a proper subset of the preceding communication until all the actions in the set have been executed. At that point, a new set is communicated if any actions remain. This makes the inference of the partial order structure unambiguous. The structural characteristic responsible for this pattern of communication is that the partial order being communicated is a totally ordered set of grouped actions which within a group are totally unordered. Such partial order structures are ideal for the communication regimen assumed in these examples.

Several benefits accrue from this restriction. From the planning task's perspective, keeping track of what can be executed next is trivial since the plan can be broken into subsets to be communicated. Further, it need only communicate the subsets of executable actions and there is no repetition in the communication of actions. Also, the execution process need only communicate back when it has finished executing all the actions in the set. The processes are more loosely coupled and both the minimization and simplicity constraint are better satisfied under this regimen.

These particular partial order structures are noteworthy not only for these communication benefits. As we saw, they constituted the conservative

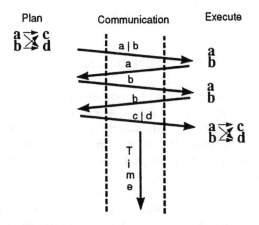

FIGURE 12.9. Communication of restricted class of partial orders.

inference when communicating the Z-full partial order. In fact they would tend to arise in any communication or mapping that groups actions, and moreover may play a role in human performance, as we will see.

Summary of Communication Approaches

The examples discussed previously placed a logical constraint on the communication, whereby the communications are restricted to the actions that could currently be executed based on another communication as to which actions had been executed. Under those constraints, there is a strong relation between the structure of the plan that is derived and the ability and ease with which the structure can be communicated. Although the particulars will change as long as there is some restriction on the communication channel there will be au impact on what can readily be communicated.

In general, this ties together plan derivation and communication. But there is a more specific linkage. The ambiguity that arose when communicating the Z partial order of Figure 12.8 is not surprising. Given the partial order $[(a, c)(a, d)(b, d)]$, there is no way to form an equivalence class over the set of actions, $(abcd)$, that will be consistent with the partial order. Consequently there also is not an HPO representation for the Z partial order. In fact, the class of partial orders in which any member of the class does not have a subgraph isomorphic to the "Z" partial order is termed "Z-less." A partial order relation P on a set A is Z-less if the following is false for any subset of A and restriction of P to that subset: $a I b$ & $c I d$ & $a \prec c$ & $a \prec d$ & $b \prec d$ & $b I c$, where I is the associated incomparability relation of the partial order.[12] It can be shown that the Z-less class of partial orders is equivalent to the HPO class of partial orders, the class of partial orders discussed earlier with respect to plan derivation using a recursive decomposition procedure (see [Marsella, 1993] for formal details).

A SIMPLE TASK

We are going to shift the discussion from abstract communication issues to how those abstract issues can inform the way data is analyzed. There is no data to present that directly addresses the issue of coordination and communication between planning, execution, and monitoring tasks per se. However, there is a rather striking relation between the earlier formal discussions and some preexisting data from a pilot study of four subjects. In that study,[13] subjects were presented (visually) 4×4 problems and then shown two solutions to the problem that were different orderings of the same fixed set of actions. The 4×4 board disappeared and the set of actions (denoted lexically as an alphabetically sorted list) was presented to the subjects. They were then asked to generate verbally as many additional orderings of the set of actions as they could that would also solve the problem. The original intent of the study was the investigation of the subject's representation of the solution under the assumption that the set of solutions the subject vocalized would be dependent on that representation. However, I make no presumptions concerning some putative fixed representation but instead consider the order in which subjects presented solutions.

Task Description

Consider the following problem (Figure 12.10).

Lowercase letters are goal locations. So F had to move down whereas P had to move in the opposite direction, up. The following solutions were presented (visually) to subjects. ML1 means tile M moved to the left and it was the first movement of M.

(ML1 FD1 FD2 FD3 JR1 PU1 PU2 PU3)

(JR1 PU1 PU2 PU3 ML1 FD1 FD2 FD3)

Note these solutions are a realizer[14] for the partial order that represents all possible orderings of these actions that constitute a solution. The partial order has the following structure:

$$ML1 \rightarrow FD1 \rightarrow FD2 \rightarrow FD3$$

$$JR1 \rightarrow PU1 \rightarrow PU2 \rightarrow PU3$$

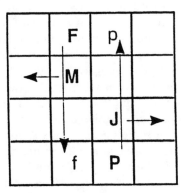

FIGURE 12.10.   Sample problem.

In this example, the lexicographically sorted list of actions presented after the solution would be:

FD FD FD JR ML PU PU PU

If you view the two solutions as a realizer of a partial order, one question, you might ask is how that order relates to the order implied by the sequences the subjects generated. Essentially, that was the question that lay behind the original study. But I am not interested in that question. What interests me is the particular order in which they generate sequences.

Task Analysis

Although they may not be aware of it, subjects in this task are essentially being asked to generate all possible topological sorts of a partial order. To perform this task correctly, a subject must have some way of determining, or insuring, that the sequences they generate are total orders of the set of actions. Likewise they must have some way of determining, or insuring, that the sequences they generate are correct solutions. These two requirements may or may not be woven together in the same procedure. Additionally, subjects must have some way of avoiding repetition, perhaps by employing some systematicity in their search of the space of sequences or solutions.

Depending on how these three logical tasks are solved, a variety of approaches are possible based on whether or not representations of the possible sequence and/or solution orders are being maintained and systematically searched. However, regardless of whether representations of possible orders are being maintained, subjects are still being asked to generate all topological sorts of a partial order. Even to write a program to do this in a systematic way is either far from trivial or results in a program that is rather time and memory intensive for such a seemingly simple task.

For instance, we can imagine what is required for a "smart" approach, whereby a (partial order) representation of valid solutions is systematically searched, without repeats. To avoid repeats, the approach must keep track of where it is in generating the set of sequences, by having some systematic way of generating sequences from the partial order. This systematicity is not achieved easily. Nor is it simple to even read a set of sequences off of the partial order. To get a sense of this, consider the problem of adding the next action to the end of some partial prefix sequence of actions that is currently being generated. An action is a candidate to be added if all the actions that must precede the action are already in the prefix sequence. To find the set of such candidates effectively means deriving a new poset, a restriction of the original poset to those actions that have not yet been generated. A candidate action to add to the sequence can be selected by evaluating this new poset. However, it gets worse if the desire is to be systematic, to avoid repeats. In that case, the choices not taken must be remembered so those choices can subsequently be made on some future sequences (specifically ones that share this prefix sequence).

On the other hand, one could use a brute force approach, whereby (a) actions are randomly selected to generate a sequence, (b) the sequence is tested to see whether it is a valid sequence, (c) the sequence is then checked against a store of previous sequences to see if it's new, and finally, (d) if it's new it is tested to see if it's also a solution (say by running an internal simulation). Of course, this is a memory and compute intensive approach for a subject to do without any external aids. There are 40320 permutations of the eight actions for subjects to keep track of. Even if the approach takes into account that there are three moves of tile F and three moves of tile P, then there are still 1120 permutations, making this a highly implausible model of how the subjects perform the task.

The way around these difficulties is some bias, some incompleteness, as to which sequences subjects generate. Even this cursory task analysis suggests that finding no bias would be phenomenally surprising.

Subject Data

Now, let's take a look at what the subjects generated. Figure 12.11 presents the initial sequences that each of the subjects generated. To reveal grouping structure, the sequences have been parsed so as to remove the direction letter, and to coalesce multiple motions of the same tile (FD1 FD2 FD3 becomes F123) or the "same" motion of different tiles (ML1 JR1 becomes MJ1). Note this does not destroy any information—it just makes some patterns more apparent.

Initial Comments on Subjects' Data

All the subjects on this problem quickly grouped the blocking tiles ML and JR (in the leading positions), even though they are not grouped in the realizers. Subject 1 produces 16 grouped responses and *then* 6 ungrouped. Subject 2 produces 1 of the realizers (number 2) and then 8 grouped for a total of 9. Subject 3 produces a total of 7 sequences, all grouped. Subject 4, the only subject to generate the original po (which in this problem requires the production of both realizers), produces, in sequence, a realizer, 3 grouped, another realizer, 6 grouped, 4 ungrouped, 3 grouped, 1 ungrouped. Note that there are 70 possible orders of which only 40 group ML and JR. Overall 43 out of 57 (approximately 75%) of the subjects' responses were grouped in this fashion, in contrast to 20 out of 70 (57%) for the actual partial order.

```
Subject 1:
MJ1   F123   P123
MJ1   FP1    FP2    FP3
MJ1   F12    P12    FP3

Subject 2:
J1    P123   M1     F123
JM1   F123   P123
JM1   PF1    PF2    PF3
MJ1   FP1    FP2    FP3
JM1   FP1    P23    F23

Subject 3:
JM1   F123   P123
JM1   FP1    FP2    FP3
JM1   F12    P12    FP3

Subject 4:
J1    P123   M1     F123
JM1   P123   F123
JM1   F123   P123
MJ1   F123   P123
M1    F123   J1     P123
MJ1   PF1    PF2    PF3
MJ1   P12    F12    PF3
```

FIGURE 12.11.   Subjects' initial responses.

However such gross measures obscure what appears to be happening incrementally. In generating the initial sequences, the subjects move along a specific path from a grouping of goal tiles (consistent with the visually presented solutions and sorted list) to fine-grain interleave of goal tile motions. In one sense this is not surprising—recall that the subjects were asked to generate as many orderings of these actions that they could. In essence, they were asked to ignore or destroy in toto any large grain structure above the level of an action and its preconditions. Nevertheless, the path they take in coalescing these reverse-direction tile motions is striking both in its similarity and its impact. Ignoring that some subjects recreate one of the solutions they saw (perhaps a misunderstanding of the instructions), all subjects first group J and M in a sequence of the form JM1 F123 P123, in essence a sequence in which the blocking tiles are grouped and each of the goal tiles is moved without interleaving of other tile's motions. All the subjects except subject four then immediately generate a solution of the form JM1 FP1 FP2 FP3 in which the clearing tiles are grouped and the goal tiles are completely and uniformly interleaved. Subject four first generates flips of the grouping structures of previous sequences (e.g., JM1 F123 P123, MJ1 F123 P123) before generating a complete interleave. In all cases, once the subjects do a perfect interleave they proceed to less perfect interleaves (e.g., MJ1 P12 F12 PF3).

Thus, subjects are iteratively coalescing independent actions into groups. First, the blocking tiles are coalesced. Once those tiles are coalesced, it leads to the coalescing of the grouped goal tile motions, F123 and P123, which are now adjacent in the sequence due to the coalescing of blocking tiles. Only after having been brought together does the consequent interleave of the motions of the goal tiles occur. So even though the various tiles move in reverse directions, which may obscure their potential grouping, the iterative restructuring of the sequences (based on the underlying partial order structure) leads to a grouping of functionally similar (or at least groupable) tile motions across subproblems—based increasingly on independence and not dependence.

In rough terms, this suggests some form of systematic island hopping in the exploration of the space of sequences. The question is: why this particular systematic pattern? I will go through three related explanations of this pattern. The first ties it into the HPOs discussed earlier, by characterizing the sequence of solutions that subjects provide as a systematic manipulation of an algebraic-like HPO representation. Although this is a quite remarkable straightforward demonstration, it is not very explicit as to why subjects uniformly perform the particular manipulation. To that end, I then go on to a second explanation that demonstrates how the sequence of manipulations minimizes the number of intermediate states that correspond to various HPOs along the path of these manipulations. The mapping from groups of independent actions to corresponding intermediate states requires fewer states than the associated full sequence. Thus, knowledge of independence along with the corresponding grouping can be exploited to reduce the number of states needed to control or monitor the generation. In addition to this minimization, this explanation also offers an interesting "automatic algorithm" interpretation of the uniformity across subject. Finally, I leave to the end the most complex discussion—how it is that these manipulations may reflect the behavior of a distributed system.

Analysis of Data: The HPO View

Consider a Hierarchical Partial Order (HPO) representation of the partial order. Recall that (par A B) means the elements in A and B are unordered with respect to each other while (seq A B) means A < B. (Note in choice of

HPO representation I am taking a slight liberty by grouping the clearing actions ML1 and JR1 separately from the motions of the tiles whose paths get cleared, F and P respectively.)

The initial partial order can be represented in an HPO as follows:

```
(par (seq ML1 (seq FD1 FD2 FD3))
     (seq JR1 (seq PU1 PU2 PU3)))
```

If we factor or redistribute the terms of the par down the next level of the hierarchy, we get

```
(seq (par ML1 JR1)
     (par (seq FD1 FD2 FD3)
          (seq PU1 PU2 PU3)))
```

And factor the par again:

```
(seq (par ML1 JR1)
     (seq (par FD1 PU2)
          (par FD2 PU2)
          (par FD3 PU3)))
```

More formally, this factoring or redistribution that is occurring at each step can be defined generally by the following relation:

$$(par\ (seq\ A\ B)\ (seq\ C\ D)) \sqsupset (seq\ (par\ A\ C)\ (par\ B\ D))$$

The symbol $\sqsupset$ signifies that the total orders denoted by the left-hand side partial order are a (proper) superset of the total orders denoted by the right-hand side. Although the prefix form of the relation ends up being a more transparent description for what follows, it perhaps will be easier to interpret this relation using infix operators. Using the infix operator $\parallel$ to denote *par* and $\cdot$ to denote *seq*, we have:

$$((A \cdot B) \parallel (C \cdot D)) \sqsupset ((A \parallel C) \cdot (B \parallel D))$$

I want to argue that this sequence of algebraic-like manipulations, this legerdemain, is roughly what is happening when the subjects perform this task (though I will argue eventually that what is hierarchical here may just as easily be viewed as communication within a distributed system). However, the above HPOs are representations of the dependencies in the solution; they are not the actual sequences that are generated. Indeed, the first HPO is consistent with any valid solution sequence and there is nothing in the last HPO that enforces FD1 before PU1 and FD2 before PU2.

So we must factor in the performance task explicitly here (this aspect of the legerdemain will not be necessary when we move to a distributed system argument). In essence, as we factor the par annotations we must also factor the "performance machine" that generates the specific behavior, given the current HPO. Since the performance requires a total order, some nondeterministic choice must be made with respect to the par annotations. So, let's assume that a performance or "execute" annotation of seq gets distributed along with the hierarchical distribution of the plan pars. This gives us two annotations over the same hierarchy,[15] as shown in Table 12.3.

Now it can be argued that this reformulation path is essentially the same as what is seen in the data. The only significant embellishment as presented is that once subject four gets to a level, he/she may generate additional alternative "execute" distributions consistent with the "plan" representation at that level or may return to a previous level. Nevertheless, the behavior still has an ordering through its space of reformulations and is consistent with the semantics of the "plan" representation.

One way to look at this reformulation procedure is that it is a very clever and perspicuous way for a system to program itself by exploiting structural grouping to insure search systematicity at the expense of completeness.

Specifically, the grouping of the plan HPO, the linkage to the execute HPO, and the systematic reformulation all overcome the difficulty of systematically generating solutions, as discussed in the task analysis section. The grouping bias in the plan/execute representations allows the procedure to keep track of where it is in generating a particular sequence. Nondeterministic choices as to which subgroup of actions to consider next are

TABLE 12.3.
Paired Plan and Execute Reformulations

"PLAN"	"EXECUTE"
(par (seq ML1 (seq FD1 FD2 FD3)) (seq JR1 (seq PU1 PU2 PU3)))	(seq (seq ML1 (seq FD1 FD2 FD3)) (seq JR1 (seq PU1 PU2 PU3)))
(seq (par ML1 JR1) (par (seq FD1 FD2 FD3) (seq PU1 PU2 PU3)))	(seq (seq ML1 JR1) (seq (seq FD1 FD2 FD3) (seq PU1 PU2 PU3)))
(seq (par ML1 JR1) (seq (par FD1 PU1) (par FD2 PU2) (par FD3 PU3)))	(seq (seq ML1 JR1) (seq (seq FD1 PU1) (seq FD2 PU2) (seq FD3 PU3)))

always at the level in the tree of the topmost par. Once the subgroup choice is made, the alterative choices are essentially hidden until the actions in the current subgroup are exhausted. The possibility of mingling the actions in subgroups is ignored. Further, basing the systematic reformulation on the group structure keeps track of where the procedure is in the set of overall sequences, the terms of the topmost pars are "factored" or redistributed. In other words, the nonarbitrariness is tied to both the simplicity of running the program for a sequence and modifying it for subsequent sequences.

Analysis of Data: The State Minimization View

As it stands, it may be hard to accept the manipulation as presented, but in fact there is another good reason for subjects to follow such a path of reformulations. Regardless of specifics as to what planning algorithm is used, planners generate plans and monitor their execution in the context of some form of world state modeling. We need only to assume that generating and monitoring are realized in a distributed fashion. Therefore, a map from actions to states is at least implicitly needed to control plan generation. And some map from state to actions is at least implicitly needed to monitor plan execution or to control reactivity. I will argue that at each step along the above reformulation path the number of states of the world that correspond to the actions is reduced and the relation between those states is being simplified. So clearly this presents a good reason to pursue such reformulation. Further, the reformulations can be realized in an essentially automatic fashion, a byproduct of iterative homomorphic (actually order preserving) mapping between action posets and world states.[16]

The details go like this. Posets of actions are generated and executed in the context of world states. The relation between these posets and states of the world is such that there may be many states in which an action can be executed. So, in the previous example, FD1 must be executed in any one of the set of states that results from executing ML1 and any prefix of actions from the sequence (JR1 PU1 PU2 PU3). But for any action, let's just map it to one candidate state, as was done in the section *Partial Order Structure and the State Space*. Recall that the state chosen for each action is one that realizes a "minimal projection into the future," minimal in terms of the cardinality of the set of actions that realize the state (as before, there actually may be more that one such state since states are realized by sequences of actions). So, FD1 can be executed in the state {ML1} (also as before, states are named using brackets around the actions that realize them). In a similar fashion, every action has such an associated state. Call that set of states the candidate state set.

Figure 12.12 represents the mapping from original action poses to states in the candidate state set. In addition to mapping every action to its associated state, a partial order is induced on those states using the original action poset's relation, so that ordering relations in the action poset now determine a derived state poset. More carefully, for two states, s0 and s1, in the candidate set, $s0 \prec s1$ iff there exists some actions, a0 and a1, which map respectively to s0 and s1, and $a0 \prec a1$. This relation realizes an order-preserving (homomorphic) map between the action poset and the resulting partial order on states. The significance of this induced partial order on the derived states will become clear presently. For now, note that partial orders are not isomorphic. Because ML1 and JR1 are executable in the same state, the initial state, those two actions map to the same state and the two posets cannot be isomorphic.

Now we can perform the same mapping for the hierarchical partial order from the second step of the algebraic reformulation presented in the previous section. Recall that partial order:

(seq (par ML1 JR1)
   (par (seq FD1 FD2 FD3)
     (seq PU1 PU2 PU3)))

The mapping for this partial order is in Figure 12.13.

Note that with the reformulation of the action poset comes a concomitant reduction in the cardinality of the state set—there are fewer states in the candidate set depicted in Figure 12.13 in comparison to the candidate set in Figure 12.12.

There is an additional interesting relation between Figure 12.12 and 12.13. The candidate state poset of Figure 12.12 induces the action poset of Figure 12.13. That is, take the candidate poset of Figure 12.12 and map each state to the actions that can executed in that state and again induce the partial order relation on those actions. That is, for two actions, a0 and a1, in the action set, $a0 \prec a1$ iff there exists some states, s0 and s1, which map respectively to a0 and a1, and $s0 \prec s1$.

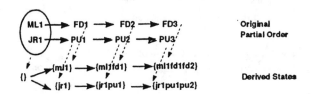

Note: Actions are circled to simplify drawing of map.

FIGURE 12.12. Mapping from action poset to state poset.

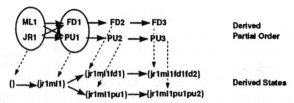

Note: Actions are circled to simplify drawing of maps.

FIGURE 12.13.   Mapping from action poset to its state poset.

Accordingly, as depicted in Figure 12.14, Figures 12.12 and 12.13 can iterativley be tied together by a composition of order preserving mappings.

If we continue this iteration (again induce another State poset from this derived action and also on), we eventually reach a fixed point when the induced ordering relation on the candidate set is a total order. At that point, the action poset will be a total ordering of a partition of the actions, where the actions in an element of the partition element are unordered. The action poset and state poset of this fixed point are as depicted in Figure 12.15.

The obvious punchline is that this action poset is the final Plan HPO in the reformulation path presented in the previous section.

```
(seq (par ML1 JR1)
   (seq (par FD1 PU1)
      (par FD2 PU2)
      (par FD3 PU3))))
```

More importantly, the corresponding state poset achieves a minima on the number of states in comparison to the state posets of all other action posets that solve this problem. So this path of reformulations realizes a hill climbing search through regrouping/reorderings of independent actions

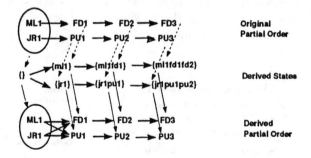

Note: Actions are circled to simplify drawing of maps.

FIGURE 12.14.   Mapping from action poset through state poset to a derived action poset.

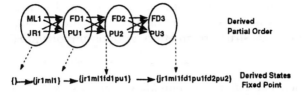

Note: Actions are circled to simplify drawing of maps.
FIGURE 12.15.   Fixed point in mappings from action posets to state posets.

that minimizes the number of states. At the least, this is significant for the generation and execution of plans that depend on state modelling.

More generally, regardless of the initial action poset, this reformulation to a fixed point always achieves a local minima on the number of states in the final State Poset. And the reformulation is automatic, even inescapable, if we accept the argument that a current action poset's state posets are the "memory" of the plan, critical for plan generation and execution monitoring, that impacts subsequent generation. With respect to this reformulation path, arbitrary plan structures are not stable. Action Posets that are Non-HPOs (not Z-less) are transformed into HPOs by the first iteration—the induced posets will always be a Z-less partial order. Any Z subgraph in the original partial order, such as partial order P at the top of Figure 12.3, will, in the induced partial order, be transformed into a graph analogous to partial order PH at the bottom of Figure 12.3. Further, even if the original poset is Z-less, the induced action poset will not typically be isomorphic to the original action poset. The final, fixed-point posets have an even more restrictive structure. The final action poset is a sequence of antichains and the final state poset is a sequence (chain) of states. (Of course, the initial action poset is still critical since the more independent the initial action poset, the fewer states that will be required in the final State Poset.)[17]

Note that the reformulation groups independent actions. The effect on the objects (tiles) these actions operate on is that they also therefore tend to group. The overall effect during execution would be that these independent action groups "move together through time," One speculative way to view the effect of this iterative mapping is that it realizes a search through a space of possible ways to synchronize the task of achieving the goal with the task of "modelling/monitoring/perceiving" state. In the process, independence in one dimension, the solution, is tied to dependence in the other, the modelling of state. That is, what the grouping bias does is tie together, make dependent, independent actions, such as the parallel motions of tiles F and D. Independence in the solution is transformed into invariance in the state description.

As presented in the previous section, this reformulation can also be modelled as a distribution of distinct plan and execute annotations over a common hierarchical structure, in effect a doubly annotated Hierarchical Partial Order.

Analysis of Data: The Communication Minimization View

Borrowing on the plan derivation work presented earlier, the HPO formulation supports an analysis of the subject behavior as an incremental process of merging of the hierarchical representations for the two independent components of the solution. The state minimization analysis reveals how the merging impacts the relationship between the actions in those procedures and states in the world and therefore suggests that the sequence of formulations may be tied to an effort to simplify the relation between actions and the monitoring of world states.

We now will undertake a third, related analysis that starts by formulating the task as a communication problem in the manner first explored in the previous section. To realize the task of communicating a valid action sequence, assume we have a planning system comprised of just two tasks, one that derives/encodes a plan of execution and another that actually executes a solution, which in this case involves simply expressing the sequence of actions in the solution. In addition, there is a communication channel by which those two tasks communicate. Figure 12.16 depicts such a two-task arrangement. On the left is the "plan" process and the partial order that it must communicate to the "execute" process. Note the partial order is the original partial, which, in HPO form, would be expressed as:

```
(par (seq ML1 (seq FD1 FD2 FD3))
     (seq JR1 (seq PU1 PU2 PU3)))
```

Depicted on the right is the "execute" process. In between, the arrows depict the communication between the tasks, each being labelled with the content of the communication. Consistent with earlier presentations, the plan process communicates to the executor which actions can currently be executed and the executor communicates which action it just executed. With respect to the temporal ordering of these communications, time flows downward. Finally, on the far right is depicted the plausible inferences that the executor could make about the original partial order, given the history of the communications.

At the bottom of Figure 12.16 is the history of communications from plan process to execute process. Note the repetition of the same action in the context of other differing alternative actions. The first and only move of tile J is communicated three times. This repetition suggests a system that

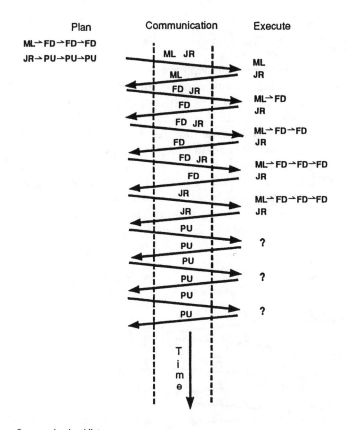

Plan   Communication   Execute

ML→FD→FD→FD
JR→PU→PU→PU

FIGURE 12.16.   Communication of original PO.

is quite neutral about how the motions of F and J are interleaved, so that alternative choices by the executer process could easily lead to the initial sequence being something like *ML1 · FD1 · PU1 · · ·*. This lack of grouping at the start is inconsistent with the data. Further, it violates several of the formal norms on communication posited earlier in the previous section. The redundancy violates the minimization constraint. Also recall we made the presumption that monitoring received the same sequence of communications from planning that were received by execution. Under that condition, the communications *(FD1 JR1)*, *FD2 JR1)*, and *(FD3 JR1)* violate the Monitoring Knowledge Constraint. The only multiple action communication that does not violate the Monitoring Knowledge Constraint is the first, *ML1 JR1*.

To avoid the formal problems and to bring this communication model more in line with the data, we only need to make the assumption that non-deterministic choice hides any further nondeterministic choices in the communication. Figure 12.17 depicts this pattern of communication. To emphasize this hiding of subsequent nondeterministic choices in this example, we represent the "Plan" partial orders in HPO in form, with the current communication underlined and in boldface. Note how once the nondeterministic choice is made to generate ML, the task is embedded in a subtree, (*seq FD FD FD*) and the alternative JR choice is hidden—and absent from the communications.[18] As a consequence, the repetition of JR1 with FD1, FD2, and FD3 goes away and the Monitoring Knowledge Constraint is satisfied. Also, the HPO and hiding of nondeterministic choice provides a rather simple solution to the task of reading a sequence off of the partial order. More importantly, this pattern of communication is

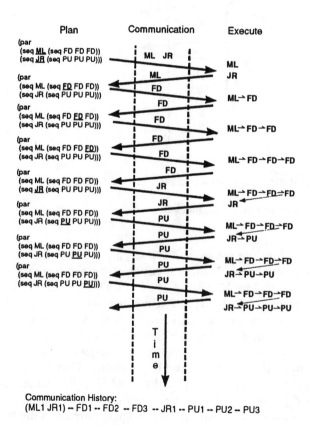

Communication History:
(ML1 JR1) -- FD1 -- FD2 -- FD3 -- JR1 -- PU1 -- PU2 -- PU3

FIGURE 12.17.   Step one: Communication of PO with hiding.

in keeping with the grouping patterns observed in the subjects and it in fact replicates the first step in the reformulation sequence:

"PLAN" "EXECUTE"

```
(par (seq ML1 (seq FD1 FD2 FD3))    (seq (seq ML1 (seq FD1 FD2 FD3))
     (seq JR1 (seq PU1 PU2 PU3)))         (seq JR1 (seq PU1 PU2 PU3)))
```

In addition, we can recapitulate within this communication model the sequence of reformulations, in an essentially automatic fashion. That is, we can presume that it is a form of iterative normalization of the communication channel that achieves the minimization of communication and concomitant reformulation. All that needs to be done to achieve this is to use the nondeterministic choice in the communication to realize the reformulation. So, in Figure 12.17, the nondeterministic choice is point (ML JR). Assume that is remembered as a grouped item and upon generating a subsequent sequence, these two actions are generated in direct sequence, creating a prefix sequence of either $ML \cdot JR$ or $JR \cdot ML$. This pattern of communication is shown in Figure 12.18. There is now a new nondeterministic choice point in the communication, (FD PU). One is chosen as

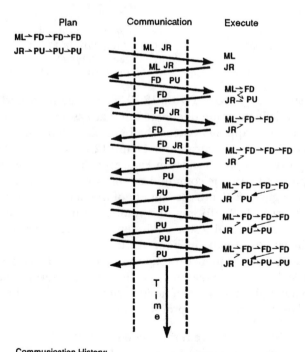

Communication History:
(ML1 JR1) -- (FD1 PU1) -- FD2 -- FD3 -- PU1 -- PU2 -- PU3

FIGURE 12.18. Step two: Cooperative communication of reformulated PO.

before, placing the communications into one of the subtrees. This essentially recreates the second step in the reformulation sequence:

```
        "PLAN"                          "EXECUTE"

(seq (par ML1 JR1)               (seq (seq ML1 JR1)
     (par (seq FD1 FD2 FD3)           (seq (seq FD1 FD2 FD3)
          (seq PU1 PU2 PU3))))             (seq PU1 PU2 PU3)))
```

I have made a (hopefully not misleading) change in Figure 12.18 by demonstrating this grouped execution by depicting a more cooperative communication. The norm for the cooperation is that the execute process, when presented with a grouped nondeterministic choice, executes both actions and then reports back only when both actions have been executed. The effect is that the communication history is even more compact than it would be otherwise.

As before, we can again assume that the nondeterministic choice point, now (*FD PU*), is grouped and executed in direct sequence, thereby realizing the final step in the reformulation sequence:

```
        "PLAN"                          "EXECUTE"

(seq (par ML1 JR1)               (seq (seq ML1 JR1)
     (seq (par FD1 PU1)               (seq (seq FD1 PU1)
          (par FD2 PU2)                    (seq FD2 PU2)
          (par FD3 PU3)))                  (seq FD3 PU3)))
```

This final step is depicted in Figure 12.19. The minimization in communication is essentially the same phenomenon that was seen earlier with the minimization of the mapping between the reformulated partial orders and the state space. Each communication in Figure 12.19 is akin to one state in the onto map from actions to states in Figure 12.15. The dotted mapping arrows of Figure 12.15 are the communications of Figure 12.19 and the circled actions in Figure 12.15 are the content of the plan-execute communications in Figure 12.19. To say this more formally, the history of communications is identical to the equivalence class realized by the onto mapping from actions to states in Figure 12.15.

Looking across the sequence of figures, the original reformulation sequence, based in manipulations of hierarchical terms, has been reframed as an iterative grouping of nondeterministic choices during communication. The key steps in this process are that:

- Nondeterministic choices are remembered
- Embedded choices are hidden
- On subsequent sequences these grouped choices are generated in sequence

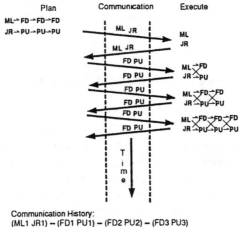

Communication History:
(ML1 JR1) -- (FD1 PU1) - (FD2 PU2) - (FD3 PU3)

FIGURE 12.19.   Step three: Cooperative communication of reformulated PO.

By these steps, a systematic and simple exploration of the partial order structure has been achieved in a rather automatic fashion. Previous patterns in the communications drive subsequent formulations. And with each step in the process, a rather strong constraint, the Monitoring Knowledge Constraint, was satisfied by essentially hiding embedded choices.

More Data Needed

The particular tile problem presented to subjects is notable for the independence, or lack of precedence relations, between the movements involving tiles M and F on one hand and the movements involving tiles J and P on the other hand. Because of the independence, the problem is well-suited for investigating how subjects manipulate independent groups of actions, any systematicity exhibited is an artifact of how subjects represent or manipulate the problem/solution and not due to the problem itself. This independence is in stark contrast to problems, like the Tower of Hanoi and Missionaries and Cannibals, where the order of actions in a correct solution must essentially be a total order. In such cases, the task itself will tend to hide any grouping biases and what those biases may reveal about how subjects perform the task.

Nevertheless, the question needs to be addressed as to how subjects perform when given more dependent solutions to manipulate. In particular, the question arises as to how subjects perform when presented solutions whose precedence relation is not Z-less. These questions are currently being considered. What appears to be the case is that prior serendipitous grouping tends to drive subsequent formulations, much as in the communication model presented here. However, more extensive data needs to be collected and analyzed to really answer these issues.

CONCLUSION: OCCAM VIOLATED

For a system to program itself, it must have, at some level, the ability to access, interpret and systematically manipulate its internal structure in a fashion consistent with its architecture. If the system can't over time manipulate this internal structure, it can't program itself. And if the manipulation is not consistent with the structure and behavior of its architecture, the "program" won't run.[19] A key issue is the nature of this ability to access, interpret, and systematically manipulate internal structure.

The regularity subjects exhibit in solving sparsely populated shading tile problems is potentially revealing in exploring this issue. In particular, the ability to exhibit a Clear-Out solution type across differing problems suggests the representation and application of a rather sophisticated strategy. The separation of goal tile movements from clearing movements suggests a decomposition of the problem into clearing and path planning subproblems. In such a decomposition, the solving of the subproblems must be coordinated, a coordination that differs during the derivation and execution of the solution. Simply, the path of the goal tiles must be known in order to plan the clearing of those paths and yet the clearing must be executed before moving the tiles to their goal locations. Moreover, subjects exhibited preferences in solving these problems, preferring the Clear-Out solutions. Recall the Clear-Out solution is marked by greater independence with respect to the order in which the goal tiles are moved, consequently the Clear-Out solutions are marked by considerably weaker partial-order representations. A general rationale for such a preference is that the independence in the decompositions enable solutions to be restructured more freely and in a fashion that simplifies the coordination between tasks.

The question of such manipulations is explored more directly in the experiment where subjects were asked to generate alternative orders of the actions in solutions that are also valid solutions. As pointed out, this is rather a difficult task to perform completely and systematically since it basically entails generating all possible topological sorts of a partial order. Subjects however exhibit considerable systematicity in the order in which they generated solutions. That systematicity could be modelled as the manipulation of a hierarchical representations of a partial order. The manipulation could in turn be modelled as the handling of either independence or nondeterminism within a distributed system. In other words, the order in which subjects generated the topological sorts suggested an algorithm realized by a rather sophisticated merging of hierarchical representations and distributed architecture.

Just as Bartleby the Scrivener (Melville, 1853) might protest, I would prefer not to argue that there is enough data to support in some universal sense this speculative, creative modelling. That is not the role I am playing here. Nevertheless, hopefully the discussion has suggested new ways to collect and analyze data as well as shone some light in general on the question of structure in problem solving. The structural descriptions of how subjects solve a problem and the dynamics of how their problem solving changes over time are individually interesting and related in extremely interesting ways. Furthermore, elucidating these issues may require changes in the models we employ. The dynamics may be an artifact of the way the components of the system work and the limitations on how they communicate, in addition to the knowledge contained in those communications. The very flexibility of the system may be due to its derivational and communication limitations since those limitations insure uniformity in the structure of its representations and communications and consequently guide how algorithms are mapped over that structure.

That is the lesson of the hierarchical partial orders, their reformulation, and their communication across channels. Whether the hierarchy is the result of derivation or the result of constraints on communication ends up not mattering—they are two sides of the same coin. Systematicity in generation of new structure may be tied to the ease of communication and manipulation of existing structure. To recapitulate the first section, HPOs were the narrative structure behind the stories the system tells itself. The HPO's modular algebraic-like structure constitutes the system's software design methodology, its model of good program design, its constraint on how arbitrary processes and data are associated that allows the system to manipulate or redesign its own representations within a distributed system.

Contrast this view of the importance of structure in general terms to two well-established approaches to modelling intelligent behavior, the PDP connectionist model and Soar. Soar and the PDP model are widely different kinds of modelling frameworks, the PDP model being a nonsymbolic description of a pattern matcher and Soar being a description of a symbol system architecture. Nevertheless, they share certain characteristics. Explicit structure is anathema to the PDP model. Furthermore, it is *a priori* extremely plastic in how it molds its behavior, in effect how it realizes a map between input and output. Therefore it proffers no innate structural constraints on how behavior is realized. It can realize arbitrary maps between input and output in arbitrary ways. Indeed, the structural relation between input and out is hidden.

And unchecked, Soar systematically destroys structure by chunking. That is the purpose of the chunking. More explicitly, the goal of the system is to approximate a knowledge level system. Paraphrasing Newell (Newell, 1990), a system is intelligent to the degree to which it approximates a knowledge level system, specifically the degree to which all its knowledge can be brought to bear in attaining its goals. This view is mirrored in the Soar architecture, whereby the chunking transforms deliberative steps, Soar's search, into chunks that are then available during the preparation phase (i.e., the rule match phase). It is in the preparation phase that knowledge can be brought to bear more immediately, without search. The preparation phase achieves this (and compensates for the increases in the number of rules due to chunking) by having an unrestricted bandwidth (the "working memory") and being massively parallel. This view, of approximating a knowledge level system, has the system trying to overcome its architecture by destroying, making opaque, aspects of the structure of the problem as it relates to its own problem solving search.

In contrast, what has been suggested herein is that the structure of the problem, the structure of the architecture and the explicitness of the relation between them may all be very important. As described, the Clear-Out strategy has a complex structural characterization that seeks to coordinate the problem solving steps involved in the task of deriving the plan as well as executing it. One way of viewing this is as a map of the strategy onto the architecture. Further, the preference for the Clear-Out is coincident with a metric on the structure of the solution, the weakness of the partial order. Finally the topological sort task suggested that the ability to express and manipulate structure and map that structure onto a distributed architecture may help explain how subjects represent and manipulate problems and the algorithms they realize to solve those problems. If these are appropriate characterizations of the phenomenon, then we might presuppose that the terms by which the phenomenon are described might be meaningful in the architecture that realizes the phenomenon.

NOTES

[1] What Pylyshyn calls, and suitably impugns, as "weak equivalence."

[2] Or impose.

[3] Prevailing wisdom especially with respect to the undergraduate subject pool of wherever a researcher may be pursuing his or her research.

[4] Or at least there is another level of the architecture that is left out of such accounts.

[5] Note the use of the term "uncertainty" is not intended to invoke images of information theoretic analysis.

[6] The data was collected in two ways. In the initial set of experiments, subjects marked their responses on a sheet of paper with a pencil. Subsequent experiments used a computer interface where the subjects saw the tile board on a computer

monitor and used a mouse to pickup and then drop the pieces to an adjacent tile location. However, I have no difficulty believing that different modes of presentation, different interfaces, would shift subjects' preference away from the Clear-Out. Nevertheless, I expect the phenomenon of regularity would in any case assert itself.

[7]Not here, not anywhere in this paper, since it clutters the presentation.

[8]A par execution order is best interpreted as any total order sequence of the $term_i$.

[9]That is, by virtue of a partial order's antisymmetry and transitivity, the following is true. If $\{a1c1\}$ and $\{c1a1\}$ are in the state set for one action then no other action's state set can contain one of these states and not the other. Thus $\{a1c1\}$ and $\{c1a1\}$ are indistinguishable in the context established by the partial order, even though they may or may not be the "same" state (in whatever is the underlying state model). And in addition if we have the names of the candidate states, e.g. "$\{a1c1\}$" as opposed to $\{a1c1\}$, the set of those candidate names and the map from the set of actions to those candidate names is sufficient to recreate the partial order and therefore the full state sets. So although there may not be a unique state that satisfies the *must* criteria, the full set of states for every action can be recreated from the candidates and the map from actions to candidates.

[10]Just so you appreciate my sensibilities, the combinations of reasoning about such sequential actions and future states of the world, especially in the case of conjunctive goals, argues against viewing planning simply as a function that is realized by compiling behavior into a purely reactive system or that is realized by a more classical purely offline approach. Not only is the size of the space of possible goals and plans too large to compile or search, but the demands that particular plans place on knowledge of future states of the world may be too great.

[11]If the concern is to model human planners, we can also colloquially argue that what we already know about the relation between structure and function in the brain argues against a shared memory approach.

[12]In effect, $a\ I\ b$ means that $a \not< b\ \&\ b \not< c$.

[13]Data collected by C.F. Schmidt and an honors thesis student with some help from me.

[14]A realizer is a set, L, of total order extensions of a partial order, P, such that $\cap\ l \in L = P$, where the intersection of two partial orders is the intersection of the set of ordered pairs that represent them. So for this example, ML1 must precede FD1 in the partial order and in fact ML1 precedes FD1 in both total orders. However, ML1 precedes JR1 in one total order but not the other and correspondingly ML1 and JR1 are incomparable in the partial order. The point of this being that a realizer and the partial order it represents are equivalent representations, computational issues aside.

[15]Recall we did something similar, albeit with a very different connotation, when expressing the Clear-Out strategy by doubly annotating the decomposition with a subproblem derivation annotation and a solution execution annotation.

[16]A map λ between two partially order sets, α and β is order preserving if for $x \prec y \in \alpha$ then $\lambda(x) \prec \lambda(y) \in \beta$ [Davey & Priestley, 1990].

[17]And as an aside, we might imagine some initial groping bias that impacts the final posets, similar to the bias seen in the algebraic-like reformulations. In particular, the "true" structure may well have more hierarchical structure. For instance, the

antichains would be antichains of chains and those chains would be chains of antichains, etc. This would realize the class HPO in what I call canonical form [Marsella, 1993]. Every level of the hierarchy would be a sequence of antichain substructures—a temporal ordering at a level of abstraction. To realize such a structure and still have the previous reformulation approach would suggest that certain partial order substructures would have to be inviolate or at least inviolate from the perspective of a level of the hierarchy.

[18]The figures also presume that this effectively erases JR from the inference that the execute process is forming which in turn removes the ambiguity in those inferences.

[19]I take these points to be essentially given, and true across symbolic as well as nonsymbolic architectures.

REFERENCES

Agre, P. E. & Chapman, D. Pengi (1987). An implementation of a theory of activity. In *Proceedings of the national conference on artificial intelligence*, pp. 268–272. August, Seattle WA: AAAI.

Bresina, J. L., Marsella, S. C., & Schmidt, C. F. (1987). *Predicting subproblem interactions*. Technical Report No. LCSR-TR-92. New Brunswick, NJ: Rutgers University Laboratory for Computer Science Research, Rutgers University.

Carbonell, J. G. (1982). Learning by analogy: formulating and generalizing plans from past experience. In R. S. Michalski, J.G., Carbonell, & T. M. Mitchell (Eds.), *Machine learning: An artificial intelligence approach, Vol 1*. Palo Alto: Tioga Press.

Chapman, D. (1987). Planning for conjunctive goals. In *Artificial Intelligence, 32*, 333–377.

Chomsky, N. (1965). *Aspects of the theory of syntax*. Cambridge: MIT Press.

Davey, B. A., & Priestley, H. A. (1990). *Introduction to lattices and order* (pp. 10–11). Cambridge: Cambridge University Press.

Fikes, R. E., Hart, P. E., & Nilsson, N. J. (1971). STRIPS: A new approach to the application of theorem proving to problem solving. In *Artificial Intelligence, 2*, 189–208.

Golumbic, M. C. (1980). *Algorithmic graph theory and perfect graphs*. New York: Academic Press.

Hoare, C. A. R. (1985). *Communicating sequential processes*. New York: Prentiss Hall.

Marsella, S. C. (1993). *Planning under the restriction of hierarchical partial orders*. Doctoral dissertation.

Marsella, S. C. (1988). *An approach to problem reduction learning*. Technical Report LCSR-TR-110. New Brunswick, NJ: Laboratory for Computer Science Research, Rutgers University.

Marsella, S. C. & Schmidt, C. F. (1993). A method for biasing the learning of nonterminal rules. In S. Minton (Ed.), *Machine learning methods for planning*. Los Altos, CA: Morgan Kaufman.

Marsella, S. C. & Schmidt, C. F. (1991). *PRL: A problem reduction learner that manages dependency.* Technical Report ML-TR-32. New Brunswick, NJ: Rutgers University.

Marsella, S. C. & Schmidt, C. F. (1992). On the use of problem reduction search for automated music composition. In Balaban, Ebcioglu, and Laske (Eds.), *Understanding Music with AI*. Menlo Park, CA: AAAI Press.

Marsella, S. C. & Schmidt, C. F. (1989). Problem reduction. Automated music composition, and interactive performances. In *Proceedings of the Second Art and Technology Symposium*. Connecticut College.

Marsella, S. C. & Schmidt, C. F. (1988). *A problem reduction approach to automated music composition*. Technical report LCSR-TR-115. New Brunswick, NJ: Laboratory for Computer Science Research, Rutgers University.

Melville, Herman (1853). Bartleby, the scrivener: A story of Wall-Street. Originally appeared in *Putnam's Monthly*, 2, 11812, 546–5576 & 609–615. Also available online at http://www.columbia.edu/acis/bartleby/.

Newell, A. (1990). *Unified theories of cognition*. Cambridge, MA: Harvard.

Pylyshyn, Z. W. (1984). *Computation and cognition*. Cambridge, MA: MIT Press.

Rumelhart, D. E, McClelland, J. L., & The PDP Research Group. (1986). *Parallel distributed processing*. Cambridge, MA: MIT Press.

Sacerdoti, E. D. (1977). *A structure for plans and behavior*. New York: Elsevier.

Schmidt, C. F. (1985). Partial provisional planning: Some aspects of common sense planning. In J. R. Hobbs & R. C. Moore (Eds.), *Formal theories of the commonsense world*. Norwood, NJ: Ablex.

Schmidt, C. F., Noice, H., Marsella, S. C., & Bresina, J. L. (1986). Preference for and transfer of problem-solving methods. Twenty-seventh Annual Meeting of the Psychonomic Society, New Orleans, LA, November 12–15.

Schoppers, M. J. (1987). Universal plans for reactive robots in unpredictable environments. In *Proceedings of the eighth international conference on artificial intelligence*, pp. 1039–1042. IJCAI, Milan, Italy, August.

Sridharan, N. S., Bresina, J. L., & Schmidt, C. F. (1983). *Evolution of a plan generation system*. Technical Report RU-CBM-TR-128. Laboratory for Computer Science Research, Rutgers University, New Brunswick, NJ. March.

Tate, A. (1975). Interacting goals and their use. In *The fourth international joint conference on artificial intelligence*, pp. 215–218. Cambridge: MIT Press.

Tate, A. (1977). Generating project networks. In *Proceedings IJCAI-77*, pp. 888–893. Cambridge: MIT Press.

Waldinger, R. (1981). Achieving several goals simultaneously. In Nilsson and Webber (Eds.), *Readings in Artificial Intelligence*, pp. 250–271. Palo Alto, CA: Tioga.

Wilkins, D. E. (1984). Domain-independent planning: Representation and plan generation. In *Artificial Intelligence*, 22, 269–301.

Author Index

Subject Index